Those Absent

On the Great Hungarian Plain

JILL CULINER

The author gratefully acknowledges
the financial support
of the Canada Council for the Arts;
and the Ontario Arts Council.

CLARET PRESS
Library and Archives Canada Cataloguing in Publication
Copyright ©Jill Culiner
The moral right of the author has been asserted.

www.jill-culiner.com

ISBN paperback: 978-1-910461-72-3
ISBN ebook: 978-1-910461-73-0

1. Culiner, Jill–Journeys—Hungary—Jewish History—20th century. 2. Central Europe—Hungarian Plain—Travel writing—Memoir—Hungary. 3. Great Kumania—Puszta—Village life—Tiszaörs—Kunmadaras (Hungary)—Social life and customs—20th Century. 4. Jews—Anti-semitism—Hungary–History. 5. Historical re-enactments–Hungary. 6. Social change—Hungary—21st century

*All rights reserved. No part of this publication may be reproduced, stored in or introduced into a retrieval system, or transmitted, in any form, by any mean(electronic, mechanical, photocopying, recording or otherwise) without the prior written consent of the publisher.
Any person who does any unauthorized act in relation to this publication may be libel to criminal prosecution and civil claims for damages.*

A CIP catalogue record for this book is available from the British Library.

This paperback or the ebook can be ordered from all bookstores and from Claret Press, as well as eplatforms such as Amazon and ibooks.

Front cover photo with courtesy from, The Memorial Museum of Hungarian Speaking Jewry, Safed, Israel http://www.hjm.org.il/

Book cover and interior design by
Bernard Tisserand - *www.bernard-tisserand.fr*

www.claretpress.Com

Those Absent
On the Great Hungarian Plain

TABLE OF CONTENTS

Prologue

PART ONE
Budapest, Gyöngyös, Beregdaróc, Beregsurány

PART TWO
Kunmadaras

PART THREE
Returning

PART FOUR
Tiszaörs

PART FIVE
The Jews

PART SIX
Change

PART SEVEN
After

Acknowledgements

About the Author

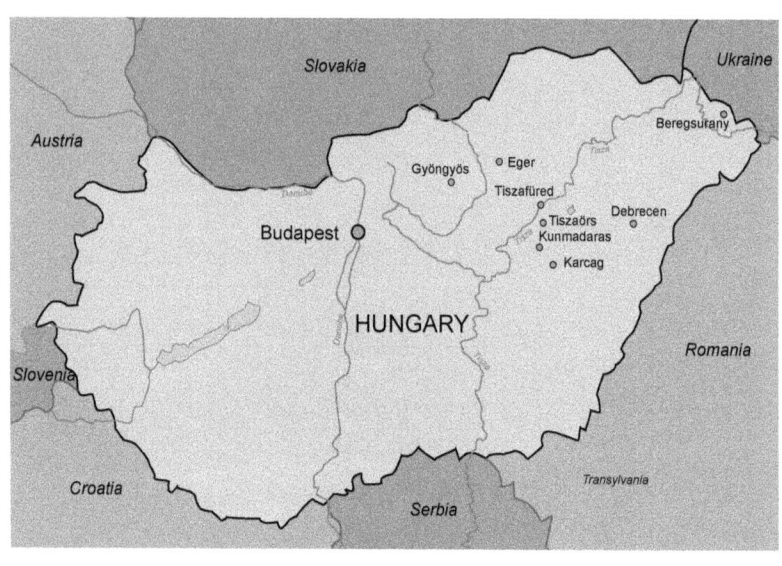

Prologue

I keep hearing that journalists should be truth crusaders, but that's not right. All you need is curiosity and the ability to convey what you see without colouring it in any way.
B. James, former foreign correspondent, UPI

The Count, a slight man with a fine moustache, possessed exquisite manners and great dignity – qualities scarce in our howling arriviste milieu. I was a scrawny and sulky child of twelve, but he was the first man to kiss my hand, thereby earning my eternal loyalty.

Along with 200,000 other Hungarians, the Count had clandestinely slipped out of his country during the 1956 Uprising. More fortunate than most, he had managed to smuggle out rolled-up paintings, those once gracing the walls of his family's pillaged and ruined manor. His was a tragic story, but it could have been far worse: under the post-war communist regime, Hungarian aristocrats had been persecuted, sent to horrific prison camps, or sentenced to death. Alive and well, but with no financial resources here in his new country, Canada, the Count was obliged to sell the precious artworks.

Thanks to an enthusiastic collector – my father's square-shaped multi-millionaire crony – the Count appeared in our life along with other colourful characters: the millionaire's buxom mistress with her rigid yellow coiffure, and a ruddy clutch of businessmen eager to insert culture into their splashy mansions. My father, although an enthusiast, lacked the funds to purchase the finest beauties – a Vlaminck or two, several Courbets and a Modigliani.

Because the Count, inhabiting a flophouse in downtown Toronto, had no place in which to store invaluable works, several came to nestle, albeit temporarily, in our house: what thief would imagine such pearls stored in a suburban lookalike? My mother, soured by my father's financial insufficiency, set out to copy the Modigliani hanging on the mauve wall above our yellow upright piano – she was an adequate amateur painter. Thus, when the original departed weeks later, her admiring lady friends believed it was still in our possession.

Back then, I couldn't have cared less about fine art, but was thrilled to bits when the Count gave me a necklace (not to be worn until I was older). It was a beautiful piece, a complicated wreathing of gold leaves studded with tiny pearls, a flowery centre with a small diamond, and one uneven pearl droplet: easy to imagine it had been worn by a Magyar princess in some forbidding castle. He also presented me with a record of traditional Hungarian music: how entrancing the sweeping melodies, how exquisite the cimbalom. Thus, he opened the world for me, and Hungary became a romantic place I longed to see.

The multi-millionaire and his pals soon purchased the Count's collection; my father acquired a few lesser paintings at a cheaper price. All was well. Until, abruptly, proud acquisition became rage and dismay. It was discovered that the paintings were forgeries and the Count had disappeared. Further investigation revealed he was no Hungarian. Instead, he came from neighbouring Quebec, worked hand-in-hand with a highly talented French-Canadian forger. Both were sought by the police. My mother's fake Modigliani journeyed from the mauve wall to the trash can; visits from the multi-millionaire and mistress ceased (four decades later, my father claimed he had also shared the brash lady's favours); and my father's business buddies no longer talked fine art.

Still, despite my itinerant life and endless mishaps, that beautiful necklace has remained with me, as have my curiosity about Hungary and my love for its traditional music.

***

The name Hungary is a misnomer, harkening back to the country's brief occupation by the Huns in the fifth century.[1] Killing their elderly, crucifying prisoners, reading the future in heated bones and entrails, scarifying their faces, flattening their children's noses and deforming their skulls into an egg shape, dressing in a mess of mouse and rat skins, wearing horns, dying part of their hair red but shaving the rest, reeking horrifically – olfactory aggression set them apart from more fastidious mortals – the Huns easily inherited the sobriquet 'barbarian'. Under the notorious Attila, known for his wild rages, they pillaged, murdered and enslaved their way across Europe. As they did, the conquered peoples emulated their fashions.

When military success flagged, the Huns retreated to the banks of the Tisza River where, after barbaric overindulgence during his wedding with the beautiful Ildikó,[2] Attila was

---
1 The Huns were possibly a confederation of nomadic warriors.
2 Attila married Enga in 413, Kerka in 421, a Gepid princess in 445, then an unnamed Hun noblewoman, then Eska, daughter of a Scythian king in 449, and Helena in 452. There were many others. Fascinated by her beauty, Attila took Ildikó (Marlisbonde) in exchange for her father's life, but died before consummating the marriage.

Those Absent

suffocated by a nosebleed. The Hun's glorious moment was over: squabbling amongst themselves, routed by resentful locals, they withdrew back east, leaving behind their name and an enticing myth of buried treasure that dreamers have searched for over centuries.[3]

In Hungarian, however, the country's official name is Magyarország (or Magyar country). Originating in the Ural Mountains, the Magyars or Megyeri, were a Nordic herding and fishing people. In around 2000 BCE, one group[4] began migrating southward. In the ninth century, settled in the area around Etelköz[5] in Khazaria, they were being decimated by incoming fearsome Turkic Pechenegs:

> *In one dense mass, encouraged by sheer desperation, they shout their thunderous war cries and hurl themselves pell-mell upon their adversaries, pushing them back, pressing against them in solid blocks, like towers, then pursuing them and slaying them without mercy.*[6]

Banding together[7] with Jewish and Muslim Khazars and Khabars, Huns, Sicules, Kalizes, Alans, Slavs, Onongurs, Avars and Bulgars, the Magyars fled to the Carpathian (Pannonian) Basin, where, under their leader Árpád, they quashed local Slav residents, joined ranks with Vikings and set out to defeat Bavarians, ravage northern Italy, the Balkans, Constantinople,

---

3   Edward Gibbon wrote: "The remains of Attila were enclosed within three coffins, of gold, of silver, and of iron, and privately buried in the night: the spoils of nations were thrown into his grave; the captives who had opened the ground were inhumanely massacred."
4   The others became today's Estonians, Finns, Voguls, Samoyeds and Ostyaks.
5   Etil: an ancient Turkic word for Volga. Etelköz is possibly 'place near the Volga' or 'by Itil', the Khazarian capital.
6   Michael Psellos, eleventh century Byzantine diplomat and scholar
7   The chiefs of one hundred and eight clans assembled in a tent, slit their forearms, let the blood drip into a cup, which a táltos, a shaman, mixed with wine. Each chief drank from the cup forging one nation by a covenant of blood. Eventually, all were known as Megyers, and the Megyer language came to predominate.

Lorraine and Burgundy. So dreaded were the Magyars, that the word 'ogre' was (falsely) said to be a corruption of their name. Finally, weakened by two major military defeats, they returned to the Carpathian Basin, settled down and founded their country.[8]

***

I had travelled in western Hungary during communist days, seen endless fields of rich black earth, met people who hinted at tales they didn't dare share, and discovered, even in tiny village bars, wonderfully talented musicians playing that heart-searing traditional music. Once, in deep winter, I happened upon a former manor in some frozen backcountry. Pressing my nose against a window's misted glass, I discovered a chandelier-lit room where elegant people waltzed to exuberant strings: it was a scene as entrancing and inaccessible as any ball centuries before.

In England, in a damp boarding house with rubbery sheets, I met Ferenc, an elderly castaway. How had he landed here? Had he fled Hungary during the 1956 Uprising, or was the reason for his exile more sinister, the result of war crimes? He confided nothing; but begging me for images of a homeland he would never again see, he wept unashamedly. And in Munich, I noticed the cynical smiles of dissident Hungarian students when their western counterparts idealized Stalin, Mao, Castro,

---

8   In Hungarian legend, two brothers, Hunor and Magor, pursued a white stag to a region of luxuriant vegetation and sweet water where they married two princesses. Their descendants were Attila, and the Magyar chief Ügyek. One night, Ügyek's wife Emese dreamt she was impregnated by a falcon-like creature, a turul, and that two rivers flowed from her breasts. Giving birth to a son, she named him Álmos (Dreamy). It was Álmos who led the Magyars to their promised land between Danube and Tisza, and founded the royal Árpád dynasty. Hungarian Nazi parties use the turul symbol; the worst anti-Semitic attacks of the interwar period were carried out by a Turul society.

Those Absent

any fashionable revolutionary leader.

In 1999, I was preparing a UNESCO-sponsored photographic exhibition for the Musée de la Résistance et de la Déportation in France: the theme was Europe's vanished rural Jews. Before WWII, nine million had lived in Eastern and Central Europe. Arriving as early traders from Greek cities along the Adriatic, Aegean and Black Seas, then as soldiers and purveyors to the Roman army, they had later joined the hordes of incoming Eastern invaders. After the collapse of Khazaria in the eleventh century, Jews were welcomed by the Kievan princes; when persecuted and expelled from Mainz, Bavaria, France, Italy, England, Naples, Switzerland and Hungary in the fourteenth century, they found a home in the Polish-Lithuanian Commonwealth. Although the Jewish world had been largely exterminated during WWII, I would travel through Central Europe and the Baltic States, search for its trace in architecture and local memory.

One stop in my journey was Hungary, home to Europe's second-largest Jewish population in 1914. Although now a popular tourist destination as well as a magnet for heritage travel, Hungary is one of Europe's least-known countries. Its long history, complicated by intermittent foreign dominance, has been obscured by fantastic myth; and its Finno-Ugric language is impenetrable to most. To further blur understanding, modern tourism satisfies itself with incessant movement, colourful showmanship and selfies taken in emblematic settings. Yet to discover, even imperfectly, an area, a country, a mentality, it is necessary to go slowly (even on foot), to tarry in places never mentioned in guidebooks or on travel sites.

I intended to spend ten days in the country, taking photos in unspectacular rural communities. But in a small town on the Great Plain, I was welcomed by a friendly local group –

the affable but bibulous Karcsi, bar-owning Ildikó, Kata, the eternal party girl, Tarzan, black-marketeer and corrupt night watchman, Janci, a musician who refused Hungarian music in favour of elevator 'noise' and Udo, the naïve Austrian. And I returned so often to hear their stories that my visits evolved into a residency of six years.

I was there at a pivotal moment. Communism had ended. Having joined NATO, Hungary was hoping to become part of the European Union. Although the former Communist, Viktor Orbán,[9] had replaced the liberal stance of his party, Fidesz, with right-wing populism and won the 1998 election, many believed this victory would be temporary only. Opposing parties such as the SZDSZ were promising a liberal western-style social democracy, one that protected human rights and guaranteed a commitment to the tenets of the European Union.[10] Surely such affirmations would triumph in a country long under Soviet domination.

Local society was an uneasy mix. Retired communist officials lived elbow-to-elbow with their victims – nobles who had lost their lands, expropriated peasants and those who had endured torture. Alongside Hungarian-Swabian survivors of post-war ethnic cleansing, there were German retirees as well as previous members of the Hitler Youth Movement; and there were returning Hungarians who, slipping out of the country in 1956, had become lucky elsewhere. For all, admission to the EU in 2004 brought change that was rapid and relentless.

The agricultural sector was unprepared for the influx of cheap foreign produce and the devaluation of local

---

9   After 1988, Orbán opposed communism.
10 The SZDSZ defended same-sex marriage, euthanasia, the legalization of marijuana, stronger borders, higher taxes on corporations and the wealthy, lower taxes for both the middle and working classes. The party also promised to increase the minimum wage, eliminate illegal immigration and accept legal immigration.

commodities. Struggling with the rising cost of food, housing and utilities, few could conceive of acquiring the flashy cars, large screen televisions, computers and big new houses advertised everywhere. Huge supermarkets were appearing, yet unable to shop in them, villagers could simply go up and down the aisles, marvel at what was being offered and dream that one day they, too, could participate in the consumer society. Because all that was familiar – traditional music, centuries-old customs and local architecture – was disappearing, reassurance came in the political promises of an authoritarian populist leader and a violent hatred of those eternal scapegoats: the Roma, and the (largely vanished) rural Jewish community.

In blending together tragic history, village life, rumour, prejudice and a search for long-vanished ghosts, I witnessed reality being deformed and forgotten. The events I describe really happened; conversations have been reproduced as faithfully as possible; and the people depicted do (or did) exist, although their names have been changed to protect privacy. But, since all is tainted by my way of seeing things, there is no guarantee of impartiality or reliability.

PART ONE:
Budapest, Gyöngyös, Beregdaróc, Beregsurány

Village Jew[11]

Upon the black heavy earth of a road which was barely traced, for here people walk where they like over hedge and ditch, our carriage-wheels rolled on noiseless as on velvet: it seemed to me I had entered into a new world, and I experienced all the delightful sensations that the charm of the unknown affords.

Victor Tissot[12]

---

11 Photo courtesy of the Museum of Hungarian Speaking Jewry, Safed, Israel.
12 *Unknown Hungary.* Victor Tissot was a nineteenth-century Swiss journalist, travel writer and philanthropist.

Those Absent

I

Perhaps nothing more precisely characterizes the peculiar stage of civilization in which the Hungarians are at present than the great importance attached to foreign travel, and the prejudice generally entertained in favour of foreigners belonging to nations acknowledged to be further advanced than themselves – in favour of English, French and Americans. As a rule, a Hungarian may be said to despise his neighbours. With him "tis distance lends enchantment to the view.' He reluctantly and grudgingly acknowledges his inferiority to the German on some points, fondly persuading himself that it is made up, or more than made up, by his superiority to others. In the case of the Italian, he is still more impressed with a sense of his own excellence. As for the rest of his neighbours, Rouman or Slav, the Magyar, in most instances, considers it derogatory to the national dignity to be placed in comparison with them.

Arthur John Patterson, [13] 1869

I sat on a sofa covered in rough silk, silver spoon in one hand and a crystal cup of strawberries in the other. To my left, windows gave out to a vast patio and a garden rich with late spring blooms. Below was the cocoa-brown Danube, and further still, roaring commercial Pest. I was in a Buda living room, not in nearby Castle Hill where camera-laden tourists clog souvenir shops, but where calm streets coil up the hillside, and smart dwellings are secreted by tumultuous foliage. The room's décor was elegant and international; no clues announced I was in Hungary.

My hosts were a Jewish couple, both lawyers. They had invited me to meet with several of their friends, Jewish and Christian, journalists and lawyers, who would give me

---

13   *The Magyars, Their Country and Institutions.* Arthur John Patterson was a nineteenth-century English travel writer.

much-needed information about the country. Yet, all were discouraging, for they thought my quest for the provincial past ludicrous. Heritage travel wasn't yet the fashion it was destined to become; Jewish rural life had been terminated in the spring of 1944.

'Don't travel to the northeast. The area around the Ukrainian border can be dangerous for a woman alone. The Russian mafia is present, and they kidnap and murder people.'

Everyone in the room nodded in agreement, but I doubted that I, a middle-aged woman in sturdy walking boots and carrying a rucksack, would be considered delectable prey.

'How are you planning to travel?'

'By train.'

'That's a bad idea. We call the trains in the east "black trains". Hijackers operate out along the lines, and you'll be robbed... or worse.'

Their concern, although touching, was irksome. Useless to insist I've lurked in far trickier places than Central Europe, that their information might be dated or pure confabulation.

'What if you run into problems?' asked one lawyer 'You can't speak a word of Hungarian.'

'Stay in Budapest. Tourists love this city.'

But I was no tourist seeking easy answers, beaten tracks and comfort. I had a well-defined project. 'I need to go to villages where Jews once lived. I'm looking for traces of their presence.'

'What sort of traces? Hungarian Jews lived like everyone else in the villages.'

'Except in the north-east, the area some call "Yiddishland".' For, in the eighteenth and nineteenth centuries, Jews from the Russian Pale and Austrian Galicia arrived en masse and settled there. Yiddish was their spoken language.

Silver spoons clicked. Chiding looks came from those in armchairs, those on the elegant settee near the window. Was the memory of that deeply religious community still an embarrassment? When Hungary's modern Jews were identifying with Hungarian nationalism and adopting Magyar language and culture, the pious caftan clad traditionalists had maintained their feudal lifestyle and remained impervious to the ideals of a secular state, equality and modern schooling.

'Tell me about Hungarian village life. What's it like today? What do you know about the Puszta?'[14] For Jewish peddlers, shopkeepers, innkeepers and negotiators had lived all along the edge of that vast lonely Great Hungarian Plain. Yet, no one in the room could answer, for none had been to the east of their own country.

'Why would we go there? We prefer travelling abroad, in Italy, France or England.'

'And in summer, we're in our country homes on Lake Balaton.' My hostess beamed. 'Everyone loves Balaton. It's beautiful.'

These declarations amused me. In the nineteenth century, vacations abroad (usually in the Austrian Empire's watering holes of Marienbad or Karlsbad) were a social requirement for this city's gentry and middle class. So was the establishment of a fine summer home at Balaton, 120 kilometres distant. Such preferences were solidly in place a century and a half later, although the lake had become a modern resort with hotel blocks, private beaches, discos, sporting events and international throngs.

'If you insist on going east, at least remove those bracelets you're wearing,' said one journalist. 'Don't look wealthy.'

---

14 Puszta, with a capital letter, refers to the flat parts of the Alföld or Great Hungarian Plain. As puszta, it can mean agricultural communities or the fields surrounding villages once belonging to a manor.

PART ONE : BUDAPEST, GYÖNGYÖS, BEREGDARÓC, BEREGSURÁNY

'They aren't silver or gold. They're absolutely worthless,' I protested.

'And your camera – it's better to go without it.'

'I'm here because I'm a photographer, and I'm preparing an exhibition.'

'People in the east are poor. Don't tempt them. Please. For your own sake.'

'Why not put off your journey?' another journalist suggested. 'In two weeks, I'll be on holiday. We'll rent a car, drive where you want. I'll translate, protect you and make sure nothing bad happens.'

Protection from nothing in particular? These comfortable city dwellers imagined the east to be a savage place;[15] to me, it seemed impossible – even droll – that a city as civilised as Budapest would still have a perilous hinterland. 'Can you give me names of previous Jewish villages that might be of interest?'

There was some discussion, and then a book was fetched. On one page was a map with little dots showing where there had once been communities. I picked one beside the Ukrainian (former Galician) border: Beregdaróc. 'This might be what I'm looking for.'

My host was scathing. 'What do you expect to find in Beregdaróc? Everything belonging to Jews will have been destroyed or converted into something else.'

'If you want destruction, start with Gyöngyös,' said my hostess. 'It's close to Budapest, and there, the magnificent synagogue is being used as a furniture store.'

I pointed to the dots along the Puszta's empty expanse. 'And here?'

---

15   It definitely was considered savage by the Pannonian Romans who lived in the west of the country several millennia ago. Raiding Iranian Iazyges peopled the East.

Those Absent

'An area to avoid.' My host turned the page, showed me a photo of a small charming building. 'This synagogue is in Kunmadaras, a town on the Great Hungarian Plain where Jews were tortured and massacred during the White Terror of 1919. Where, in 1946, there was a blood libel and a pogrom.'

'A post-war charge of ritual murder?' For I knew of the horrific blood libel and pogrom that had taken place in Kielce, Poland, in which two Holocaust survivors were shot dead, and forty were murdered with bayonets, beaten or stoned to death.[16]

'Exactly. Someone in Kunmadaras claimed the Jews kidnapped a Christian child because they needed blood for kosher sausage. The townspeople went on a rampage, pillaging and killing survivors of Auschwitz and forced labour camps.'

I begged for information, but no one could tell me more. '

No Jews live in the town now, and you won't be welcome.'

'It would be interesting hearing what people remember.'

My host didn't hide his exasperation. 'You think you'd feel comfortable doing that?'

In my notebook, I jotted down the names of the three places that had been mentioned: Kunmadaras, Beregdaróc and Gyöngyös.

My hosts' son, a university student, drove me to the train station. 'You're very brave,' he said.

'Certainly not.' I knew I was taking no risk. 'I'm simply curious.'

---

16   At the same time, a pogrom broke out in the Hungarian city of Miskolc. Influenced by anti-black market propaganda, 25,000 workers marched into town and killed two Jews who were supposedly selling flour above the legal price. The next day, the same mob captured and killed the Jewish police officer who had tried to protect the victims. In September, another pogrom was narrowly avoided in the town of Hajdúszoboszló.

PART ONE : BUDAPEST, GYÖNGYÖS, BEREGDARÓC, BEREGSURÁNY

II

There is a wound in the wood at each Jewish door
A gaping hole where the neighbours tore
The mezuzah out and left a wound,
Inflicted by the neighbour's hand.

Rokhl Korn[17]

My train left the beautiful Budapest station of Keleti, entered the less scenic suburbs with their monotonous rows of communist housing blocks, passed scrubland with rotten shanties made of cardboard, plastic sheeting, and corrugated iron perched beside gullies filled with garbage and polystyrene packaging. Finally, we were rattling through meadows and acacia-lined villages. But where were the traditional whitewashed adobe houses I had seen in the 1970s? Many had vanished, victims of heavy-handed standardization; replacing them were squat villas. And in the great expanse of sunflowers and maize, only occasionally could I spot the once ubiquitous sweep-wells: gallows-like apparitions with arm-like poles stretched high.

We groaned to halts in country stations where waves of people marched across the open tracks, or squeezed into my seedy compartment. Furtively, I sought the trace of exotic ancestors in their features; was it my imagination that made cheekbones unusually high and eyes tilted? But I wasn't the only voyeur: although no one was welcoming, all observed me openly and with apparent mistrust. Yet, in this country where hatred towards 'aliens' constantly resurfaces, after millennia of migration and invasion, Hungarians are as genetically mixed as any humans.

Now I, a peaceful invader, was crossing the country, searching for vanished people, but also for a glimpse into a long-gone

---
17   Rokhl Korn, 1898 -1982, was a Polish-born Canadian Yiddish poet.

world, one described by nineteenth-century adventurers who found exotica when it was still available. I would avoid the usual tourist lures: horse-drawn wagon tours; circus performers and actors disguised as sheepskin-clad herdsmen, whip-cracking horsemen, costumed dancers or fierce cowboy csikósok; I would give pseudo-rustic csárdák (hostelries) a wide berth.[18] Once the dens of shepherds, Transylvanian salt traders, robbers and cutthroats, today they welcome rainbow-coloured tour buses and hawkers of 'local' handicrafts manufactured in Romania and China.

Thanks to the written instructions of a polyglot ticket seller in Budapest, I left the train at the right place, boarded a red and yellow branch line omnibus heading for Gyöngyös. But, by the time I arrived, it was late. The sun had vanished and a niggling wind scattered dust, plastic bags and candy wrappers along the uneven pavement. I had no idea how to begin my search for the Jewish past other than finding the synagogue, but the lowered heads and unfriendly faces of those leaving the station discouraged enquiries (and what language would I use?)

At a loss, I followed them; they, at least, knew where they were going. Yet, all soon turned left or right, entered houses and apartments. The deserted streets were gloomy, or perhaps they felt that way because it was Sunday: everyone snug at home, safe behind drawn curtains, food waiting on the table. Only I remained on the street outside, a lonely chilled traveller trailing through an unknown town.

What if those solicitous Budapest lawyers and journalists had been right? Perhaps I really was on a fool's errand. What, aside from weedy cemeteries and ruined synagogues, could I hope to discover? How could I take photos of nothing?

---

18   Although Hungarian plurals add the letter 'k', I have, for simplification, anglicised most by adding 's'.

I reached the central market square, a bleak empty expanse. Trees shivered, the sky darkened a tone or two. Feeling increasingly dreary, turning this way and that, not knowing which street to follow, I suddenly realised that the huge, rather imposing building right in front of me was the synagogue.

It had been greatly modified. Now a furniture and textile showroom, its walls were covered with vulgar, gaudily painted advertisements; its stained glass had been replaced by display windows.[19] Yet, the Star of David was still there, topping the cupola, soaring proudly.

Vainly, I circled the locked building several times. Perhaps I could find Jewish houses – in Hungary, Christians and Jews had lived side by side – so I began looking at doorposts, searching for tiny holes or painted over places, hints that mezuzahs[20] had once hung there. Found nothing.

Here was a religious building: Catholic. Perhaps I'd find a welcoming priest who would speak a language I could understand. He'd invite me in for a cosy chat, recount the history of buildings, of the town, the Jews, the peasants, and make residents come alive with words.

I knocked on the door, waited, knocked again. This evening, no one was home.

---

19 In 2022, the building was being renovated for use as a cultural centre.
20 A small case containing a parchment scroll and fixed to the doorpost by some Jewish families.

Those Absent

III

The plaits of her magnificent black hair are interlaced with red and green ribbons, and hang like two silken bell-pulls down her back. Her slender figure is full of feminine grace. Our curiosity makes her rosy lips part and smile, and if she opened her door to us, it was because, in this old-fashioned country, hospitality still opens its doors to a stranger.

Victor Tissot

I travelled northeast on ancient groaning trains. Despite the warnings of my Budapest acquaintances, I encountered no unscrupulous robbers, no cunning hijackers. But station waiting rooms were filled with dozing elderly folk in lumpy clothing, ragged bundles at their feet: they were the new homeless, the victims of capitalism.

When the train line ended, a weary, rattling bus carried me to the town of Beregdaróc. Afternoon sun touched all with gold, and I wandered along bumpy lanes, snooping, peeking, searching for traditional art: holes above doors where birds could settle and protect the household;[21] doorposts, gables and gates carved with spirals, rosettes and circles celebrating the sun; life-size idols with globe heads representing the moon.[22] But in this village of modern villas, there were none: few Finno-Ugrian relics have survived renovation.

After settling in the Pannonian Basin, early Magyars kept up their traditions, sundering dogs to seal bargains, invoking spirits to guarantee clan victory, nailing bodies to coffin floors to hinder their use by ghosts, naming children after the dead to ensure eternity, burying fishermen in their boats, warriors with

---

21 In ancient Finno-Ugric belief, the world was hatched from the egg of a sacred wild duck. The deceased continued to exist in an afterlife of eternal happiness, protected by the semi-divine Big Bird.
22 Those still in existence have been handed down in families.

their saddles, bridles, and the heads, flayed skins and leg bones of their horses.

But the Catholic powers saw the advantage in Magyar conversion. If this Asiatic tribal society became a civilised Christian monarchy, it would provide a bastion against other fearsome eastern invaders. Lured by Catholic Europe's economic prowess, the tribal leader Vajk received baptism at Christmas 1000 CE, and was recognised by the pope as István (Stephen), Hungary's first king.[23]

His clansmen, loyal to their traditions, resisted conversion for two hundred years, and only after horrific persecution did Christianity triumph.[24] The Magyar belief in a tripartite division of life uniting the underworld with the earthly and celestial, was transformed into the trinity; holy oak trees became oak crosses; places of sacrifice near streams or rocks called *egy* or *igy*, became churches, *egyház* (egy-house). Those making sacrifices, leaving offerings or avoiding religious service were fined and beaten into church; those doing business or hunting during religious ceremonies lost their horses. To end the nomadic lifestyle, burial was restricted to the ground around churches, for clansmen would never abandon deceased ancestors who received a share of each harvest.

Beregdaróc isn't large, and I quickly reached its end at a jagged patch of vegetation punctuated by lopsided stones. Camera in hand, I struggled through thigh-high weeds. I was in a Jewish cemetery, and I'd found it quite by accident!

In the 1770s, when Poland's dismemberment[25] and partition began, many Jews headed for this corner of Hungary, first

---

23 Vajk opted for Western, not Eastern, rites although some tribesmen in the east of the country chose otherwise.
24 Today, Hungarian populists consider their nation the fortress of Western Christianity and civilized Europe.
25 By Russia, Prussia, and Austria.

Those Absent

from Moravia and Bohemia, then from overpopulated and impoverished communities in the Russian Pale and Galicia where they could comprise forty percent of a town's population. They found themselves in a country where only one or two Jewish families lived in each scattered village, where religious needs depended upon peripatetic rabbis who travelled by horse and cart along the rutted lanes.

By 1941, forty-eight Jews were living in Beregdaróc, a town of 1,300. Had there been a small synagogue or prayer house here? I'd find out soon enough for each local woman (certainly no exaggeration) had come out of her stuccoed home to stare at me over her wrought iron garden gate. Taking advantage of the general nosiness, I questioned all in English, German, sign language, and the two words of Hungarian I had learnt: *zsidó templom*. Well … at least everyone understood I was looking for a synagogue, but although friendly enough, all seemed perplexed.

One, determined to be helpful, led me to the war memorial. 'This is something worth seeing,' she seemed to say. She patted the stone, ruthlessly ripped out an audacious flowering weed that had dared poke up near the cement base. Another pointed at a house down the street: *'Deutsch, Deutsch,'* she shouted. *'Historia.'*

Relieved to have someone to converse with, I marched over to the indicated dwelling and rang the bell. Out came an elegant man, and he did speak German. 'Yes, I'm an amateur historian. Yes, there was once a synagogue. Come, I'll show you the building.'

At the war memorial, we crossed the road, headed down an alley, and stopped at an inauspicious building, slightly larger than a garden shed.

'This was it. The synagogue.'

I walked around the hut looking for traces of its former use. There were none. The historian waited. 'There were no Jews left after the war. These days, we use it as a dairy.'

'Does anyone remember the local Jews?'

The historian looked away.

Evening was coming on, and I had no plan other than finding a field to sleep in when it got dark. For lack of anything better to do, I entered a dingy, rather smelly *kocsma*, a bar, near the weedy cemetery. The men, although drunk, seemed friendly, and all knew what I was up to: word travels speedily in minuscule places. A lewd creature with puffy face and colourful blood vessels was particularly insistent: he clearly considered our coupling inevitable and wanted to buy me a drink. In lieu of conversation, he shouted – the usual way of addressing a foreigner who understands not one word of a language. The others watched, a blurry sea of snaggle-toothed grins in the murky room. The one-eyed barman observed impassively.

Suddenly, a well-dressed young man burst into the kocsma, came to a full stop in front of me and said in perfect English: 'My name is László. I'm the local priest. The barman telephoned, told me you were here. I'll take you to my house. You'll meet my family, have dinner and spend the night. Staying longer in this bar would be a bad idea.'

Meekly, I followed him into the street.

'First,' said László, 'we will visit my beautiful church. The community is growing quickly now that communism is over.' He swung open the door, and we entered.

'Very nice,' I said, although it wasn't spectacular.

He was proud of the building. 'Not just nice: beautiful. Look. There, it is beautiful, yes?'

Those Absent

At his house, his wife Erzsébet and their two children stood in the entry. A generous dinner waited on the table. 'All local specialities. Blood sausage made by us.'

No use explaining that I'm vegetarian. These kind people would have been most offended at refusal. There were other foods as well: crackling bits, ear and snout-like things, unidentifiable chunks. Not a vegetable in sight.

'You will have our bed tonight,' said my generous host. 'It is big and comfortable.'

'And you? Where will you both sleep?'

'On the floor in our children's room.'

'Hospitality has limits. I have a sleeping bag. I'll stay in the garden.'

Husband and wife were shocked. 'No. You must take our good bed. You are a guest.'

I had to smile. Was this yet another hint of tradition? In earlier centuries, main rooms of rural Hungarian homes contained a 'best' bed, a showpiece article of furniture heaped high with feather mattresses and beautifully embroidered cushions. Believed to offer protection from the evil eye, the bed was to be used by honoured guests only, or by women in the few weeks after giving birth.[26] Everyone else slept on temporary trestle beds or in the barns.

Argument continued for quite some time, but I was determined to win. 'Then let me sleep on the floor in the main room. I'll be leaving at sunrise, long before you're awake.'

Both husband and wife seemed disappointed by this imminent departure, but I needed to be back outside, uncovering secrets, walking along lanes bordered by wildflowers and rustling with small creatures.

---

26 Each time a new mother left the safety of the bed, a broom was put in her place to foil malevolence.

PART ONE : BUDAPEST, GYÖNGYÖS, BEREGDARÓC, BEREGSURÁNY

'Why not come and live here in the village?' Erzsébet asked. 'We need an English teacher. A French teacher too. Perhaps you'd like the job? You won't be paid. You must have your own money to live on.'

Those Absent

IV

The Jews are found all over Hungary also and are looked upon with almost as much scorn as the gipsies, with the difference that they are feared. The great distinction between Jew and gipsy lies in the money-making and money-saving aptitude of the former, his reticence, and the fact that he rarely lets himself go.

Geraldine Edith Mitton,[27] 1915

*A*t dawn, I left Beregdaróc on foot, passing open fields and orchards, heading toward the next village, the slightly smaller Beregsurány. Perhaps I would find a trace of the thirty-nine Jews who had lived there in 1941.

Their ancestors hadn't found immigration easy: border officials granted Jews only temporary stay, imposed exorbitant entry taxes, restricted the goods traders could carry, spontaneously invented any pesky hindrance. Many incomers with no official papers[28] had been forced into perpetual wandering, and they joined the bands of vagabonds, beggars and robbers in forests or Puszta swampland. Others specialised in illegal but necessary tasks: receiving, spying, informing and lockpicking.[29] But if life was difficult in Hungary, it could be worse elsewhere: in Ostfriesland, under the laws of 1710, Jewish beggars could lose their children, be flogged, branded, condemned to forced labour or hanged.

In many of these villages in Hungary's northeast, Jews maintained a traditional, Hasidic or Orthodox way of life. Their

---
27 *Austria-Hungary.* Geraldine Mitton, 1868-1955, English novelist, biographer, editor and travel writer.
28 Many itinerants were the victims of the population limiting Famiiants Laws in Bohemia, Moravia and Silesia.
29 Jewish *Schnorrjuden* and *Betteljuden*, had been roving over Europe for centuries. The 1510 *Book of Vagrants, Liber Vagatorum,* mentions the many Hebrew words in vagabond vocabulary.

insularity and indifference to the world around them provoked a general hatred for the Jewish presence. All were dubbed "Galicians." Not every Jew was bad, said the anti-Semites, only Galicians[30]. Today, "Galician" is still a euphemism for Jew in anti-Semitic diatribes.

On this late spring morning, despite the early hour, the world was wide-awake; expensive cars passed, Mercedes, BMWs, all filled with men, all with Ukrainian license plates – the border was a few kilometres distant. They cruised slowly, the occupants looking at nothing in particular but watching everything. The scrutiny was, after a time, unnerving, so I clambered over a fence, veered through an apple orchard and leapt over a narrow stream. Soon, a meandering lane appeared, one that would take me, I hoped, to Beregsurány. And, without warning, I came upon another Jewish cemetery, weed-filled, forgotten.

Beregsurány is a long string of a village where bungalows squat along a drowsy main road. Only rows of cherry trees lent charm and offered shade from the shimmering sun. Finding no building resembling a synagogue, I began questioning everyone I saw.

'There never was a synagogue here.'

Some insisted, in simple German, there had never been Jews. 'In the cities, in other places. Not in Beregsurány.'

'There's a Jewish cemetery right outside town,' I protested to no avail.

I went into the school; perhaps a teacher or school director knew local history. The first person I met in the hallway was a French teacher who, unfortunately, spoke almost no French. I was determined to use him for the bit he did possess. Gangling,

---

[30] Once an independent Slav country, Galicia, (in today's Ukraine) became part of the Polish-Lithuanian Commonwealth. After 1790, it was the poorest, most undeveloped region in the Austro-Hungarian Empire

Those Absent

achingly shy, he desperately agreed to question other teachers. I waited, kicking my heels until his return.

'No one has ever heard of Jews living in Beregsurány.'

My enthusiasm sank into discouragement. There really was no information to be had. During the communist regime, it was forbidden to mention the Holocaust. Today, people are uninterested in a disgraceful history.

Between 800,000 and 900,000 Jews lived in Hungary when Fascist Germany occupied the country in 1944. Already in the grip of defeat, the Germans knew that without Hungarian cooperation it would be impossible to eradicate the community. But after World War I and the trauma of losing one third of the country under the Treaty of Trianon, Hungary had adopted right-wing authoritarian rule well before Germany. Far from resisting, the government saw the advantage in confiscating Jewish real estate, furniture, jewellery, artwork, businesses, industrial establishments, livestock, stocks, cash and bank accounts. Within three months, over 500,000 Jews had been murdered. Even the SS plenipotentiary Edmund Veesenmayer was astonished by local enterprise:

> *'Only the zealous and active participation of the Hungarian police enabled us to achieve this task.'*[31]

I went to the bus stop and stood there for a long while, hoping a bus would miraculously appear – it was impossible to understand the posted timetable. The sky was a glazed bowl; the tarmac road simmered. Hungry, I was incapable of identifying a restaurant. Thirsty, I was unwilling to lurk in yet another doubtful drinking dive. I was discouraged, frustrated.

Suddenly, here was the French teacher again, madly pedalling

---

31 *The Politics of Genocide*: The Holocaust in Hungary. Randolph L. Braham, 1994.

his bicycle in my direction and waving one arm. *'Suivez, suivez!'*

He led me back down the endless main street to a house at the village edge. Stopping at a gate, he called out. Several people appeared. 'Can I help you?' asked an ageless blonde.

'You speak English!'

'Of course I do. I left here in 1956, and now I live in Florida. It's the first time I've been back to see my family.'

Hardly believing my luck, I asked her about Jews.

'Certainly, there were Jews in Beregsurány,' she said. 'When I was a little girl, I knew all the Jewish children. We played together. The community wasn't large enough for a synagogue, but a room in that house across the street was used for prayers. It was a Jewish house then. Now it belongs to my family. Do you want to look inside?'

It was an ordinary square building with a deteriorated roof. In place of wallpaper, flowers had been hand painted on the walls. The rooms were empty. There was no sign of anything.

'Come. I'll show you something else.'

I followed her out into the garden, and fighting our way through stinging nettles and snagging brambles, we reached the back.

'Look in here.' She threw open the door to a narrow, windowless space with a dirt floor: an oubliette of sorts. A grotto. 'Here's where four Jewish families were locked up in 1944, mothers, fathers and children.'

So this had been one of the many holding places for Jews before their transfer to ghettos set up in factories, brickyards and barracks, and before their deportation to Polish extermination camps.

The woman from Florida closed the door, and we returned

to the road. 'It was shameful. One day, all the Jews were gone. Vanished, just like that. Nobody told us anything,' although she must have seen villagers laughing, hooting and jeering when her Jewish neighbours were force-marched away.

'How did your family come to possess this house?'

'After the war, the Jews didn't return.' Her tone was dismissive, as if the answer were a complete one. 'Now my family wants to sell. Are you interested in buying? It's not expensive, around two thousand American dollars. That's not much for a nice Jewish house in a lovely, quiet village. What do you think?'

PART TWO:
Kunmadaras

Kunmadaras synagogue

The truth surfaces like oil on water.

Yiddish proverb

Those Absent

V

Approaching a village, we observed a vast concourse of people gathered together on its outskirts. A fair is being held, and the ground is inundated to such an extent that the booths are actually standing in water, a day or two's rain having been sufficient to cause it to lie on the surface, for the soil in this district is already saturated with moisture, in consequence of its proximity to the Theiss [Tisza]. Accustomed to this state of affairs, the people of both sexes, nothing daunted, hold up their petticoats and paddle through the water like ducks. Here and there, in the little patches of green that, like wet islands, rise above the water, are sellers of pottery displaying their wares, and a colporteur his tracts, whilst, standing about in groups, are Jews, dragging their long togas in the mire, and gipsy children taking mud baths. Away beyond the fair, with its booths and wet islands and general slush and slipperiness, are thousands of horses, cattle, and pigs – pet pigs, affectionately watched over by buxom Magyar females, ankle deep in water.

Nina Elizabeth Mazuchelli,[32] 1881

*I*n a shivering two-carriage train, I crossed onto Hungary's Great Plain, the Puszta, a word that means wasteland. Yet, once called the 'sea of grass', it had been the refuge of wild boars, deer and aurochs. In 1241, Mongol invaders set up their white felted yurts[33] here and tarried over the winter, venerating spirits of earth and water, sacrificing prisoners and eating the fermented cabbage that is the ancestor of sauerkraut. Perhaps they were soothed by the waving grasses, billowing clouds and endless wind; by a mélange of harshness and beauty so similar

---

32   *Magyarland*. Nina Elizabeth Mazuchelli, the British wife of an army chaplain, was one of the first women to travel in the Himalayas.
33   Covered by felt, painted with lime or powdered bones, decorated with paintings of grapevines, trees, birds and animals, some yurts were more than nine meters wide, and thirty head of cattle were needed to pull them along.

to their own. When spring arrived, instead of moving westward to slaughter Europe, they turned and went home.[34]

Centuries later, this was swampland where villages perched on misty islands, and inaccessibility offered a haven to bandits, outsiders, and military deserters. Intense summer heat provoked fabulous mirages – great forests, castles, churches, shivering seas – that inspired much folklore, superstition and fear.

Today's Puszta is much changed: the Tisza River, shortened in the nineteenth century, has been diverted into irrigation canals. There are no longer annual floods, modern villages are not islands, mirages have been tamed by air pollution, and much of the land is used for industrial farming. But wary deer, storks, rabbits and hares crouched in the remaining marshland and watched our sluggish train pass.

Despite modernisation, there was still considerable mystery in the countryside. Take those compelling high mounds interrupting the unrelenting flatness. Although called *kunhalom* and falsely attributed to thirteenth century Kuman settlers, they are far older, dating from the Copper, Bronze, and Iron Ages. Their purpose varied over time: some earth castles were inhabited tells. Others, the burial mounds of nomadic Indo-Iranian Scythian or Sarmatian royalty, contain sacrificed humans and concentric rings of slaughtered horses. Used as border markings, guard posts or elevated heights for the transmission of signals, these wonderful mounds have been much abused in modern times. Ploughed, flattened, only an amendment to the Nature Protection Act in 2003 would finally protect them.

---

34 Perhaps to join the race for succession in Qara-Qorum when the Great Khan Ögedei died after a drinking binge, or because grazing was insufficient for their immense cavalry. The Mongol Empire, said to be the safest in existence, guaranteed freedom from religious persecution, exempted teachers, lawyers and artists from taxes, encouraged and protected traders. When sea trade replaced the silk route, the Empire lost its advantage. Shattered by internecine strife, decadence and ignorance, it broke up into violent insular Khanates.

Those Absent

We paused at cracked platforms where no travellers boarded and none descended, where cement buildings with shattered windows testified to modern-day vandals. I once caught sight of low mud cottages rotting in tangled elderberry, perhaps serfs' abodes, for a ruined manor stood nearby, surrounded by the abandoned buildings of a communist collective farm: several hundred years of social history in one view.

Leaving the train in Kunmadaras, I hitched my pack onto my back, followed a well-trodden dirt path leading away from the station (all the while observed by an expressionless face in a window) and arrived at a tarmac road. To the left, a church spire poking up from distant greenery hinted at the town. I felt a rush of atavistic excitement: I was in the heart of Great Kumania, land of the Kumans,[35] a people so ferocious they had routed the violent Pechenegs,[36] before being, in turn, slaughtered by Mongols in 1237:

> ...*in the country of the Comans, we saw piles of human bones and skulls everywhere, heaped as though they were piles of rubbish...*[37]

Joining up with persecuted Jász (Iazyges or As),[38] like the Pechenegs a century before, the Kumans sought asylum in Hungary. King Béla IV, with great reservation, finally agreed – those savage Pechenegs had certainly frayed local nerves. Forty thousand Kuman rowdies arrived and made a nuisance of themselves, letting their vast herds of long-horned cattle

---
35   A people originating on the eastern bend of the Huang-ho or Yellow River.
36   In the 11th century, the Pechenegs, considered a violent eastern scourge and once slayers of the Magyars, sought asylum in Hungary after being massacred by terrifying Kumans. Asylum was granted; the Pechenegs arrived and were perfectly obnoxious until settling down. Their descendants became serfs.
37   *Histoires des Mongols, Enquête d'un Envoyé d'Innocent IV dans l'Empire Tartare, 1245-1247.* Jean Du Plan Carpin.
38   Perhaps cousins or descendants of earlier Iazyges, a people so ferocious, they kept Roman legions at bay.

trample cultivated fields, munch gardens and orchards, and crush vineyards. Finally, when the king was absent, jealous nobles massacred the Kuman royal family. Enraged, the Kumans slaughtered a swath between the Danube and Tisza, then they and their Jász allies departed for Bulgaria: never mess with barbarians.

Only after the Mongols murdered forty percent of the Hungarian population, did the Kumans and Jász return as military support. To assure them of his loyalty, King Béla arranged a marriage between his eldest son and the Khan's daughter, who was baptised and re-named Erzsébet.

> At this wedding feast ... the Kumans ... made an oath, according to their custom with their swords on a dog that had been sundered in two, that they would defend the lands of the Magyars as would the King's own supporters against the Tartars and barbarian peoples.[39]

They settled on this Puszta. Keen consumers of horseflesh, they, too, buried dead kings with loyal servants and sacks of gold, immolated favourite horses and, as protection from curses, pestilence and hailstorms, dotted the countryside with horse skulls on posts:[40]

> I saw one person who had died recently; around him was suspended the skins of sixteen horses, four of each in the direction of the cardinal points on their high stakes.[41]

Such quaint traditions have, happily, vanished, but not the towns bearing the Kuman name: Kunhegyes, Kúnbaracs, Kúnszentmiklos and Kunmadaras.

Kunmadaras is a crossroads, yet it's nowhere. Surrounding

---

39 *Histoires des Mongols, Enquête d'un Envoyé d'Innocent IV dans l'Empire Tartare, 1245-1247.* Jean Du Plan Carpin.
40 Even as late as the mid-twentieth century, a dying man would be taken into the courtyard to bid farewell to his favourite horse – perhaps all that was left of the old tradition.
41 *Voyage dans l'Empire Mongol,* 1253-1255. Guillaume de Rubrouck.

Those Absent

fields are swampy and flat. Under the intense light, young sunflowers smeared the foreground with brilliant yellow; acacias and sleek poplars scratched an azure horizon with celery green. Bulrushes luxuriated in the stagnant water of ditches, and thousands of hopeful frogs piped an eerie flute-like mating tune.

I passed more houses modified from traditional long shapes into villas, saw curtains twitch. Some individuals popped out of doors and gawked at me, while those propped on makeshift benches cut short conversations. But there were still no robbers or hijackers, no sly-eyed pillaging locals coveting my camera or metal bracelets. Instead, everyone seemed quite distrustful of me, although my imagination might have been doing over time: I was obviously foreign, and an unaccompanied woman with a bulky backpack was probably a rare sight. I was, of course, more leery than they: in this town, Jews had been massacred twice.

I arrived at a main square. On my left was a stone with a Star of David and an inscription in Hungarian that I was unable to read: a memorial to the 1946 pogrom? What else was left of the Jewish community? A synagogue? A cemetery? In 1941, Kunmadaras was home to 273 Jews – a fairly large community. But that wasn't unusual. At the end of the nineteenth century, only twenty percent of the country's Jews lived in Budapest. The rest lived in small provincial towns and, unlike the deeply religious Jews of the northeast, were well assimilated.

The sun was slipping past red tile rooftops: too late to begin a search. Now what? A gaggle of children pointed at me, whispered. An ancient crock, loose-jawed and trembling, got off his bicycle and gaped. I was weary, even discouraged. Did I really hope to get information about a pogrom that had taken place sixty years earlier? Wanting nothing more than to escape the rubberneckers, I craved a meal, something to drink, and a room for the night (I only sleep in fields when less an object of observation.) So I marched on through town and came to the end of it: no hotel or guesthouse to provide a roof for the night, no restaurant anywhere. Merely a field with cows, a traditional sweep-well and, on the left, a shabby, evil-looking bar, a kocsma, out of which low lascivious male laughter floated on a reek of stubbed-out cigarettes. Not my sort of place, really.

An elderly woman with orange hair was monitoring my every movement from a window, so I went up to her. *'Sprechen Sie Deutsch?'* I asked.

'Deutsch!' Her face beamed with inexplicable joy. *'Deutsch! Deutsch!'* She motioned me to wait right there. Then, ripping open her front door, she rushed into the street, clamped her arm around my waist and steered me into that awful bar, that Auerbach's Keller.

In the dim light, I perceived a voluptuous middle-aged woman with mounded dyed black hair at the counter. *'Sprechen Sie Deutsch?'* I asked hopefully. She answered in incomprehensible Hungarian. We stared stupidly at each other.

Behind her were rows of bottles, posters of vast-bosomed women in unhitched bras, a girlie calendar, a few fake woodcarvings in resin and a rockstar poster. Unusual-looking men with high flat cheekbones and long, drooping moustaches stared at me from the three tables in the tiny room: Kumans, these men were definitely Kumans. Other Kumans in remarkably tattered, stained clothes drunkenly pumped coins into two burping slot machines. All wore lumpy, shapeless headgear, modern versions of the high peaked felt or fur caps adorned with buttons that once established clan identity. As far as I could see, Kuman clansmen no longer shaved the front of their heads, nor did they braid their back hair into multiple pigtails and knot them together at the neck. None wore traditional caftans.

Those Absent

'Can I help?' a man asked in German. Hatless, sporting no moustache, short-legged, soft-bellied, he perched on a stool in front of a counter made of peeling yellow plastic.

I turned to him with great relief. 'I'm looking for a pension, a hotel, a room for the night.'

'Not in Kunmadaras. You'll have to go to Berekfürdő, eight kilometres away.'

After the day's trying journey in hot crowded trains, the endless waiting in stations where overhead loudspeakers pierced the air with ear-shattering electronic noise and unintelligible destinations, an eight-kilometre slog on foot sounded like a thousand.

'Have a seat,' said the man, visibly amused by my dismay. 'Would you like a beer?'

'Why is your German so excellent?'

He laughed. 'Because I'm Austrian.' His name was Udo and, although he lived in Vienna, he had been coming to Hungary for the last twenty years to fish, and to spend good drinking time with his best buddy, a local man nicknamed Tarzan. 'I love Kunmadaras. It's so different from Vienna. There, friendliness is superficial; here, people are sincere, sweet, emotional and open.' His expression was dreamy, his round blue eyes childlike.

I took a slug of cold beer – exactly what I needed since bed and board weren't immediately available. 'Perhaps not as sweet as all that,' I said. 'Don't forget the pogrom.'

His dreamy smile faded into consternation. 'I never heard about a pogrom.'

'That's why I'm here. To get information about the Jewish Holocaust survivors who were massacred in Kunmadaras in May 1946.'

'Impossible. That couldn't have happened. Everyone is so kind.'

'Like the kindly Austrian grandmothers who welcomed Hitler in 1938?'

He was silent for a minute or two. 'I don't speak Hungarian, but I'll introduce you to a friend of mine. Karcsi speaks German, and he'll confirm there's never been a pogrom. He'll be showing up soon.'

So we sat, sipped beer, grinned mutely at the landlady whose name was Ildikó, and exchanged getting-to-know-you information until Karcsi arrived with his friend, Bálint. Both men had been guest workers in Germany and Austria, and both spoke German. In their late forties, they wore another version of tribal headgear: baseball caps.

'She claims there was a pogrom here in 1946,' said Udo.

The men, uneasy, told me to follow them. Leaving the counter, we went to sit in the bar's empty back room where plastic flowers in fake Grecian urns topped wobbly tables, and an incongruous string of Christmas lights formed a glowing heart on the wall.

'We heard about the pogrom, but we have no information,' Karcsi said, his voice low. 'Jews, pogroms, the camps, we couldn't talk about those under the communists.' Officially, the war had been waged between fascists and anti-fascists, and the anti-fascists had won.

'Is the Kunmadaras synagogue still standing?'

'There never was a synagogue in Kunmadaras.'

'Of course there was,' I said. 'I saw a photo of it in Budapest.'

Karcsi shook his head in denial. Bálint was slumped in his chair, clearly bored.

Those Absent

'Do you like Gypsy music?' Udo asked me. 'Why not come with us? We're going to eat in the town of Abádszalók and hear music.'

I was starving, and I would have loved to hear what he called Gypsy music, but I didn't know these men at all, and night had come on. 'I have to find a room.' Drearily, I thought of the eight-kilometre walk.

'Don't worry. I'll drive you to a pension later.'

And because I never have the heart to refuse an excellent offer and lack a nose for keeping out of trouble, I left the bar with these three men, and climbed into Udo's car. We drove twenty kilometres over lonely bad back roads, arrived at an inn where, under an ancient wisteria vine, four ancient Roma played heart-breaking melodies on a violin, a viola, a bass and a cimbalom.

Udo ordered a huge wooden plate of food for us all to share. And schnapps. And wine. We all did a *Bruderschafts* toast – linking arms, kissing on cheeks – that allowed us to *duzen* one another (use the familiar thee, thy and thou in German), and we became chums.

Perhaps because we were truly – with the help of much *pálinka*[42] (Hungarian schnapps) – the best of chums, or perhaps because there was nothing to lose with a stranger, when we drove back over the empty road to Kunmadaras, Karcsi said, 'I'll ask my mother about the pogrom. She was a schoolteacher back then. And tomorrow, I'll take you to the Jewish cemetery of Kunmadaras and the synagogue in Karcag.'

'We'll drive there in my car,' said Udo with enthusiasm.

Bálint stayed silent. He didn't offer to accompany us.

---

42 Fruit brandy. The best is brewed in villages using fruit fallen from trees and left to ferment in barrels in back gardens, after which it is brought to the official local distillery for completion. This pálinka is, however, for home use only. The pálinka sold in kocsmas is a far less pungent industrial product.

PART TWO : KUNMADARAS

VI

The truth has charm, but it's shy.

Yiddish proverb

*U*do and I had another drink in a café in Berekfürdő, a spa community with modest holiday villas lining unpaved dirt roads. It was a strange place, that café: two workers were busy cementing up an interior doorway even though it was one in the morning. What was going on? The patron who spoke some German explained that the café's toilet was being claimed by the shop next door.

'There's a lawsuit, and the courts will decide who the rightful owner is. That's how things go in new capitalist Hungary.' He was, understandably, disgusted.

Outside, on the sidewalk, a man at a synthesizer pumped out American elevator music, added one or two Hungarian tunes, old melodies. But distorted by electronic whine, backed by a relentless techno pump, they provided only a faint memory of beauty – rather like this café itself, an older building now smothered under the ubiquitous, communist cement. In the absence of a toilet, beer-logged men relieved themselves along the neighbour's outside wall.

Udo talked about his life, his four children. Married at eighteen to his pregnant girlfriend, his mother was pleased to hand him over to a second mother. Life had been narrow, and adventure had come from a television screen. Bored, he built matchstick dream ships in his spare time until his wife's protests about dust discouraged him. He'd attended night school, studied art, gone into advertising and was presently in charge of public relations for a printing company.

He loved Hungary's chaos, so different from the obsessive

Those Absent

Viennese cleanliness. Yes, he admitted, he took great care of his car, washing and vacuuming it once or twice a week. He voted for the right, yet claimed to be free of prejudices: his first girlfriend had been half-Jewish. But why had the United States and Western Europe condemned Kurt Waldheim?

'Because Waldheim tried to refute his nazi past,' I said, although reality is a weak tool against indoctrination. 'He openly disseminated anti-Semitic propaganda during the war, but denied knowing that, a few kilometres away from where he was stationed in Yugoslavia, Serbian civilians were being horrifically massacred, and Jews were being sent to factories as slave labour, or to death camps.'

'But he became Austria's Ambassador to Canada and Secretary-General of the United Nations. And Pope John Paul II awarded him a knighthood,' said Udo, stoutly defending his former president. 'If he hadn't been a worthy man, he wouldn't have received such honours.'

By the time we left the café, the pension was closed for the night. Udo invited me to stay in the house he rented from Karcsi's mother. 'There are two rooms, eight beds.' It had started raining, and thankfully, he wouldn't hear of my sleeping in the fields.

In the morning, we returned to Ildikó's bar where Karcsi was waiting for us. Like the other Kumans present, he was knocking back glasses of breakfast pálinka chased by beer. We got into Udo's car, drove to the surprisingly large Jewish cemetery of Kunmadaras where gravestones were gripped in an inaccessible tangle of brambles. On a large memorial stone were the names of those who had perished in Auschwitz; quite a few were preceded by the title 'Doctor' – surprising for this insignificant town in Great Kumania, an area closed to Jewish settlement until 1867.

PART TWO : KUNMADARAS

We then drove to Kumania's main city, Karcag, twenty-five kilometres away, to see the synagogue. Impressively large but not elaborate, it stood on a street of neutral-looking communist-era housing blocks. To the right, a still-functioning open-air market harkened back to days when many sellers had been Jews. A short distance away, an empty lot of shattered brick indicated vanished buildings. What sort of buildings?

The synagogue's gate was locked, so I clambered over a sagging bit of chain-link fence, peered into the high windows, and saw long, hanging lamps, quite elegant. Was the building still being used? Were there still Jews here? But the faded ochre plaster fell in chunks from outside walls, and near the roof, high round windows were boarded up. Visibly ill at ease, both men stood at some distance.

We drove back to Kunmadaras. In the middle of town, Karcsi told Udo to stop beside a fluorescent-lemon house surrounded by an iron fence.

'Here's where the synagogue was.'

I stared at the awful villa. 'What happened to it?'

'My mother said it was pulled down in 1956.'

Back in Ildikó's bar, Karcsi ordered a round of pálinka. 'One Jew still lives here in Kunmadaras,' he said.

I felt the heady excitement of a detective stumbling upon an important clue. 'Who?'

'Mr Kohn. Do you want to meet him? He's eighty-six years old. Everyone likes him. He's a good man. His wife converted to Judaism when they married in the 1930s.'

Kohn lived in a tiny house right around the corner, fifty metres from the main square and the memorial with the Star of David, seventy meters from where the synagogue had once stood. Stick thin, he wore thick-lensed spectacles, but they were of no use: he was blind.

'Shalom,' I said.

'Shalom,' he answered. He didn't seem surprised by the greeting. But he spoke only Hungarian, and we had to converse through Karcsi. The room into which he admitted us had a rough plank floor, a worktable and a few ancient electrical machines. On one wall was a large photo. 'My mother,' said Kohn.

Karcsi indicated tools on the worktable. 'Even though he can't see, he repairs bicycles to make a little money.'

'Can he tell me about the 1946 pogrom?'

Dutifully, Karcsi translated.

'I know nothing,' Kohn answered.

'How did it begin? What happened after?' I disliked asking questions via Karcsi.

'There's nothing I can tell you.'

There was nothing he wanted to tell me. Did he prefer to forget? Perhaps the presence of Karcsi bothered him. Patiently, we stood there. Kohn was also patient; he was waiting for us to leave.

***

Karcsi invited me to meet his mother, the retired teacher. She could tell me about the Kunmadaras pogrom. She had been a young woman when it happened.

When we arrived at her house the next day, a banquet of homemade specialities waited on a long table: the traditional tepid soup with its thick layer of half-melted fat; blood sausage prepared with lard and rice; fried pork rinds; thick slices of raw white pork fat on larded bread; fried pig's ears. Also, fortunately, homemade pickles and homebrewed wine.

'Eat,' said Karcsi's mother. She, a soft-eyed woman, piled my plate high, and sensing my reticence, seemed hurt. 'You must taste authentic local food.'

Only after dinner was finished, did she mention the pogrom.

'It was started by people from somewhere else, from another town.' She shook her head, regretful, even ashamed. 'They arrived in a truck and began killing Jews. It was a terrible thing. The people of Kunmadaras are kind. They'd never do something like that. No one hated Jews back then. No one hates them now either.'

Because, aside from Kohn, there were none left?

VII

We had to stoop as we descended the steep stairs which led to the ball-room, whose walls were as black as those of a chimney, and whose only flooring was the trodden earth... and...I could not get out of my head the sickening scene of the low, dimly-lit cellar, with its gipsy musicians playing furiously on their violins, their white teeth shining under their large moustaches as they smiled, and its abandoned, half-drunken men and women, dancing their csárdás with fury as intemperate as though they were possessed by demons.

Victor Tissot, 1881

*I*dikó announced she would give a dinner in my honour – how often did Canadians show up in Kunmadaras? I was lucky, Udo said, for she was a most excellent cook. When we arrived at the kocsma that evening, she was hard at work over a hot plate. Helping her was close friend Kata, an exuberant blond in her late fifties dressed in a skintight top and mini-skirt.

All the scratched and rickety tables in the back room had been pushed together, covered with disparate cloths, and set with unmatched plates and unrelated cutlery. The air was fragrant with hot oil, fried garlic and spicy paprika, and huge serving plates were piled high with garlic-stuffed paprika chicken, breaded chicken stuffed with cheese, sugared noodles, fried fish caught that afternoon in the Tisza River, as well as a large tureen filled with fish soup sprinkled with paprika. It bothered no one that, in the worst environmental catastrophe since Chernobyl, Romanian mining discharge had recently polluted this river with heavy metals, cyanide, copper and zinc, thereby killing a great number of fish as well as cattle, foxes, otters and birds.

Other guests soon arrived, a few local friends, and a noisy

group from Püspokladány, some thirty kilometres distant: the usual party crowd, Udo explained. After considerable tippling at the bar, we all lurched our way into the back room with its glowing Christmas light heart and began feasting.

There was no question of discretion, certainly none of refinement: diners gobbled and sucked, pausing, occasionally, to dab with wrists at greasy juices seeping down chins. It was a throwback scene harkening to Brother Heribald IV's tenth century description in the Ekkehart Chronicles, when the Magyars invaded the (Carolingian, later Swiss) Saint Gallen monastery:

> *The Magyars drank a great quantity of wine that they brought with them, tore and devoured with their bare teeth the half-raw shoulder blades and other joints of cattle that they had slain. After the feast, they would cast the gnawed beef bones, in sport, at one another.*

And this modern banquet, although a private one, was also provocatively public. Customers who had been drinking in the front room – men with long, drooping moustaches and lumpy headgear, tired-out women in wilted housedresses – were not invited to join in. But lured by the aroma of browned herbs and hot foods, they clustered in the broad open doorway and, like hungry servants of a great house watching their masters feast, noted our over-filled plates, heard the clack of cutlery, the belches, slurps, grunts, then the moans of sated delight when dessert appeared. If I felt uncomfortable that I, a mere visitor, a non-paying guest, was the privileged recipient of generous excess, none of the others took the slightest notice of those excluded.

Drinking continued unabated: vodka (Kata knocked back at least eight of those), pálinka, a bitter herb alcohol called *Unicom*, beer, a ghastly chemical wine stored in clear plastic jugs. Then all stood, shoved tables and chairs against the wall, dimmed the lights, and turned up the sound on the jukebox in the corner. Time for dancing.

Here again were the old Hungarian tunes, but distorted by rock and techno. Yet all, those in the bar, those in the back room, knew the words, and they sang along, even as they danced – that word designating an elementary but highly energetic jumping from one foot to the other.

I was forced to join in, for no one was allowed to stay seated in Ildikó's back room, but after a while, exhausted from the mindless hopping about and keen to avoid the noxious groping fingers of a lusty little man from Püspokladány, I escaped to the bar. The moustachioed men were there still, markedly unsteady on their feet. Bálint (he hadn't been invited to the feast) was also present, and swaying drunkenly.

'Did you get the information you wanted about the pogrom?'

'I was told the perpetrators weren't from here.'

'That is correct. The Jews were killed by retreating German soldiers.'

'There weren't any German soldiers here in 1946.'

'Russian, then.' He turned, began talking to someone else.

The door opened, and three people entered, a man and two women, all dark-skinned, dark-haired Roma. There was a definite shift in the atmosphere. Ildikó's affable face became hard and unwelcoming. The gathering of men fell silent; even Karcsi's thick moustache bristled as he assumed an aggressive fighting stance. One of the Roma women strutted up to the bar, ordered drinks. Ildikó, mean-lipped, poured them out ungraciously.

'Everyone hates Gypsies in Hungary,' Udo murmured. 'Everyone.'

PART TWO : KUNMADARAS

The music was still blasting out from the back room and Kata, clearly a woman fond of jolly times, was bobbing and bumping around the dance floor with the itchy-fingered man. The Roma woman at the bar began snapping her fingers in time to the music. Then, turning, she looked at me and smiled. She was used to the blatant hostility, I realised. She never expected anything other than enmity.

She carried the drinks to the table where the other two were sitting, put down the glasses, and held out her hand. It was an invitation to dance. I accepted, of course, determined to defy local antipathy, and together we began moving. Her steps were far more sophisticated than silly hopping, to be sure, and aware she was on display, she executed trickier turns yet. The other Roma woman stood, joined us (the man was far too drink-sodden for such activity).

Ildikó watched with disapproval; the general displeasure of all was palpable, but the partying had not stopped. In a short time, everyone was ignoring us and laughing amongst themselves. The evening's easy atmosphere seemed to have been restored.

Nothing like music and laughter to kill hate, I told myself and knew, at the same time, how fatuous that thought was.

Those Absent

VIII

Popular absurdity has even gone the length of suspecting them, the Gypsies, of being cannibals; and though it is true they are everywhere accused of being thieves, nevertheless their thefts are trifling. Hunger sometimes impels them to shake an apple tree or to wring the neck of a goose; that is the utmost extent of their robbery, they never steal an object of value; nor are brigands found amongst them. They never steal children except in nursery rhymes. What a miserable acquisition the care of the sickly offspring of our towns would be to a people who have such quantities of children, so strong and so handsome, of their own!

Victor Tissot, 1881

'In Hungary, we don't like Gypsies,' said Karcsi, downing his umpteenth breakfast schnapps in the kocsma. 'There are too many. The Hungarian population is decreasing, but Gypsies never stop having children. Soon there will only be Gypsies here. They don't work. They steal chickens, fruit, vegetables, bicycles, anything they can get their hands on. In winter, they don't buy wood to heat their houses. They just go into people's gardens and saw off fruit trees at waist height. Can't be bothered bending down.'

'They steal everything,' said Ibolya, a brutal-looking, squat woman with short-cropped hair and an aggressive jaw. Occasionally employed in Germany in homes for the aged, her German was reasonable. 'My bicycle was stolen right outside this bar. I knew who took it too – a Gypsy. Two days later, what happened? That same Gypsy passed me on the street riding my bike. I recognised it, because the brakes were faulty and I'd attached a piece of cord to the line. Except the bike wasn't the right colour. He'd painted it green. I raced over, grabbed it. He denied he'd stolen it, but I wouldn't let him get away.

As we pushed and pulled, I noticed my hands felt sticky. Why? Because the green paint was still wet!'

'I've had three bicycles stolen by Gypsies,' said Karcsi, downing yet another schnapps. 'The last time, I knew exactly who did it. I went to his house with a few friends of mine, but the bicycle was gone. One hour later, and it had already been sold.'

'They have broods of children and get money from the government. Then, instead of paying for the school bus or school supplies, they spend the money on alcohol.'

Everyone in the kocsma – those who understood German – grunted with approval. By now I'd learned the word for Gypsy, *cigány*, and saw how its utterance provoked sneers.

'Is it easy for them to find work?'

'Who'd hire them? They're lazy. And these days, they're arrogant too.'

'Some of Hungary's most brilliant musicians have been Gypsies,' I said. 'They've had an enormous influence on the development of Hungarian classical music.'

Karcsi sneered. 'You want to hear good music? Go listen to the Hungarian musicians who play every evening in Berekfürdő, the town where you're staying.'

'You won't find Gypsies there either,' said Ibolya happily. 'If they show up, the police drive them out. If tourists saw any, they wouldn't rent the summer houses.'

Like Jews, Gypsies[43] (the Roma) were once blamed for the Black Death, cholera and other epidemics, and accused of kidnapping Christian children, of being in league with the devil, of cannibalism, of fraud ('the Jews rob us from above, the Gypsies from below.')

---

43   A misnomer, one arising from the incorrect belief that the Roma originated in Egypt.

Those Absent

Originating in northwest India as a conglomeration of many peoples – Tandas, Lohars, Gujjars, Rajputs – they were brought together as a warrior caste to fight Muslim incursions in the sixth or seventh century. Because of degenerating economic conditions, they began migrating through Armenian, Persian and Byzantine lands. Arriving in Europe long after the system of land use had been established, they were excluded from agriculture. Some settled on noble estates, others moved from village to village, one forest glade to the next, working as swine and horse herders, leatherworkers, woodworkers, metalworkers, smiths and makers of adobe bricks for house construction – this last is still a Roma occupation today.

Under communism, when mass-produced goods replaced handmade products, traditional work vanished. Expelled from villages, resettled in newly created urban tower blocks, the Roma were employed in factories and mines. Today, those factories are gutted, and the mines are defunct.

Sixty percent of Roma live below the poverty level, and their high birth rate causes resentment. Fewer than one-fifth of Roma children regularly attend elementary school; half drop out before the age of fourteen. Sent to Roma only schools, or placed in Roma classes, inferior education results in high unemployment. Even those with trade or vocational skills are shunted towards manual labour and paid less than non-Roma.

***

*E*ach morning in Berekfürdő, I watched a horde of bathrobe-clad holidaymakers waddle out of the disparate communist-era holiday villas and head for the spa baths, huge picnic hampers banging against their sturdy legs. The barrel-shaped women, the men with bellies of vast dimension, all spent the day soaking in the various pools: one where tepid water is chest high; one shallow but intensely hot; and one deeper and cooler, where, if there were room, a little paddle might have been contemplated.

When hungry, all delved into the hampers, pulled out thick loaves of white bread, glistening raw pork fat, sweating sausages and a plethora of sugary goods. For those still peckish, a mere wobble away were food booths where pork morsels sputtered in pork fat, cakes sweated under phosphorescent icing, and soft drinks, frothing beer or strong pálinka offered succour.

The country's baths are an Ottoman legacy, but by the seventeenth century, Hungarian nobles were opening their own, often luxurious, springs. The public flocked to them, as did all manner of quacks and sawbones, tooth extractors, healers of suppurating sores, administers of purgatives and appliers of leeches: the floors of these 'health emporiums' were a mess of blood, hair and infection. Today, perfectly clean, more popular than ever, the waters claim to cure sclerosis, post-operative ills, and to render the overweight sleek.

In the evenings, the modern holidaymakers repaired to tables outside the cafés on the main street and listened to live music. This, too, was the tail-end of a tradition: once itinerant musicians – Roma and Jews dressed as Roma – roved the countryside with violins, flutes, bagpipes or cimbaloms strapped to their backs, and entertained nobles, travellers and villagers. Others climbed into carriages and serenaded passengers for a few coins. When winter set in, they installed themselves in an inn's fusty nook and waited out the cold.

The most brilliant Roma musicians were part of an exclusive caste. Denied access to Hungary's music conservatories, they demonstrated their virtuosity at aristocratic balls and select dinners in elegant restaurants and hotels. When well paid by hopeful suitors, they would serenade marriageable women

Those Absent

under their bedroom windows.

Some made foreign marriages, enjoyed wealth and social success, but not all fairy tales end happily. The violinist Jancsi Rigó planned to marry a Belgian countess, however she abandoned her gypsy lover when common sense intervened. Violinist Elek Vörös captured the heart of a Parisian lady who was prepared to divorce her millionaire husband; but when she arrived in Hungary, she discovered her paramour already had a wife and many children.

Not everyone appreciated Roma musicians. Famous violinist Ede Reményi[44] was hateful:

> *If we want our national music to be spoken of with respect in educated circles abroad, we must strive, above all, in our homeland to take our fine music out of the hands of the many frothy, chaffy, tastelessly gaudy, dilettantish wild and virtuoso Gypsies, whose style is an affront to a deep sense of beauty, and to elevate it from the stinking morasses of the centuries in which they had sunken and still keep on sinking it through their distorted procedures.*

In this modest spa town where no Gypsies could enter, there were no Gypsy musicians. Karcsi's idea of good music was outmoded western pulp played on synthesizers and geared to the Hungarian tourist audience: Beatles, Sinatra, Mantovani, elevator music. All were complemented by electronic oom-cha-cha. From time to time, a musician veered into the traditional, but when he did so, there were boos, insults, howls of protest from the 'modern' holiday crowd. Traditional music with cimbaloms and violins was restricted to restaurants catering to foreign tourists and traditional dance halls.

Such rude behaviour is not new: 'Gypsy' musicians were ever expected to cater to the public's whims: to play while standing

---

[44] Franz Liszt's student, Reményi introduced Brahms to Hungarian music, and he was soloist to Queen Victoria and Emperor Franz Joseph.

on one leg; to stop and start on request; to mirror the reveller's mood, be it joyous or mournful; to submit to any humiliation. As brilliant and talented as many certainly were, they were members of a low caste.

Those Absent

IX

The square is crammed with buyers and sellers. Here anything can be exchanged, anything bought and sold. A soldier is hawking army bread, and another, army linen. A Jew is selling old umbrellas and frayed collars; a Jewess, old dresses. The customers put on straight away the articles of clothing they have bought. Others are bartering: they hand over some old rag or other for a roll of bread or a packet of cigarettes, and many a man leaves the market without his coat but the richer for a bottle of brandy. Trade here is pushed to the very frontier of decency; you can barter anything, that is to say, but your trousers (for, according to the law, you aren't to appear in the market without your trousers).

Sholem Asch,[45] 1917

'When the Russian Air Force had their base here in Kunmadaras, those were good times,' said Tarzan, a hugely fat man with long, drooping moustaches, and the over-developed biceps that had gained him his nickname. 'You could get anything by trading in those days, caviar for pálinka, vodka for wood, chocolate for diesel fuel.'

Tarzan knew. He had been a big shot back then, a man respected because he was friends with the occupying Russians, had an 'in' with them, could get his happy black marketeer's hands on anything not tied down, and a good deal of anything that was.

'We lived better when the Russians were here. Now that they're gone, people are poorer. There's no restaurant here because no one can afford to eat out, there are no hotels, there's nothing going on. Back then, the population of Kunmadaras was 8,000; today, it's 4,000.' He looked tragic, although the emotion didn't reach his eyes; those remained hard, calculating.

---

[45] *Motke the Thief.* Sholem Asch, 1880-1957, Polish-Jewish novelist and essayist.

PART TWO : KUNMADARAS

'In the good old days, I smuggled caviar into Vienna.'

'Which he sold on the black market.' Udo winked with sly complicity, for his own Viennese apartment had been Tarzan's base.

'Fine Russian caviar, and Russian champagne.' Tarzan chuckled. 'The good old days.' Those days were over. Townsfolk now considered Tarzan a traitor, someone who had traded with Russian communist occupiers.

Tarzan, a non-Roma, Mariska, his Roma second wife, their two grubby young children and Imre, Tarzan's adult son from a previous marriage, all lived in a cinder-block box of a house at the shabby end of Kunmadaras, on the back streets of the Roma quarter. There was a front yard of sticky mud, rubble and smashed toys; in one far corner, a huge and doleful Rottweiler on a pitifully short chain passed his life in a metal barrel. Rooms inside the house were filled with defeated sticks of furniture, and rotting clothes were tossed into corners.

It was a scene of reeking, filthy poverty, although Tarzan had a decent job as night watchman, working shifts all over the country. While he was gone, Mariska frittered away the household money on slot machines. Because bills were left unpaid, it was Udo, the good Westerner, the loyal friend of twenty years, who helped out, handing over the cash for electricity and water. He also brought huge bags of barely-used clothing, family rejects he managed to rescue before his wife's sharp scissors could cut them into shreds (she would never let 'parasites' profit from an Austrian's hard-earned salary). Tarzan never did pay back the money Udo lent him. That didn't matter. Tarzan was his best friend.

'He does me favours.'

'Such as?'

Those Absent

Udo's fuchsia-stained face was moist. 'He introduces me to attractive women.'

'That you pay for?'

'Well… only once.' He squirmed. 'Tarzan introduced me to a nice girl. I thought she liked me, and I took her out to dinner, then brought her back to my room. The next morning, she told me how much I owed her. I hadn't expected that.'

We sat in Tarzan's kitchen on a hideous, upholstered 'cosy-corner' bench at a nearly new kitchen table – both recent gifts from Udo. But in Tarzan's house, all degraded quickly. The table was already battered, sticky; from a fat-encrusted stove mere inches away, a seething pot of offal, paprika and onions sent jets of greasy sauce onto the cosy-corner's flower print cushions.

Tarzan and Udo conversed in a strange German mixed with Russian, Hungarian, English and nonsense words, a passe-partout language concocted over the years. Tarzan was complaining about Mariska in a sad, self-pitying way: he couldn't control her loose-fingered relationship with money; he didn't know if she was faithful to him. When he was away, she returned to Roma society, to her pipe-smoking mother's house. 'I only stay with her because of the children,' he said mournfully.

This was clearly untrue. It was a statement made to save face. In reality, Tarzan was fascinated by Mariska's great beauty and enslaved by her indifference. He was also a jealous man, and when I offered to take Mariska's photo, he became cold and forbidding.

'I don't want her to get ideas.'

Tarzan and Mariska had met during his successful days when, apart from smuggling caviar, he had deep-fried sausages and other fatty meats at his popular, fast food stand. Attracted by such material success, Mariska had sashayed up and down the dirt road, flashing him looks rich with seductive promise. He soon abandoned his alcoholic first wife, who never left her bed, and took up with this woman, twenty-five years his junior.

But the fast food concern was no more, and caviar smuggling had ended with Russian military withdrawal. When Tarzan's status declined, so did Mariska's. She found days of household chores and parenthood a bore. Now, her luxuriant black hair falling to her waist, she lounged in the doorway of the oily kitchen. She knew no German, no Russian and no English, but watched us intently as though, by mere observation, she could understand the conversation. She would not sit with us on the cosy corner.

'Can you tell me anything about the pogrom of 1946?' I asked Tarzan. I was determined to question everyone I met. Someone had to know something.

Tarzan examined a smudge on the far wall. 'I heard about it.'

'Have you any details?'

'No.' He turned to Udo, as if seeking help. 'Do you remember when we went drinking with the Russian soldiers?'

'Hard drinkers, those Russians,' said Udo to me. 'We'd go out to their cabana on the edge of town, and they'd fill our glasses with vodka. As soon as we finished one glass, we had to drink another. And another. There was no way we could refuse.'

Dewy-eyed, Tarzan pulled out more anecdotes, warm, sweet morsels, all that remained of the glorious past. 'Money grew on trees back then.' He sighed with deep melancholy, before, again, becoming perky. 'Of course, there are still deals to be made. Good deals. If you're clever enough.' He recounted how,

Those Absent

as night watchman, he siphoned off diesel fuel from company trucks, spirited away sacks of animal feed, then sold the booty here in town.

'You come, see where I'm working. It's near Kunhegyes. A big company. I'll show you around. And when you want animal feed or diesel fuel, come to me. Tarzan's the man you need to know.' He chuckled. Sobered. 'Still, it's not the same. The Russians, everyone liked them. They were fun. You could trade with them. Do real business.'

Udo wanted to show me where the Russian's cabana stood, where so many amusing nights had been passed swilling down vodka. We drove down a dirt trail, parked, set out on foot into the brackish green swampland. Mosquitoes and midges swirled around us in a crazed, starved frenzy; a beautiful black snake nonchalantly crossed our path before slipping into the rushes.

Little of the cabana remained: a few rotting poles, a collapsed thatched roof. All was sinking slowly into a moist, weedy tangle.

PART THREE:
Returning

Nearly one half of Hungary's arable land is cultivated by the servants of the Puszta. In morals, customs, outlook on life – in the very way they walk or move their arms – this social stratum differs sharply from any other. Hidden, tucked away, beyond the villages even, they live in complete isolation. Due to their day-long labours, not excluding Sundays, they hardly ever leave the Puszta. To seek them out in their habitat, I submit, is a more difficult undertaking than to study a Central African tribe – on account of the long distances, the bad roads, the peculiar Hungarian conditions, and also their primordial distrust of outsiders.

Gyula Illyés,[46] 1936

---

46   *Ceux des Pusztas*. Gyula Illyés, 1902-1983, Hungarian poet, novelist and spokesman for the oppressed peasantry.

Those Absent

X

A very strange being indeed is the Magyar peasant, mysterious as his country's history; he has sympathy with gloom and melancholy reveries, and is fond of brooding in a seeming lethargy when his heart is ready to kindle with all the fire of a crusader. When free from his daily labour, in his happiest moments, he is marked by sudden transitions. Apparently happy, he quickly becomes sad, soon to burst forth into exultation, only to plunge again into grief, which always marks the end of his frolicsome episodes. He is not easy to cheer with incitements, which put heart into other people, for he does not readily respond to this sort of thing. There is a saying that the 'Hungarian enjoys life with weeping eyes'.

Geraldine Mitton, 1915

*I*n November, while I was in Austria photographing what was left of the vibrant pre-war Jewish community, Udo phoned. He was going to Kunmadaras for a holiday. Was I still interested in getting information about the pogrom? If so, we could meet in Vienna and drive to Hungary together.

It was another Puszta that greeted us: minus golden sunflowers and military lines of corn, fallow fields were sodden, and wispy fog tickled frozen grasses and blackened reeds. I was pleased to return, for I had fond memories of this bleakly majestic flatland, of Ildikó's shabby, welcoming kocsma and the easy friendships.

Most compelling for a curious (even nosey) person was being allowed to penetrate this unfamiliar, exotic microcosm: Hungarian provincial society. I knew that such cursory admittance could never help me understand the past or find a vanished Jewish world. For that, much time, patience, and at least a rudimentary understanding of the language would be necessary, but I was willing to take up the challenge.

We advanced cautiously along the uneven roads, for

Udo's car was laden with family rejects: a huge television, a play station, practically new jogging suits, children's clothing, sweaters, skirts, a heavy fine winter coat, a cocktail table and yet another cosy-corner seating arrangement. All was destined for best crony Tarzan. And if Tarzan was waiting for us on the shattered lane in front of his house, the entire Roma neighbourhood was equally present: older women sitting on the hard, cold ground, their feet dangling in ditches; hormone-driven young males smoking cigarettes; females lounging, weight on one hip, shaking back dark glossy curls; unsteady, weathered men ravaged by alcohol.

Tarzan greeted me as a dear friend, kissing me on both cheeks, ushering me into that greasy kitchen of his. Mariska, not in the least welcoming, remained standing in the doorway, her eyes mocking.

Nothing had changed since my last visit: the two children were as filthy as before; clothing was still stuffed into corners; the black pot was ever on the hob, and its contents, a pong of fat, entrails and paprika, burped enthusiastically. Tarzan and Udo, beamingly pleased to be together, conversing in their mad mixture of cartoon sounds and assorted languages, understood each other perfectly.

After forcing down an artificial cappuccino, we trooped outside to unload the car whilst the indolent Mariska remained in her doorway. Imre, Tarzan's eighteen-year-old son was hardly more useful: sly-looking, lethargic, he slipped outside, lifted a box, put it down again, lit a cigarette, skulked back into the house. Certainly, Tarzan and Udo didn't require my help, but lugging things through the sucking mud of the littered yard seemed a more pleasant activity than sitting on the oily cosy-corner and being stared at by Mariska and Imre.

Those Absent

When all the goods were safely stashed, Tarzan, Udo and I walked a few streets over to a kocsma. Which is when I opened my purse and discovered my wallet was missing. Hadn't it been in my handbag when we'd arrived at Tarzan's house? Of course, it had. But where had my handbag been while we were unloading the car? On the cosy-corner in the kitchen.

'Mariska,' Tarzan hissed, and he barrelled out of the bar, heading for home. Udo and I followed, but the house was dark. Mariska and Imre were nowhere to be found. We searched everywhere, inside the house, under the cosy-corner, in the yard, inside Udo's car. The wallet was gone.

'Mariska.' Tarzan's face was pale with fury. 'She took it. I'm sure she did. When we were busy bringing in the furniture. She steals. She steals everywhere she goes. Even steals the child support we receive, spends it on slot machines.'

'You can't say a thing like that about your own wife,' tempered Udo, the very man who had been paying Tarzan's outstanding bills for years.

'This time she's gone too far, stealing from my friends, I'll kill her. I'll get the wallet back first. I can't stand it anymore, living like this. She doesn't even take care of the children properly. She's a bad woman.'

'Perhaps you shouldn't accuse Mariska,' I said. 'There's no proof.' I noticed he hadn't questioned the honesty of his son, Imre, who'd certainly had both time and opportunity to search my handbag. It was a distressing, embarrassing situation. He wouldn't really kill Mariska, would he?

'I'll get the wallet back for you,' said Tarzan. 'I promise, you'll have it tomorrow.' He stormed down the road.

***

PART THREE : RETURNING

*T*arzan was a sad creature the next day. We met him in another kocsma, one around the corner from his house where, according to Udo, he passed much of his time. It was a rough and frowsy neon-lit place, reeking of alcohol, cigarette stubs and urine. The owner was hard-faced; the drooping men and women around the gummy counter were serious drinkers.

Tarzan clacked three glasses of rotgut down on our table and watched us with melancholy puppy-dog eyes. 'I asked her again and again. All night, I asked her. Mariska claims she didn't take the wallet. I held a gun to her head, said I'd shoot her if she didn't confess.'

'You did what?' I was appalled.

'No one steals from my best friend's friend.'

'Please, it's not worth violence.'

'She lies,' said Tarzan.

'Maybe she's telling the truth.' I'd already cancelled my bankcard, would have to replace my driver's license, and write off the cash I'd been carrying.

'Perhaps,' said Tarzan glumly. But he was also looking somewhat relieved. 'Anyway, it's not in the house. I searched everywhere. When she steals things, she takes them to her mother's. Once there, you never see them again.'

'We'll forget the whole thing,' said Udo gallantly, as if the wallet had been his, not mine.

'You really mean that?' asked Tarzan.

'Of course.'

Instantly, the puppy-dog despondency vanished, was replaced by concupiscent triumph. 'Making up was good.' Tarzan's snigger was lascivious. 'She knows how to please me, do the things I like.' He pointed to his crotch. 'Tarzan's an old man, but down here, everything's in working order.'

By the time we left him, he was truly happy.

Udo was uncomfortable. 'This isn't the first crisis in our friendship. Two years ago, I came to Hungary with my eldest son. Tarzan was out of town, but we invited Mariska and Imre to come for a pizza in Kunhegyes. I didn't realise you can't do things like that here. The pizza restaurant was partly a disco, and the kids liked that. When Tarzan heard about it, it was as if I'd asked his woman to go on a date with me. Afterward, Mariska lied to him, said I'd tried to seduce her. I found myself in a dangerous situation. Tarzan wanted to kill me.'

'What happened?'

'We worked things out. Tarzan is my best friend. I love him, and he loves me.'

PART THREE : RETURNING

XI

The dance opens with a stately promenade; then, as the music quickens, each couple takes a twirl or two, and breaking away brusquely from one another, continue a series of pantomimic movements, now approaching coquettishly, like parted lovers desiring reconciliation, then, as if the lady thought she had given sufficient encouragement, she retreats with rapid but measured steps, while her partner pursues, and gradually gaining on her again seizes her waist; they whirl swiftly round two or three times, and then breaking away, recommence the pantomime as before. What makes the csárdás unrivalled as a spectacle is its variety. One seldom sees two couples performing exactly the same figure at the same time. While two separated partners are doing their steps with their backs turned to one another, another couple between them are spinning round in ecstasies of reunion.

Arthur John Patterson, 1869

*I*n Ildikó's kocsma, Karcsi and the modern Kumans were still in position at the tables, at the bar, and at the slot machines: women in shabby trousers, topped by frazzled blouses, topped by housedresses of faded colour, topped by tired cardigans; moustached men in ragged work clothes and odd headgear. Many greeted me as if I were a beloved friend of long standing, one who had 'come home' to Kunmadaras.

'A Canadian coming here to a small Hungarian town? Well, that's something! Hungarians, they go to Canada and never return. Now you are one of us.'

The ineluctably stylish younger people were more blasé: Enikö, Ildikó's exotic and beautiful daughter, a direct descendant of eastern hordes with slanting eyes and jet-black hair; Gabika, an artificial-looking anorexic girl who dreamt of modelling.

Those Absent

The two young women played at boredom when a gaggle of youths sporting trendy haircuts meandered into the kocsma, lounged in front of the jukebox and feigned equal indifference.

Kata, her blond hair frizzled into fashion circa 1962, sat at the back table and read palms, simpering as she traced men's lines with her forefinger. They all looked mighty chuffed when she finished: evidently, their futures held great promise. Women were less fortunate. With them, Kata shook her head in sympathetic grief.

Soon, two strange-looking and shaggy men arrived in the bar, cowherds, the genuine item, not the colourfully clean stuff of tourist brochures. Like their forebears, they spent days, sometimes nights, out on the Puszta in lean-tos of twigs, reeds, and ragged cloths near sweep-wells that are, traditionally, half a day's walk from each other.

Not so long ago, such herdsmen, living outside village life and norms, were believed to possess special powers. Many swore they had seen swineherds miraculously pull piglets from the sleeves of their sheepskin cloaks, had heard ghostly bagpipes when in their presence. Herdsmen were adept at manipulating the evil eye, casting spells and avoiding attacks by dogs. They knew better than to beat to death or hang creatures of ill omen – spotted dogs and black cats – thereby putting at risk their stock and family members.

After enough pálinka, these two – perhaps less magical – herders slung their arms about one another and burst into drunken but harmonious ancient song, effectively drowning out the jukebox's commercial pop. Ildikó was disparaging. The others grinned with condescension. Only Udo and I tarried, enchanted. Seeing our rapture, the tipsy herders sang more lustily.

The show ended with the arrival of Ildikó's husband, Józsi, the musician. In he strutted, a portly, clean-shaven man with grey-streaked hair and prominent eastern cheekbones. His was truly the entrance of a star: head high, narrow eyes glancing left and right in anticipation of applause. And those in the kocsma were certainly admiring.

'He's a wonderful musician,' Karcsi gushed. 'Famous, too.'

Józsi greeted Udo enthusiastically, bent low and kissed my hand. 'Welcome,' he said in German. 'Welcome to the land of my ancestors.'

'You're a musician,' I said.

'Yes.' His smile was falsely modest.

'What instrument do you play?' I asked, hoping for a violin, a cimbalom or a contrabass.

'Synthesizer.'

'Hungarian music?'

Józsi snorted. 'What is Hungarian music? It's garbage. I play good music. World Music. Film themes, pop tunes: Beatles, Sinatra. Modern Hungarians want World Music.'

'Traditional Hungarian music is beautiful. It's loved all over the world,' I said.

But Józsi, a modern man, was disdainful: 'No one wants that stuff, believe me. I've lived here all my life. My family has been in Kunmadaras for eight hundred years. I am a true Kuman. A pure Kuman. You know what a Kuman is?'

'Of course I do,' I said. 'But pure Kuman? No one can say they are pure anything.' The end of Kuman identity was long ago forecast by the conversion and marriage of Kuman Princess Erzsébet to Magyar King Béla's son. Like the Pechenegs before them, the Kumans eventually settled down, intermarried,

Those Absent

adopted local attire, customs, settlement structures and Christianity.[47] By the mid-1700s, their language had vanished, although, in a moment of widespread ethnic nationalism, a faulty Kuman version of the Lord's Prayer was put into print, and pseudo-Kuman dances appeared.

'We Kumans have always kept ourselves separate as a people,' Józsi insisted. 'And we were never serfs, but independent.'

Ever polite, I nodded. Yet, just that morning, I had read that fourteenth-century Kunmadaras had been a vast estate belonging to György Madaras, a Jász-Kuman descendant, and once-proud Kuman clansmen had become his serfs.

The 'civilising' of Hungary meant cutting clan property into units ruled by noble chiefs. The king's kinfolk and the church took possession of great stretches of land, built forbidding fortified castles and replaced slaves with serfs. Slaves had been easy to come by in the days of war and pillage, but when the Vikings, notorious slave takers, settled down to farming, the supply dried up. Slaves didn't reproduce sufficiently anyway, and raising them from babyhood to usefulness took time. They were exchanged for society's poorest: herdsmen, impoverished freemen, Slavs, Pechenegs and Kumans with no claim to land.

Mere possessions, barely considered human, branded like livestock and condemned to eternal bondage, serfs cultivated a noble's fields, owed him military duty and yearly fees. Were a noble evil, his serfs lived in misery. A serf could take flight, claiming sanctuary at the gate of a more humane lord, but if captured before reaching safety, he was tortured, his hair burnt off and his nose slit.

In 1514, György Dózsa, squire, soldier of fortune with

---
47 Whereas the Jász resisted integration longer by living in outlying *tányas*, small, isolated farms. As late as the early twentieth century, they still dressed in traditional costumes that differentiated cattle, sheep and geese breeders.

a reputation for valour, was appointed to organize a crusade against the Turks. His soldiers were serfs. While drilling them into discipline, he heard their grievances: the nobles had not supplied them with food or clothing, but, as harvest approached, had ordered them back to the fields. If they resisted, their wives and daughters were mistreated.

When the Turkish campaign was cancelled, Dózsa lost control of his men. Joined by townspeople, they rampaged over the country, burning castles and manors, impaling and crucifying thousands of nobles. Mercenaries from Venice, Rome and Bohemia quelled the rebellion, and György Dózsa was condemned to sit on a red-hot iron throne. His starved followers devoured his carcass. And just then, when the rift between noble and peasant was at its widest, the Ottomans attacked.

***

Autumn meant *szüret*, the moment when new grapes are harvested and pressed for wine. It also meant a feast at Karcsi's mother's house.

'Tonight, music. Józsi play music. Good music,' said Kata, ever the fun girl.

'Józsi plays modern music,' I said. 'I like the older music.'

'Gypsy music. People no want. Only in one kocsma is music with accordions, violins, cimbaloms. People dance… csárdás.' She stopped in the middle of the dirt path between two rows of grapevines, took my hand and led me in a dusty dance, one step forward, one back, one sideways, sideways again. 'Csárdás dance in kocsma.'

'What kocsma?' I asked. Her truncated pidgin sprinkled with the odd German word wasn't easy to understand.

Those Absent

'Before. Ten years.' She waved one hand. 'Outside town. Now gone. People like modern.'

Ten years? Not so long ago, and I'd missed it. But even as early as 1907, the writer L. Schlosz witnessed the growing disregard for Hungarian culture and predicted the doom of Jewish and Roma musicians.[48]

The only locals invited to Karcsi's party were Ildikó, Kata, one or two others, for szüret is a family gathering. Noisy relatives from the west of Hungary had arrived, and packed into the glassed-in veranda, they were stacking plates high with pickles, cakes and fried, boiled and ground chunks of the just-slaughtered family pig, then heading for trestle tables in the ancient vaulted wine cellar. From a little niche in the stairwell, a flushed and tipsy Józsi pounded out *Strangers in the Night, These Boots Are Made for Walking,* and *California Here I Come* on his synthesizer.

'What would you like me to play?' he called to me.

'Hungarian music.'

'Hungarian music is shit. I play World Music.'

'What's really important is that this tradition of szüret remains,' said Udo with starry-eyed optimism. 'Don't worry. Hungarians won't modernise too much. They're too smart for that.'

When sated, we all lumbered back upstairs to the glassed-in terrace with its floor of white industrial tiles. Józsi and synthesizer followed: time for dancing. What steps does one do to *My Way* with an oom-cha-cha beat? No one seemed to know. So, hand-in-hand, we formed a human chain and wove mindlessly between and around the wallpapered pillars.

---

48 *Mitteilung zur Jüdischen Volkskunde.* Schlosz, L. Rimaszombat, 1907, volume 3.

PART THREE : RETURNING

XII

Apart as the Jews have kept themselves after centuries of degradation, and still impressed with the stamp of their national physiognomy, they have nevertheless become Europeans, naturalized by the many interests and pursuits, which they have in common with those who surround them.

Theresa Pulszky,[49] 1850

'Ildikó's landlady has something to tell you,' said the brutal-looking Ibolya who was friendly enough when in the mood to practice her German. 'I'll translate.'

The red-haired elderly landlady – she who had first pulled me into this bar – was perched on a stool and watching me with excited eyes. 'I thought you'd be interested. This kocsma was a Jewish bakery before the war. There were many Jewish-owned shops here in town, a shoe shop and a grocery. The ironmongery on the main street belonged to a Jew, the barbershop on the corner was Jewish-owned, and further along was Jewish Farkas' shop '.

'And where are those Jews now?'

'Some didn't come back after the war, the others left town. The family that owned this bakery died in Auschwitz, and the communists took over the building. Later, my husband and I bought it.'

What was the Jewish baker's name? What did she know about him? But either Ibolya's translating skills were unequal to the task, or the landlady had nothing else she wanted to share. Smiling, she said in pidgin Hungarian, 'Many Jews before. Good people. Good, good.'

---

49 *Memoirs of a Hungarian Lady.* Theresa Pulszky 1819 – 1866 was an Austro-Hungarian author, translator and musician. Forced to flee Hungary during the Revolution of 1848, she took up residence in London.

Those Absent

I prowled through the kocsma, but there was no sign that it had been Jewish-owned, there were no holes in doorposts where mezuzahs might have been placed, and nothing showed it had been a bakery.

'Why are you asking everyone about the pogrom?' asked Ibolya who had followed me. 'Everyone knows it happened during the war. That's when Jews were killed by the Germans.'

'The pogrom took place after the war,' I said.

Ibolya smirked, certain she was correct. 'It was during the war.' Convinced I'd got it all wrong, she asked Ildikó for a pen and paper. Handed both to me. 'Write the date.'

I jotted down, May 21, 1946.

'No,' she said. Crossed out 1946 and wrote, 1944. I shook my head, and she replaced her smirk with a belligerent scowl. 'There was nothing in 1946. The Jews came back. Nothing happened to them after that.'

'There's a memorial in the middle of town, and you pass it every day. We can go look at it now.' Outside, it was dark but, by the light of street lamps, it would still be possible to read the words carved into the stone plaque.

Ibolya left me, went to the far end of the bar and began chatting to others. The subject was closed.

An hour later, to my surprise, she came back to where I was sitting. 'Shall we go to the memorial?' She was smug. Had she discussed the subject with the others? Had they also said the pogrom had taken place in 1944?

We pulled on our coats and went out into the night, crossing the road at the town hall, going up to the memorial with its Star of David. I sat on the parapet, while Ibolya went to the tablet. She peered at the inscription, then sat down beside me.

'You have to understand,' she said. 'People hate Jews because they're all rich.'

'You think I'm rich?'

'Of course not. Not you. You are pure Jewish?'

Whatever 'pure' means. 'Yes, I'm Jewish, and there are poor Jews in the world, too. There always have been. Jews are as rich or poor as everyone else.'

'That's not true. Jews are rich. Always. Even back then.'

'Education was important to Jews. They knew if they educated their children, they might have a better chance of getting a good job, earning a decent living.'

'Kohn. Look at Kohn,' she said.

'Kohn is a poor man.'

'No!' Her snicker was triumphant. 'Kohn is rich. Everyone in Kunmadaras knows.'

'He lives in a simple house. To make extra money, he repairs bicycles although he's blind. How can you say he's rich?'

'It's all for show. He has piles of money hidden away. He lives in that house so people will think he's poor, but he's rich like all Jews. Look at this country. Who runs it? The Jews. They're the politicians. They own the banks. They own the big companies. They're professors in the universities. They control everything.'

'There are certainly some Jewish politicians and bankers and professors. There are far more Christian bankers, professors and politicians.' I was wasting my breath. Her hatred wasn't the result of rational thought. Jews were accused of controlling the economy when most lived in poverty; they were hated communists at the same time that they were hated capitalists. For Ibolya, non-Jews are the victims of Jews, a sentiment born of resentment: she'd been left behind by birth, luck and education. Someone had to be responsible.

Those Absent

'The Jews want to destroy our society,' Ibolya insisted. 'In Hungary, we're controlled by Jews. Jews always do better than Hungarians.'

'Why do you think that happens?'

'Because they're smarter than we are, that's why.'

I tried not to laugh. 'Then you should be pleased that smart people are running your country.'

We returned to the bar. Years have passed, and Jews, aside from Kohn, were gone from this town. But the jealousy remained.

***

After long cohabitation in Khazaria,[50] Jews were an accepted people in early Magyar society. Holding high positions in economic institutions, minting the kingdom's coins, when the foreign Crusaders invaded, King Koloman sent out armies to quash them.[51] After such a strong show, those persecuted elsewhere flowed into the country. This was much to Koloman's convenience, for the hefty Jewish protection tax filled his coffers.

With the death of the last Árpád king in 1301, papal pressure brought an end to tolerance. Under zealous Anjou rulers, there was persecution, then expulsion. When Jews returned in 1381, Catholic hatred was firing the medieval mind: Jews, yellow-skinned or dark and swarthy, didn't resemble human beings.

---

50 Turkic Khazaria stretched from the Caspian to the Black Sea. A buffer state between the Islamic and Christian worlds, the Khagan (king) and ruling class adopted Judaism in 740 CE. In 970, the Rus under Svyatoslav, Prince of Kiev, joined with Pechenegs to shatter Khazaria – a great mistake. One year later, Pechenegs murdered Svyatoslav and drank a toast from his skull. Khazaria struggled on, but the diaspora to Byzantium, Central and Eastern Europe had begun.

51 One Khabar descendant, Samuel, was crowned third Hungarian king in 1041, and his name suggests he might have been Jewish. Khazars soon blended into the European population, and if they remained Jewish is unknown (Arthur Koestler claimed they did). There are traces of Khazarian residence in Hungarian vocabulary; Szombat the word for Saturday means Sabbath.

They had massive heads, enormous mouths, protruding eyes, pig bristle eyelashes, huge ears, crooked feet and asymmetrical bodies. Their hands hung below their knees; their skin was covered with shapeless warts. They were cheats, jealous, lazy, dirty, mean, weak and repulsive. Instruments of the devil, they refused pork because they were pigs. They lived longer than Christians, suffered less from cholera, leprosy and smallpox. Jews consumed Christian blood and used it in their rituals. As John Chrysostom (347-407), considered one of the eminent Church doctors, wrote, in his *Eight Homilies Against the Jews:*

> *The Jews sacrifice their children to Satan... they are worse than wild beasts. The synagogue is a brothel, a den of scoundrels, the temple of demons devoted to idolatrous cults, a place of meeting for the assassins of Christ, a house of ill fame, a dwelling of iniquity, a gulf and abyss of perdition.*

Locked into ghettos, forbidden to own land, excluded from guilds, Jews could excel in one field: money lending. Because a Jewish occupation, usury became a sordid word, yet Christians, even Church officials, secretly practised it and used Jews as fronts. The wealthiest moneylenders loaned to aristocrats, to the royal and ecclesiastical courts; petty lenders – many were women – made enough to feed their families. In a world where liquid cash was a rarity, possessing it could mean survival. But when official coffers were empty, when Christian debtors were disinclined to repay loans and shopkeepers wished to destroy Jewish rivals, charges of blood libel and profanation of the host were levelled.

Did Jews revolt at this ill treatment? No. God loved them but punished them as a parent would a wayward child. They were to remain humble, keep their eyes to the ground. As Rabbi Moïse of Evreux instructed:

> *Only your heart should reach towards heaven.*

Those Absent

***

We returned to the kocsma, found Karcsi sitting in the back room. Ibolya and I joined him.

'Ibolya tells me that Kohn is rich and has piles of money hidden away,' I said.

Karcsi stared at her for a minute, then asked in German, 'Rich? Who told you that?'

'Everyone knows it,' she answered calmly. 'All Jews are rich.'

Karcsi said something to her in Hungarian, but Ibolya riposted in German. She was certain she would win the argument, and she wanted me to hear it. 'Look at Kohn's daughter. You've seen the big house she lives in. If Kohn isn't rich, how can his daughter live like that?'

Karcsi leaned forward, his face red. 'She went to university, and she works two jobs, that's how. She runs the grocery store in the day, works as an accountant in the evening. If you work hard, you make money. That's how it should be.'

They lapsed into Hungarian, and I could no longer follow. Karcsi was angry. Yet, even without his backing, Ibolya remained obdurate. She had centuries of hatred on her side.

PART THREE : RETURNING

XIII

The soldiers' [of the Ottoman armies] discipline under arms is due to their justice and severity, which surpasses that of the ancient Romans. They surpass our soldiers for three reasons: they obey their commanders without question: they seem to care nothing at all for their lives in battle: they go for a long time without bread or wine, being content with barley and water.

Paolo Giovio,[52] 1521

*H*aving promised Tarzan we would visit him at his place of work, Udo and I drove out in a higgledy-piggledy way, passing through one village after another. All had multicoloured square villas with PVC windows and roll-down shutters, shattered pavements and slinking strays with jutting ribs.

In a weedy field in Kunhegyes, I found an abandoned synagogue. Heavy beams propped up an outside wall; wooden doors sagged open; rows of benches waited for long-dead worshippers. Dating from the 1880s, it was beautifully decorated with painted lions, flowers and scenes of a fanciful Promised Land. The building could still be saved, I thought. Its beauty could be easily revived. Perhaps there were no longer Jews here.

Beyond villages, the frozen steppe rolled unhindered to a grey horizon, was interrupted only once by another ruin, that

---

52   *La prima parte dell'historie del suo tempo.* Paolo Giovio, 1483-1552, Italian physician, biographer and prelate.

of a high tower half-hidden by a smudge of leafless trees. What was that place? We would ask Tarzan.

In his capacity as security guard, Tarzan passed the time in a hut beside a dirt yard swept by wind and covered in icy puddles. Alongside warehouses stood a few trucks, antiquated models, battered and grimy. Tarzan emerged when we pulled up, and I could see that, on duty, he was a changed man. No longer affable or jovial, he was a man with a position of responsibility, a stern watchdog of the most determined sort. Nothing sneaky would get past him, you could see that by the hostile set of his flabby jowls. Barely polite, even to Udo, his very best friend in the whole world, his eyes, always cold, were slits of pit-bull suspicion. His head was arrogantly thrown back, and his mouth turned downward with haughty disapproval.

'I'll give you a tour,' he said stiffly. 'Of course, you'll want to see everything.'

Discomfited, Udo and I made polite noises.

Tarzan led us into the first building. 'This warehouse is filled with sacks of animal feed.'

Udo and I admired the piled bags and mumbled, 'hum-m-m,' in unison.

Tarzan took us back into the yard and stopped before the trucks so we could best appreciate the view. 'These vehicles transport sacks of feed.'

'Whooh,' we said.

We shuffled on to the second warehouse, also filled with sacks of animal feed. Then a third. Each time Tarzan expected a reaction, so turning this way and that, frowning appreciatively and nodding wisely, we emitted more onomatopoeic noise.

This, of course, was the same place from which Tarzan

filched diesel fuel, siphoning it out of the trucks in the evening when no one was around; these were the sacks of animal feed he spirited away and sold privately in Kunmadaras. Did the company even suspect their watchman? Did they realise things went missing? Perhaps this was an accepted practice: one dog eating its fill at his master's table, then strutting about the yard and keeping hungry homeless mutts at bay. Tarzan came to a halt at Udo's car. Clearly, hospitality was over.

'We passed a tower on the way here,' I said. 'A tall, ruined tower in a line of trees, only a few kilometres away. Do you know what it is – or was?'

Tarzan was uneasy for a minute or two. He had no answer to this question, yet felt he had to offer something impressive. 'Roman,' he said finally.

'Roman?' I said, embarrassed for him. 'The Romans weren't out here.' Emperor Tiberius invaded western Hungary in 8 BCE and created the state of Pannonia. In its up-to-date cities, there were heated floors, houses with running water, temples decorated by mosaics, frescoes and statues. But this Puszta remained a wild land inhabited by fierce Iranian Iazyges.

'Roman,' Tarzan confirmed. 'Definitely Roman. No question about it.' He wasn't about to be contradicted by a foreigner, especially a female foreigner.

As we climbed into the car, Tarzan watched with an absent expression. He was thinking hard. 'Maybe Ottoman,' he added before I closed the door. 'Either Turkish or Roman.'

A teensy leeway of almost 1,500 years.

Udo turned the car around, edged toward the entry gate. Tarzan followed, motioned for me to open the window. 'You'll meet my daughter, Zsuzsa. She lives in Budapest, works as an executive in a bank, and she's also doing a doctorate at the

Those Absent

university. She speaks six languages: German, French, Italian, Hungarian, English, Russian and several Gypsy languages too. When she comes to town, I'll introduce you.'

We drove back out to the line of trees, found a dirt lane over the flatness, passed two outlying farms, *tanyas*, with their jumble of barns, chained dogs of indeterminate breed, rusting cars, tractors and bales of hay. Not a soul around. The track headed ever straight, toward the tower perched on a rocky mound surrounded by dead shrubs, dried thistles and brambles. Udo parked, and we began picking through the scrub, clambering over rocks, climbing. Thick walls revealed themselves. Had we really found a trace of Ottoman occupation? A mosque, a tower, an outpost of some sort? Something magnificent?

For when Ottoman armies passed through the Balkans, they did so with dazzling splendour: thousands of camels[53] carried arms and ammunition; horses were covered by silver cloths studded with gold and precious stones; and mounted warriors held jewelled scimitars. Infantrymen, willing to fill moats with their bodies, wore waving plumes; and the formidable fighting Janissaries followed.

The battle for Hungary lasted a mere two hours. On August 29, 1526, King Lajos I drowned in the Mohács marshes; 200,000 soldiers were massacred, another 100,000 were taken to Istanbul[54] as slaves. The ancient Kingdom of Hungary was divided into three: King Ferdinand I of Austria retained the western and northern sections; Suleiman the Magnificent occupied Buda and incorporated the Kingdom's central wedge into the Ottoman Empire; Transylvania became an Ottoman vassal state.

---

53 Thirty thousand camels were used in the taking of Belgrade.
54 Originally Byzantium, renamed Constantinople in 330 CE, changed to Istanbul by the Turks in 1453.

Libraries and palaces were demolished; baths, mosques and prisons sprang up in their place. Crops were destroyed, animals driven off and fertile fields tumbled into wasteland. Entire villages were burnt, Kunmadaras amongst them. Others, abandoned by their inhabitants, crumbled, disappeared forever.

Hungry soldiers, serfs and looters employed by the nobles, roved the countryside, marauding, torturing peasants to reveal hidden herds in woodland and swamp, kidnapping travellers and holding them for ransom, preying upon one another and annihilating the local population. By the 1560s, most of the nobility, deprived of their estates, had fled to Habsburg Hungary. Many of their peasants followed.

Destruction continued along the frontier lands for well over a century, and life was hardly better in Austrian-dominated territory. But within Ottoman Hungary, there was positive change, despite the negative light in which it is often seen. Turks were so foreign – although many were converted Slavs[55] who had been kidnapped or given (sold) as child tax – and domination by non-Christians was a humiliation. However, peasants and serfs soon discovered that, liberated from seigniorial obligations, they had the freedom to move from one place to another, could become artisans and traders. Augmented by incomers[56] – Serbian, Croatian and Bosnian Slavs, Romanians and Ruthenians – the population increased. Towns were allowed to maintain autonomy in internal affairs, and peasants demonstrated a capacity for self-government and commerce. Within a few years, many rebuilt communities were

---

55 Converted to Islam, they became members of the Sultan's slave family and received an excellent education. The most intelligent became diplomats; the brawniest, toughened by games of prowess, became elite Janissaries. Many administrators, grand viziers and members of government were slaves; Sultans took slaves as concubines; and some sultans had slave mothers.

56 New residents were welcomed by landowners who needed to replace serfs who had run away or died in battle.

Those Absent

doing far better than before.

There was neither religious nor racial persecution. Jews and Protestants, tolerated as believers half way along the religious path, were under the protection of Islam in exchange for the poll tax they paid. The Roma joined Ottoman armies, and freed of Catholic persecution, the Protestant reformation spread rapidly. Yet Catholic influence was still felt: authorities of Habsburg Hungary levied taxes in an area extending several hundred kilometres into Ottoman territory, and bishops collected tithes.

With the Cossack massacres in Poland and anti-Semitic persecution elsewhere in Europe, more Jews arrived in Ottoman Hungary. Because they had suffered in Christian lands, Turks did not suspect them of allegiance to the Sultan's enemies. In great demand as doctors, merchants, long-distance traders, interpreters and tax collectors, Jewish craftsmen could belong to guilds and be lacemakers, glassmakers, leatherworkers. Soon Buda was the most important Jewish community in the Ottoman Empire.

Ultimately, favouritism and corruption weakened the Ottoman army. Provincial pashas sought personal enrichment, and the tribute of Christian children to be trained as soldiers was no longer exacted with regularity. Eventually allowed to marry, Janissaries and Sipahis[57] conspired for the admission of sons into the military; and idling in harems, degenerate Sultans became the pawns of female intrigue. Anarchy, murder and palace intrigues plagued the Turkish capital; Christians undermined the once invincible court.

In 1683, a vanguard of allied Polish, Bavarian and Saxon armies broke the Ottoman siege of Vienna. Two years later,

---

[57] Janissaries (infantrymen) and Sipahis (cavalrymen) were rivals. Janissaries were former slaves; Sipahis were freeborn.

Buda was captured and most of its inhabitants massacred. The 1699 Peace of Karlowitz ended Ottoman rule in the Carpathian Basin, and the Habsburg Monarchy became the dominant power.

Many Jews departed with the retreating Turks, and they settled in the great Jewish centres of Istanbul, Salonika and Sarajevo. Those who remained – peddlers, ribbon and scarf sellers, buyers of skins, sellers of silks, cloth, crops and foreign goods – suffered Habsburg persecution. Accused of having aided the Turks, they were slaughtered or taken captive and held for ransom. There were expulsions and accusations of ritual murder. In Pösing, rather than pay his debts to local Jews, Franz, Count of St. Georgen and Pösing had thirty burned at the stake. Although Karl III ordered Christians to halt the violence in 1715, it was to no avail.

Ottoman withdrawal came too late for the restoration of most monastic architecture, and any remaining traces were almost totally destroyed under communism. Standing inside this ruin on the Puszta, I knew it had not been Ottoman and certainly never Roman. Lovely, albeit roofless and long abandoned, it had been a magnificent church, perhaps a monastery or convent. Impossible to know. There were no answers to be gleaned from the frozen plain, and floating on the air was the sense of loss that haunts places with no tales left.

XIV

It did not take me long to learn that she had come to town as a maid a year and a half before, and had since gone wrong. Yet she was not dressed like an ordinary street-walker... She must have felt that she had been born for better things than to become the wife of a peasant or servant, and she had certainly succeeded, as far as circumstances would permit, in rising above her original station in the world.

Géza Csáth,[58] 1910

*T*o demonstrate his loyalty was unalterable, and that he bore no rancour for my missing wallet, Udo invited Tarzan and Mariska for a luxurious dinner in the Abádszalók restaurant. There, they could hear a 'Gypsy' orchestra — wouldn't they enjoy such a treat? Yet neither showed gratitude. On the contrary, they seemed to take the invitation as their due. They even dragged sullen son Imre along.

If indifference flavoured the meal, bad behaviour spiced it: all three guests declared the food inferior, Tarzan belittled the waiter, and when the lead violinist came to chat with Udo who had been his fan for years, Tarzan was rude.

'Don't you think the music is wonderful?' Udo begged with teary sentimentality. 'It's authentic Gypsy music.'

Imre, always insolent, briefly opened his mouth in defence of techno. Tarzan was mocking: 'I'll give you a cassette of authentic original Gypsy music. The real thing. You'll like that more.'

I had my doubts. Even Mariska, although Roma, was too young to have heard that older music made by sticks tapped on the ground, spoons, slapped hands, rhythmic grunts and fantastic vocal imitations of instruments. If those sounds still existed

---

58   *The Red Haired* Girl. Géza Csáth, 1887-1919, Hungarian psychiatrist who, addicted to morphine, was discharged from the army during WWI. After murdering his wife, he committed suicide.

anywhere, it was in recordings made by ethnomusicologists.

The restless boredom of Tarzan, Mariska and Imre discouraged dallying. Dinner quickly over, we piled back into Udo's car and headed back to town. Everyone was silent. What was there to say? Until, passing through the centre of Kunmadaras, Tarzan shouted, 'Stop!' He was staring wild-eyed into the night, pointing a trembling fat finger at a shiny red Mercedes convertible parked outside a kocsma.

'Zsuzsa! She's here! My daughter Zsuzsa from Budapest has arrived.' And heaving his great bulk out of the car, Tarzan clumped toward the bar. 'Come on! All of you,' he ordered over his shoulder.

Mariska and Imre left the car slowly, dragging their feet. Her complacency lost, Mariska seemed wary.

'Zsuzsa is the daughter who speaks six or seven languages?' I asked Udo. 'The one who works in a bank and is doing a doctorate at the university?'

'She's his only daughter.'

Inside, Tarzan, Mariska and Imre were already seated at a table. With them was a most astonishing-looking young woman. Her eyes were ringed by thick lines of black, blue and gleaming gold, her collagen-fattened lips were ruby red, and dyed, jet hair was piled high in tortured stiff swirls. She was not overjoyed at seeing her family.

But the men standing up along the bar were mesmerised. Aware of their attention, she languidly changed her posture, leaning back slightly but provocatively, forcing vast artificial breasts to strain at their casing of skintight elastic and push for freedom over the plunging neckline. Crossing one thigh-high booted leg over the other, a tiny band of fabric, no more than a hint of skirt, rucked high.

Those Absent

This was not a woman who worked in a bank.

Tense, out of his depth, Tarzan fought to maintain his wise man-of-the-world image, although a constant and nervous twitching at the corner of his mouth betrayed an indefinable emotion. He introduced me to Zsuzsa with great ceremony. She gave me a perfunctory nod, for her interest was directed towards a white-hot youth sliding into the empty seat beside her.

'You can speak to her in English or French,' Tarzan said to me. 'Go on. Speak to her in German. Anything. She speaks many languages.'

The burning young man stared at Zsuzsa's profile. She graced him with a nanosecond's glance, tossed her head, surveyed the bar to see if interest there was still undiminished. Then lowering her lids, half-smiled.

'Talk to her in French,' Tarzan insisted. 'Go on. You'll see.'

She wasn't in the least interested in me, in conversations in foreign tongues, or in Tarzan, her father. We were, frankly, spoiling her game.

'Talk to her,' said Tarzan.

I leaned forward to catch her attention. 'Do you speak English?'

Almost imperceptibly, she shook her head.

'Français? Deutsch?'

Again, she shook her head.

'You see?' said Tarzan, refusing to understand her negation. 'I told you she could!' He ordered a round of drinks from the barman, convinced Zsuzsa and I were deep in conversation.

Then I looked at Mariska. She was staring, with undisguised fascination, but also amusement, at Zsuzsa. She understood perfectly what was going on, and she was thinking hard. Of course she was. Weren't she and Zsuzsa almost the same age? Yet Zsuzsa was a creature from another world, a glamorous world of elastic togs and spiky-heeled boots. Those were a far cry from the sad, second-hand jogging suits and lumpy trainers that comprised Mariska's wardrobe.

Wasn't Mariska also beautiful? As beautiful as Zsuzsa – far more so. Yet Zsuzsa possessed a mouthful of perfect white teeth, a flashy red Mercedes, a life in Budapest with freedom, romance and glamour. What did she, Mariska, have? Rotted broken teeth, oversize Tarzan, two grimy children, and a cement hovel with a trash-filled mud yard in the Roma section of town. Linking her life to Tarzan's had meant one step up the social ladder in Kunmadaras. It had raised her above her pipe-smoking mother and layabout siblings. But it was just another dead end.

The boiling young man put his hand on Zsuzsa's thigh, a tentative gesture. She smiled, refused to look at him. Ignored me, Imre, Udo and Mariska. Ignored Tarzan. She wasn't here to be the dutiful daughter.

Those Absent

XV

The evening was as calm as one on which, ten years before, when there was also a full moon, this house... was attacked by brigands... 'My predecessor,' my host said, 'when the affair happened, was sitting just where you are, smoking his chibouk and taking his coffee. From that time we have never kept any money in the house, and our doors are locked, as they used to be even in towns during the Middle Ages, at night-fall... Good night... and if you dream of bétyars, be sure to remember that there are bars of iron outside all the windows, and two doors, of which one is plated with iron, guns in my room, and a big dog in the court-yard.

Victor Tissot, 1881

Snow fell. The summer cottage in Berekfürdő could only be heated by means of a hoary, seriously frightening gas radiator. Yet, despite the limited comfort, I had no desire to leave. I was enjoying my (temporary) life here, and warmth could be accessed by plunging into the steamy spa baths, or tramping over the austere hinterland. And one fogged morning after Udo's return to Vienna, I set out over the powdery white fields, headed for Ildikó's snug kocsma, eight kilometres distant.

Kunmadaras was a stark world in black and white; sound was muted by cold. Down misty roads, people were stick figures, gingerly negotiating ice or disappearing altogether. In the kocsma, Ildikó merely nodded when I entered, for vociferous negotiation was taking place with a toothless man in a fatty felt hat and blood-splattered rubber boots. Beside him was a bucket of something wet, malodorous. I couldn't understand what was being said, but Ildikó's high, cackling chicken voice was rebellious and determined; the edentulous man's yelp was equally so. Finally, Ildikó went into the back of the kocsma, returned with a commodious plastic basin. The something malodorous was plopped into it.

What was it exactly? It shivered there, yellowish, whitish, greyish. Ildikó grinned in pleased triumph; the toothless man peered at me, mooed like a cow, pointed to his stomach, sliced one finger across his throat. So I came to understand that he had butchered his cow, and the wet, stinking mass was innards. Soon Kata arrived, and the two women washed the thing, added fresh water and vinegar to the basin, and then abandoned it to soak for a day or two under the Christmas light heart in the back room. The smell in there was just awful.

'Yum-yum. Good. Cow good-good. Yum-yum.' said Kata in the excessively silly pidgin she always used with me. Yet Hungarian, with its fourteen vowels complicated by dots, slants, double slants, its consonant clusters, tricky conjugations, incomprehensible sentence structure, wildly unfamiliar vocabulary, complex suffixes and irritating habit of stating things twice in each negative sentence, was defeating me, despite my diligent swatting.

At least I didn't have to eat that gory thing in the tub. I'd never convert the locals to vegetarianism here in cattle country, where drovers once walked lumbering herds of white bovines all the way to Nürnberg, Frankfurt, Augsburg, or Italy – Venice alone required 15,000-20,000 oxen per year. If demand was lacking or the price low, drovers and beasts trudged home again.

'*Buli*,' said Ildikó. '*Péntek*.'

'Party,' said Kata in translation. 'Friday night party.' She pointed to the soaking entrails, rubbed her stomach. 'Yum-yum. Eat-eat Friday. Party. Eat, yum-yum.'

Thankfully, I had an excuse for not attending. I had no car, and there were no evening buses or trains from Kunmadaras to Berekfürdő. Why risk staggering over ice-bound fields at night?

Those Absent

But before I could open my mouth, Kata added, 'You sleep me house. Must!'

***

*K*ata's house had belonged to her deceased husband's family. According to Hungarian law, Kata's two (absent) adult children presently owned it. Although widows couldn't inherit the home, they maintained the right to reside in it during their lifetime.

Traditional in layout, the long front terrace, glassed in and painted enamel blue, contained a flickering television and a bed populated by an assemblage of stuffed animals and dolls. The main door opened into a high-ceilinged kitchen, and in a living-cum-bedroom, more bears, rabbits, puppies and dolls sat on shelves, chairs and occupied a bed. Some were perched on the top of a larger television, and a privileged bunch in an armchair could even watch the set.

'Love television,' Kata said, her hand on her heart. 'Love movies. Me, romantic.'

She wanted to show me the rest of the house, so we returned to the icy garden where we were greeted by two real dogs, one yapping and tiny, the other huge and yellowish – Hungarian dogs are never permitted to come indoors. Attached to the house were barns: the highest for cows and horses, a lower one for pigs, the lowest for fowl. Since Kata had no farm animals, and Kunmadaras was no longer rural, the first barn had been converted into a summer kitchen where homemade jams, bottled vegetables and pickles sat on shelves, dried tomatoes and grapes hung from a wire. Vengeful winter wind was blowing, but Kata wouldn't starve.

We made ourselves ready, heating water in the wood-burning boiler, scrubbing our cheeks pink, smearing on lipstick and mascara. When we set out, Kata locked her doors and front gate, but the television in the terrace was still flickering.

'Always on,' said Kata. 'Day, night. Gypsies. Streets, night. Gypsies look-look. Who home? All night dogs bark, woof-woof. Kunmadaras Gypsies dangerous. Steal.'

The party gang had arrived at the kocsma: the locals, the friends from Püspokladány, the fumble-fingered man. Again, we sat at the tables in the back room; again, outsiders filled the open doorway and watched, a crescent of heads. I merely moved the sad remnants of cow around my plate, but the rest tucked in, smacking, slurping and sucking. Over-eating done, the jukebox was again cranked up. Again, echo-chamber techno boomed; again, the hopping began. I soon grew bored and wondered how long we would have to stay. Then Casanova arrived and, briefly, things livened up.

Lean, swarthy and dashing, an authentic lady-killer, Casanova never appeared with the same beautiful woman twice, a prowess that dazzled Udo as much as Casanova's aristocratic blood. 'He's a real noble,' Udo had said in great awe (how proud he was that his grandson had been born in the same hospital as Caroline of Monaco's daughter.) What did it matter that Hungarian aristocrats were once so common, they comprised five percent of the population,[59] that titles mean nothing in modern Hungary, that mention of aristocratic descent is, today, considered eccentric?[60]

Did Casanova descend from well-to-do peasants, or burghers affluent enough to buy a patent of nobility? Perhaps his family had belonged to the impoverished caste dubbed 'seven plum tree nobles' or 'bootless nobles' – peasants or serfs who, having

---
[59] Hungary was only surpassed by Poland where nobles made up 9% of the population.
[60] Titles and distinctions of nobility were abolished in 1947. This was confirmed by parliament in 1990.

Those Absent

fought against the Turks, had been rewarded with a title. This inexpensive honour was distributed with such liberality, that all peasants in some boggy, boot-sucking villages were ennobled. Even Udo's anachronistic fervour was somewhat quashed upon learning that Casanova worked as a trucker, possessed no manor, and lived with his mother in a 1960s bungalow.

That evening, Casanova decided I was to be his partner, and he charmed me with great determination. Dancing with him had its positive side: there was no vulgar jumping about, for he twirled me around the ragged linoleum floor with elegant ease. After a few dances and a mighty quantity of alcohol, his gestures became more intimate: with gentle fingers, he curled back a lock of my hair, let his hand rest possessively on my shoulder. But, oddly, when ordering drinks, they were for himself. The rest of us bought rounds for each another, but not Casanova. Did he expect me to pay for the gift of his company?

'Tonight, we will sleep together,' he announced.

'No,' I said, wanting to be kindly but firm. 'I'm staying at Kata's house.'

'No problem,' he said confidently. 'We will be together at Kata's house.'

He insisted until my refusals made him cantankerous. Standing, he coldly and elegantly bowed, kissed my hand and disappeared into the night.

At midnight, the atmosphere changed. A ruddy fellow with a fine handlebar moustache made an appearance. He, a musician, was wending his slow, pálinka-doused way home after playing at an affair in the nearby town of Tiszafüred. Another glass or two down the hatch and he fetched his accordion. Heaving it into place, he began playing Hungarian melodies of infinite sorrow that hug Klezmer, Gypsy notes and Ottoman whine.

Ildikó lit candles and turned off the overhead neon. Everyone began singing, searching for half-forgotten lyrics. Kata's lovely voice could be heard above all: high-pitched, certain and traditional. She sang, wept, wiped away tears, sang on. The words, standard Puszta themes, conjured up aged mothers, vanished sweethearts, fallow fields and lost homes.

In truth, this heart-tugging music, far from being an ancient rural throwback, is a nationalistic nineteenth-century creation. Composed in Budapest by professionals (many of them Jewish) who had never been anywhere near a barn, a farm or a sweep-well, it was enthusiastically adopted by peasants and aristocrats alike. All claimed it was the true Magyar sound, a remnant from the glorious Ugric past.

The accordionist changed tempo and everyone began dancing again, Ildikó, Karcsi, Kata, Zoli, and the excellent music inspired complicated and lovely movements. An elderly, alcohol-sogged Roma man appeared, managed some fancy steps with knee and heel slapping accompanied by wild cries. This is it, I thought. This is the sort of thing I've been snuffling around for. Here's how things must have been before commercial mass culture destroyed all with its kamikaze certainty.

Then, abruptly, it ended. A group of ultra-fashionable young men swaggered into the kocsma and, indifferent to what was taking place, began pumping coins into the jukebox. The scream of electric guitars, the angry slash of American hard rock, drowned out the accordion and signalled the triumphant re-entry of the twenty-first century.

The accordionist put down his instrument, his face impassive. Ildikó returned to her usual place at the bar. The neon lights clicked back on. Kata began a conversation with the drunken postman she was currently in love with.

Those Absent

'Don't you mind?' I asked the musician in German. I was angry and ashamed at the cavalier treatment he had received. 'Everyone was singing. It was beautiful.'

'It's always like this now,' he said mildly. 'The young don't want traditional music. They don't care. They want the modern, commercial world. That's how things are.'

Time dragged on endlessly after that. Hard rock continued to rip the air; the crowd of friends disappeared homeward – gone are the days when folk wrapped themselves in their cloaks and slept on kocsma tables. To my great relief, at three in the morning, a yawning Ildikó finally informed the youths she was closing, for she opened again at seven. They shuffled out ungraciously, faces resentful.

Kata and I waited while Ildikó emptied the slot machine, dumped the coins into cloth sacks, carried them outside into the frigid night, dropped them on the ground, hauled down a steel grate, secured it with heavy chain and severe-looking lock. Those sacks contained a considerable amount of money, but the windswept streets were perfectly empty: no infamous Puszta robber of yore – a *bétyar* – was in sight, and no dangerous Gypsy. Yet all in town must have known that Ildikó closed the bar each evening with identical sacks of money. She bid us goodnight, got into her antediluvian Wartburg car and rattled away.

Arm in arm, singing loudly, quite tipsy, Kata and I reeled along the main road, turned left, passed a strange wheeled pump, turned left again under frozen trees, and reached her house. The two dogs, their fur ice-coated, were waiting for us and, in the veranda, the television was still flickering its welcoming bluish light.

Despite the hour, Kata insisted on showing me photos of her

daughter, and there were a great many to be got through. The daughter, a handsome blond woman, assumed fashion model poses or clowned for the camera. Here she was before leaving for Mexico with a boyfriend; here she was in Canada, where she lived.

'Miss her. Me sad. Daughter soon come back. Soon, soon. In few weeks.'

Kata then pulled me into a bedroom, pointed to the wedding band she still wore, pointed to another photo on a dresser: her deceased husband. She made the sign of a cross, pulled a sad face, although I didn't get the feeling there much genuine emotion behind it: he'd been dead for ten years and looked a stern character, humourless and scrawny. She then directed my attention to a tall urn, again pointed to the wedding ring, again simulated wretchedness. I nodded, uncomfortable. What is correct etiquette when meeting someone powdery in an urn? Mutual appreciation is out of the question, so is conversation.

Perhaps wanting me to be on more intimate terms with what was left of the man, Kata lifted the urn's lid, indicated I was to peer inside. Which I did, ever a polite guest. At the same time, she peered with me. Then shrieked. For there, stuffed inside, was a thick pile of paper money. Kata's hand flew to her mouth. She blushed, made flustered gestures. Then doubled over, laughing. She'd forgotten about the money she'd hidden there. So the dear departed husband was still in charge of the family budget.

Throughout the rest of the brief night, Kata's dogs barked. I lay in bed listening to them, listening to the neighbour's dogs barking across the street and next door, listening to the dogs down the road barking. Woof-woof-woof in the dark, an off-key chorus of canine melody. Valiant, creative beasts they were and,

Those Absent

according to Kata, meticulously keeping sly thieving Gypsies out. But, aside from the barks, I heard nothing, no human voices and no stealthy footsteps.

Provoked, curious, I left the luxury of the warm bed – once, twice, three times – peeked out the window. No one to be seen, no men bent on plunder, not a human afoot. But slinking through the snowy night streets were dogs. Dogs of all shapes, all sizes. Night dogs. Strays. Terrified beasts that, by day, cowered in fields, copses and dark tangled places on the Puszta. By night, they invaded these streets, skinny craven beasts, terrified and unwanted, shot when seen. They padded through while humans slept, snuffling for scraps, vanishing at dawn and the sight of early risers.

PART THREE : RETURNING

XVI

Love's arrival is not announced by heralds, as if he were a king; nor by a burst of rage, as if he were a seven-headed dragon, with his mace flung ahead of him... he comes quietly, almost stealthily, and the heart is seized with a sacred lunacy, it becomes an overflowing cauldron of boiling, bubbling feelings, and the soul exudes poetry, just as the forest soil after a downpour brings forth an abundance of mushrooms in token of its fertility.

Kálmán Mikszáth[61]

*T*emperatures dropped further, and even in Ildikó's kocsma, the atmosphere was icy. A tight knot of women, bundled into heavy coats and woollen hats, hunched around a miniscule electric heater, whispering, snickering, and ignoring me. When I managed to catch Kata's eye, she jerked her head towards the back room. 'Mariska. Tarzan Mariska. No Tarzan. No good.'

How I wished she'd stop using pidgin. 'I don't understand,' I said sourly.

'*Szerető, szerető,*' clarified Ildikó in that overly loud voice used to communicate with foreigners. She jeered, pursed her lips, made smacking noises. But, by now, even I knew szerető meant lover.

'She's a bad woman. You can't trust a Gypsy,' added Ibolya with glee. None of these women liked Mariska, and she knew it too. I'd seen her in Ildikó's kocsma once, accompanied by Tarzan, and the hostility had been flagrant.

Just in case I was still incapable of understanding, Kata mimed a couple in each other's arms, kissing. 'Tarzan bye-bye. Other town. Work.'

'He'll kill her when he gets back,' Ibolya gloated.

---

61   *The Deaf Blacksmith.* Kálmán Mikszáth, 1847-1910, Hungarian novelist, journalist and politician. Although a member of the lesser nobility, his satirical novels were highly critical of the aristocracy.

Those Absent

'Ruined Tarzan's life. Doesn't take care of her children properly,' said Ildikó, forgetting she was supporting two layabout sons and their own broods of unmanageable children.

'Takes his money, spends it all,' said Ferike, who, as everyone knew, hated Tarzan.

But I was sceptical. Mariska and a lover? I had to see for myself. Why shouldn't I? If Mariska were seeking discretion, she wouldn't have waltzed into enemy territory. With no hesitation, I went to the doorway of the back room and peered in. All the lights had been turned off, and the Christmas heart illuminated the place, but feebly. There was a dark blotch in one corner – perhaps two people pressed tightly together. I returned to the bar, hardly wiser.

Half an hour later, two people emerged into the main room's dour silence and paused, blinking, in the neon's ugly glare. Yes, it was Mariska all right, and her paramour was a beautiful Roma man, lithe, dark-eyed, with coppery skin and delicately drawn features. Mariska, too, had been transformed by love's tinsel. Gone, the sluggish body and expression of ennui. Voluptuous and enticing, she wore tight white jeans and a soft red sweater. And, although it was impossible to overlook the impolite gathering's sneers, the beautiful lover's protective arm around her shoulders rendered her immune to insult.

Why come to Ildikó's of all places? To show everyone she was more than the mother of slobby Tarzan's children? To demonstrate that love had given her identity, and that society's condemnation had no weight? That the rest of us were no longer powerful, merely dull and incombustible? And why deny her a triumph? To show a little solidarity, I went over, kissed her on both cheeks as always. 'Good luck,' I said.

Their point made, the lovely couple went out into the sweet

PART THREE : RETURNING

dark night, taking their magic with them. Leaving behind sharp tongues and sour disapproval.

'Gypsies! Never trust a Gypsy. They take. Always taking.'

But there was envy there, too.

***

A week later, Tarzan sat in the kocsma I jokingly called his 'office,' that rough place of leering drunks and cheap alcohol, where stale cigarette smoke curled into hair, crawled under fingernails, itched its way into seams. He was a pale, defeated man, but best friend Udo had arrived and was on hand to comfort him.

Naturally, Tarzan didn't have a good word for Mariska. At any mention of her name, as though a truly nasty stench had crept in, he raised his left hand, pinched his fatty nostrils shut with thumb and forefinger, raised his right hand, closed his fist, mimed pulling a toilet chain and made a gurgling, flushing sound.

'There are other women in the world, women who would be happy to be with you,' said Udo for the fifteenth time.

Tarzan wasn't listening. 'I don't miss her. Trash, that's what she is. It's my two children I care about. They're with her at her sister's house. But as for her…' Once more, sausage fingers pinched fatty nose, arm pulled imaginary chain, slack wet mouth made noise.

Would do better to lose some weight, I thought uncharitably. Give the pretty Gypsy man some competition. Not that Tarzan had a ghost of a chance.

'I want my children with me. She doesn't care about them. I go see them at her sister's house every day and I bring them food. That way, they're fed decently. She never gives them meals, never cooks.'

'Then go to the sister's house, get the children and bring them home,' Udo said. 'If she doesn't care about them, find another woman to raise them, one who'd be happy with you.'

'I have to work. I don't have time to take care of two young kids.'

Perhaps bringing them food was Tarzan's excuse to see Mariska, hang around, try to convince her to return. Who knew? For my part, I hoped she wouldn't. I wished her romance, passion and beauty. Those things made a prettier picture than tawdry domesticity.

Sitting by Tarzan's side was a massive hulk of Homo sapiens. 'A good man,' Tarzan said. 'My best friend, just like you, Udo. A man I trust. Strong. You should see how strong.'

I didn't doubt that for an instant. The hulk's thighs were astoundingly broad and tightly meaty; his hands and fingers were dangerous lumps of flesh. Minus the bolts and other hardware, he was Frankenstein's monster with the same dead eyes in an expressionless face. Like Tarzan, he knocked home pálinka, one glass after another. A man with an astounding capacity for drink.

'You live in Kunmadaras?' I asked, attempting polite social palaver in bad Hungarian. I was pretty tired of watching Tarzan simulate toilet flushing.

'Yes,' Tarzan answered for him.

'Yes,' echoed the Monster.

'He's strong,' said Tarzan.

'I'm strong.' The Monster nodded sagely.

'He had a terrible accident a few years ago,' said Tarzan, putting on his sorrowful face and expecting, perhaps, to drum up my mothering instincts.

PART THREE : RETURNING

'Terrible accident,' said the Monster. 'Holding high voltage wire. Got connected. Went right through me.'

'High voltage electricity went right through him,' said Tarzan.

The Monster nodded his colossal head. 'Live electricity. All through my body. Can't let go, can't drop the wire. Stuck on. Standing there high up. Whole hour there, holding the wire, juice going through me.'

'Until someone came and turned off the juice,' said Tarzan. 'And he fell, dropped like that, right down on the ground.'

'And lived,' said the Monster. 'Still alive. Juice went through one hour.' Sluggishly, he mimed the whole incident so we could all capture the full drama of it.

'Did damage though,' said Tarzan.

The Monster bobbed his head sluggishly. 'Damage.'

'Terrible,' I said, and wondered what he'd been like before the accident.

'Mariska,' said Tarzan, trundling back onto the beaten track. He shook his head, pinched his nose with pudgy fingers, raised his arm, pulled the invisible chain, and made the sound of a flushing toilet. 'Monday night. Next Monday. You both come.'

'Come where?' asked Udo.

'Ildikó's. I meet with Mariska on Monday night to negotiate. I want lots of people there.' Tarzan contemplated the Monster with evident satisfaction. 'He's coming, too.'

Of course he was.

***

On Monday night, the tables had been pushed together in Ildikó's back room – not for a feast but a showdown. The

Those Absent

Christmas lights were not twinkling; the back room was neon-lit and garish. On his side, Tarzan had gathered a daunting clique from the middle-class: a dignified older couple, several well-dressed, respectable-looking men. Less conventional, less classy, but infinitely more threatening, was the Monster. Tarzan had cleaned-up nicely and, in suit and tie, was steady, arrogant. Mariska had one person on her team, not the beautiful lover, but her sister, a worn-out, stringy Roma. The atmosphere was disagreeable.

The rest of us, palpitating quidnuncs, were exiled to the front room: Udo, Ibolya, Ildikó, Kata, Karcsi, Enikö, Annuska, Ferike and the other habitués. Not active participants in this witch trial, we were there as peanut gallery.

'What's going on?' Never a fan of purges or blood sports, I was peevish.

'They're negotiating their future,' said Karcsi, who seemed to be an emissary, for every ten minutes, he went into the back room, listened for a bit, brought back news. It seemed an oddly public way of working out a marital problem. But what did I, poor foreigner, know?

'Is it about who gets the children?' I asked.

'No, of course not,' Karcsi said. 'They're negotiating Mariska's return.'

'Return where?'

'Return home. To Tarzan.'

'Nonsense. She won't do that. She's in love.'

'Tarzan has money. Mariska doesn't. They're negotiating what he'll give her.'

'Not everything is money,' I scoffed. I didn't believe him for a minute. He, like everyone else, wanted to think the worst of

PART THREE : RETURNING

Mariska. She needed money? I began working out what kind of work she could do: what if she set up a second-hand clothing stall in the market? Udo always brought good clothes and furniture from Vienna. She didn't need Tarzan. I'd help her get started.

For the moment, there was nothing to do but ruminate, and the back-room confrontation dragged on endlessly. Finally, we heard chairs scrape. Mariska and her scraggly sister were the first to appear in the doorway. They glanced around the bar, hesitant, uncertain, and then quickly went out into the night. The others filed up to the counter, conversing in low tones.

Karcsi came over to me, smirked. 'Like I told you, she's going back to Tarzan.'

'She wouldn't do that.'

'The terms have been decided upon.'

'What terms?'

'The financial conditions for her return. What Tarzan is willing to do for her, give her, buy for her. That's all she wanted in the first place.'

'I can't believe that. What about her lover? Why doesn't she go live with him?'

'Oh, him.' Karcsi was scathing. 'That Gypsy! He's home in Kunhegyes with his Gypsy wife and six children. He has no money. He doesn't work. How could he live with Mariska?'

XVII

The silkworm shall weave your garments,
The fairies will smile upon you,
Their benediction will give you love,
And may God come to your help in all places.

Hungarian lullaby

Customs officials showed up in Ildikó's kocsma, poked around a dank cupboard-like room, and found bottles of local pálinka. No chemicals, no artificial flavours, this was the real thing: undeclared bootlegger's produce. Ildikó was fined a huge sum, too huge for a woman with a family to support. If she couldn't come up with the cash plus a considerable chunk for baksheesh, the kocsma would close.

Udo, in his role of 'wealthy' foreigner, pulled out notes, handed them over, but Ildikó, at her counter of peeling plastic, remained mournful. In corners, habitués muttered sourly while the inner circle, Kata, Ibolya, Enikö, István, Annushka, Bálint, bent into a huddle. Then Karcsi came to where Udo and I sat, announced we were going to the baths.

'At this time of night?' It was already ten o'clock.

Kata went home to fetch a few women's bathing suits. The serious drinkers were shooed away, the lights were put out, the door closed, the steel gate slammed down. Some stuffed themselves into Udo's car, others into Ildikó's chugging Wartburg, and off we went.

These baths were some eleven kilometres distant, on the inky Puszta's edge, near the village of Tiszaörs. In summer, this was another holiday settlement of dirt roads and wooden houses; now, out of season, all was icy, silent, shuttered. Blanketed in a haze of hot sulphurous steam, a surly moustached genie stood

PART THREE : RETURNING

by the entry to the baths, surveying all with reptilian stealth. Karcsi approached him, began endless and complicated negotiations, and then handed over a hefty roll of forints.

We changed into the suits Kata had brought, and almost invisible to each other in the thick haze, went to soak in hot brown-flecked water that smelt of burnt rubber or long-steeped Lapsang Souchong tea. Until the swarthy genie again materialized. With him was another man, dark-haired, arrogant and self-important. He pointed to Udo, to me, said, in German: 'You will come drink fine wine.' Then, both men evanesced.

Although this had not been an invitation but a command, Udo, ever trusting, was enthusiastic. 'What an adventure!'

With Karcsi and Ildikó, we changed back into dry clothes, went out into the night. The genie was waiting for us.

'What about the others?' I asked. All the cloak and dagger mystery made me suspicious, but not admitted into the Arcanum's complexities, we were, *nolens volens*, to follow and obey.

Dulled by swirling vapour, stars were wobbling smears, and we cautiously picked our way along unlit lanes, stumbling, sliding. Passing the rows of summerhouses, we came to a wall of dead reeds and frozen marsh, where a brightly illuminated house waited, voluminous and unlovely. The genie swung open its pretentious front door, led us into a room of textured plaster walls where, under the glare of a rococo chandelier in factitious gold, the self-important man waited at a wooden table so highly varnished, it resembled plastic.

'Sit,' he commanded.

The genie placed himself at the door, arms crossed, legs spread: a sentry? Or a barrier. Another man, a meek lackey with lowered eyes, appeared with glasses and a bottle of wine.

Those Absent

'We will drink,' said our host. Raising his glass, lifting his chin, he smiled with great condescension at Udo, at me. 'Tonight we will drink many wines. The finest. The best. I am a connoisseur. I know my wines.'

His was a harsh, rubbing voice, and on he went in sometimes-incomprehensible German thickly laced with brag. Wasn't this a magnificent building? He'd had it built to his instructions, and he knew how to get things done. That's why the 'boss' trusted him, and the 'boss' was an important man indeed, one of the most important men in Hungary, a number one top-level politician (who remained nameless). And he was number one's number one man, because he knew things, was clever and intelligent. He told of compliments received, flatteries, personal power and great sums of money. He took care of things, he insisted. Again. And again.

Being a passive audience to boastful twaddle quickly became tiresome. I glanced at Ildikó sitting across the table; her face was expressionless. This could only be tedious for her, for she understood no German. Even Karcsi couldn't possibly follow such effusion, but under his baseball cap, he looked cowed, obsequious. From time to time, he stood, helped the silent serf uncork bottles and bring fresh glasses, for each new wine demanded its own.

But Udo's face glowed. He didn't mind being talked at. He was impressed by our host's insistence on his own consequence, on the importance of 'the highly-placed politician', whoever he was, and talk of the politician's immensely influential (unidentified) buddies. Wasn't this a unique Hungarian evening? Hadn't he been singled out to mingle with the mighty? Such things never happened to him in Vienna!

What about the others? Some time had passed since

PART THREE : RETURNING

abandoning them in the baths. Were they desperate, waterlogged, their skin corrugated from long soaking or had they been evicted from the comforting heat? Surely, they were waiting for us. What else could they do? Without Ildikó's Wartburg or Udo's Camry, they had no way of getting back to Kunmadaras. Another bottle, perhaps the seventh, was uncorked. I put my hand over my glass. 'Not for me, thank you. And I think it's time to leave.'

'But we will drink much more,' snapped the host, visibly annoyed. We were not to escape so easily. Why were we there? Did he need us, two inauspicious foreigners, as public? Were we, for the privilege of being in the domain of the powerful, to drink ourselves into oblivion? Perhaps he had more lascivious plans for impressionable and tipsy guests. He barked at the lackey who skittered away, came back with six more bottles. 'The best. And after that, there are more. I know my wines. You will never taste such fine wines again.'

'When we drink one after the other, it's impossible to appreciate quality.' I stood.

Udo glanced at me, conflicted. He wanted to bask in the hint of power, tarry in this lofty microcosm, yet even he was ill at ease.

'It's freezing outside,' I said. 'Our friends are waiting for us to bring them back to town.'

An irrefutable argument. Udo rose, so did Karcsi. Ildikó, ever inscrutable and passive, remained seated. Seeing our determination, our host only begrudgingly ordered the genie-cum-sentry to open the door.

I looked back at Ildikó. She smiled faintly and waved goodbye. Without her, we went back into the wintry night, followed the lanes back to the baths. The others, chilled to the bone, were huddled together in the bath's locked entry. What would have become of them if I hadn't insisted on leaving? Gratefully they packed themselves into Udo's car. Enikö was crying noisily, and Karcsi, awkward, embarrassed, comforted her.

'He was an interesting man, don't you think?' Udo asked with his usual naïve fervour. 'He's obviously someone powerful.'

***

*T*wo days later, we went to Ildikó's kocsma. In high spirits, she drew beers for us both, poured out two glasses of Unicom, then hustled us into the back room. There was something she wanted to show us, something *jó*. Something wonderful.

There, in pride of place, stood a new huge jukebox. Glowing strobes of blue and green flashed from its great plastic face, and when Ildikó slipped in a coin, Hungarian techno jerked out, the bass notes deep, intense.

'What about the inspectors and the fine you have to pay?'

'No problem. Problem finished.' She waved one arm and imitated someone holding a paintbrush. 'Soon all beautiful here in kocsma. Soon. Renovation begin. *Szép*. Beautiful!'

PART THREE : RETURNING

XVIII

It is extremely difficult at first to distinguish the pure Magyar type, since more than half the inhabitants of Buda-Pest are Jews, and Jews trying to conceal the fact, who have already adopted Hungarian names, and caught some of their courtesy and cleanliness. The violent sweeps of a Hebrew woman's figure usually betray her. Indeed, many of these ladies, being touched with an Oriental laziness, have come to resemble gigantic torsos on legless feet. With the men, we found that as a rule, a tall, well-grown, straight-featured specimen, not very dark, with hair ridiculously closely cut, and clothes à l'Anglais, would prove to be a Magyar, while the swarthy, black-eyed, thick-lipped beings, of our earlier notions, were Hebrews. Hungarians themselves have developed to a remarkable extent the power of scenting a Jew, or even a strain of Jewish blood, and feel towards them very much as dogs do towards rats.

Margaret Fletcher,[62] 1892

*K*ata left a message for me at Ildikó's kocsma: I was to go to her house immediately. Her daughter, also named Kata, had arrived from Canada.

The younger Kata was a tall, strapping young woman with a heavy blond ponytail and ready smile. Her English was excellent, and she had adopted modern new age chitchat: 'I don't eat animals because we're all part of the cosmos, and our souls are their souls.'

She worked in a fitness centre, had a new boyfriend who was a partner in his family's lucrative building business. The young couple would soon live together in a large, modern apartment. Life was looking good. 'Each time I come back, my mother hopes I'll stay, marry a local boy, have babies, but I'll never do

---

62 *Sketches of Life and Character in Hungary.* Margaret Fletcher, 1862-1943, British feminist, founder of the Catholic Women's League.

that. I'm too much of a rebel. Besides, everything I want is in Canada: big new houses, nice cars.'

Sitting beside her was Juli, once her closest friend: 'It's awesome seeing her again.'

Juli, a passive, beautiful, dark-haired woman, held a tiny baby, and she watched Kata with all the admiration due a star from a dazzling galaxy. Hovering solicitously near Juli, was a considerably older, somewhat shopworn man: her husband.

'This baby is just too gorgeous,' young Kata gushed with pouting envy, but the reunion didn't seem a comfortable one. The couple soon stood, prepared to leave, Juli with evident regret, even resignation, her husband, hesitant and awkward, as if unable to believe he possessed two such jewels. Certainly, he must often have feared fortune's inconstancy.

Once they were out of earshot, young Kata lamented her friend's fate. 'Can you imagine what it's like, marrying a man forty years older? I understand why she did it. He's rich. They live in a huge new house, and she has an adorable baby – that's about the best you can do when you live in Kunmadaras. But I feel sorry for her. I have nothing to say to her.'

The reason I'd been summoned, she told me, was to meet her grandmother, who was also named Kata (the pet name for Katalin). 'She heard you were asking about the Jews in Kunmadaras, and she wants to talk to you. She asked me to come along and translate.'

'She wants to talk about the pogrom?'

Young Kata looked sincerely confused.

'Haven't you heard about the Jews who were murdered here in 1946?'

'No.' Uninterested, she shrugged. 'I'm only translating.'

PART THREE : RETURNING

Grandmother Katalin lived a few streets away from the square and the memorial stone. Still spry and droll at eighty-six, her traditional house was surrounded by a large garden that, in summer, would be rich with flowers, vegetables and fruits. She was particularly pleased with her whitewashed, solid stucco outhouse.

'I built it myself, without help from anyone.' She grinned. 'My husband had just died. I was angry with him for leaving me, and I had all this pent-up mad energy, so I built an outhouse to express how I felt.'

Inside the house, we travelled back a century. Here were antique crocks, embroidery, paintings, rag rugs, a larder filled with home bottled fruits and vegetables. Katalin also showed me her handiwork: the paintings and many clever constructions that, in western society, would be lauded as excellent examples of folk sculpture or art brut. Kata was proud of her mother's artistic energy and imagination, but not young Kata, her granddaughter.

'Sure, all the paintings and objects are cute, but aren't they sort of weird?' Although convinced of her own iconoclasm, the youngest Kata was a conventional young woman.

'You want to know about the pogrom,' grandmother Katalin said when we were seated beside a gutted television filled with fantastic creatures and impossible blooms.

'I've asked people what happened, but no one wants to tell me anything,' I said.

'It was terrible, disgusting, but it should never be forgotten. I was a young woman back then, but I remember the Jews. A few had survived the deportation and the camps, and they returned to this town where they'd always lived. Why shouldn't they have? This was where they belonged. But not everybody

Those Absent

thought that.

'The pogrom started in the market. Back then, it was held in the little park where the roses grow, across the street from the memorial stone. I wasn't there, but I heard that one Jew was selling eggs, and a local woman started shouting that he was charging too much. Then another woman said the Jews had kidnapped two Christian children, and the townspeople went crazy, beating the Jews, going into their houses, and looting.

'When the violence stopped, the Jews stayed hidden for days. They didn't dare go outside. A Jewish family lived next door, in the house that's on the right. In the evening, when it was dark and no one could see me, I went out and left a plate of food on their doorstep. If I hadn't, if a few others in town hadn't done the same, the Jews would have starved. But we didn't dare go talk to them. Those were hard times. We were all afraid.'

'Why is everyone saying that people from somewhere else started the pogrom?"

'Because they pretend no one here was responsible. But it was people from Kunmadaras, all right, I know who they are.'

'What happened after?'

'The Jews left. Some went to Budapest, others left for Israel or America.'

'Not Kohn.'

'All except Kohn.'

'And he won't talk about the pogrom.'

'He has to live here. His wife converted to Judaism in the 1930s. Everyone likes Kohn.'

'Why did it happen?'

'Because people were jealous.'

PART THREE : RETURNING

'After the Holocaust? The camps?'

Grandmother Katalin leaned forward in her chair. 'It wasn't only the Jews who suffered in those days. We Catholics suffered too. The communists persecuted us. And so many Hungarians were taken away to the gulag and never heard of again. We hold a church ceremony for them every year.' She stopped, shook her head, deeply troubled.

Those Absent

XIX

Homestead, my homestead, homestead on the plain:
Knee-deep in lake mud goes my bullock's tread.
Bullock, for clover you must suffer pain
And I must suffer with you for my bread.

Hungarian Folksong

*U*nder the granite-grey sky, I sat in the frozen little park. How often I had tarried here, waiting for evening, for jolly times to begin, for conversation of any sort although I could barely follow it, for any clue that would unlock the past. And this same pretty park with its winter-dormant roses was where the pogrom had begun.

To my right was the elegant town hall, a leftover from Austro-Hungarian days; in front, was the plinth of a now-vanished cement statue of Stalin; across was the memorial stone with its Star of David. To the left of the small, box-like police station was another nineteenth-century imperial throwback: an official building, low, long and ochre. And where the synagogue had stood, was the citron yellow house with white icing trim. What stories did these stolid buildings hide? Nothing is ever what it seems.

I appreciated the slower way of life, these jumbled shops, the ugly bars where all met, the mucky roads, weedy sidewalks and the tangled misty fields without town limits. I relished the friendliness and hospitality. But I was a well-behaved foreigner from an 'acceptable' country, Canada, and was based in another 'respectable' country, France. What if I hailed from a poorer or more 'foreign' part of the world, Africa or Asia? Or if I announced Roma parentage?

I also knew that hidden by the party crowd's gaiety, there was a more sombre picture. Kata's merry-widow determination

PART THREE : RETURNING

to collect lovers compensated for years spent with a violent husband, for the abuse of a drunken son who showed up too often. Józsi pumped his own earnings and much of Ildikó's into slot machines, and she longed to leave him. Beautiful daughter Enikö with her sharp wit and dramatic gift, would never study theatre for, working in the kocsma, she helped her mother support indolent older brothers and their children. Karcsi, like Bálint, was deliberately drinking himself to death.

And one afternoon, when walking along the back streets with Karcsi, I'd seen a merry group of laughing women. With them, sashaying with a deliberate swing, was Mariska, arch and confident.

'The other Mariska,' Karcsi gibed. 'There is one Mariska when Tarzan is around, and here is the other Mariska.'

***

'Have you been able to get any information about the pogrom in Kunmadaras?' Bálint asked as we stood at the counter in Ildikó's bar.

'Yes, quite a bit.'

'From Kohn?'

'No. He doesn't want to talk about the pogrom.'

'Because he knows nothing.' Bálint smiled with calm satisfaction. 'Kohn wasn't here then. He'd been sent to a work camp. The German military carried out the pogrom in 1944. They came in trucks, killed people on their way to the train station.'

Karcsi was listening to the conversation. I had told him what I had learnt from Katalin, but now he simply nodded assent.

'Karcsi, you know that's not true,' I said, angered by his defection. 'Both of you do, even if you're pretending you don't.

Those Absent

Local people carried out the pogrom. All I need are the details, and I'll be sticking around until I know everything!'

'It's only rumour,' said Bálint. 'That story has gone too far. I once worked in Vienna, and I stayed in a pension run by a Jew. He'd heard about the pogrom, and when he saw from my papers that I was from Kunmadaras, he treated me as if I were responsible. I was born years after it happened, but he charged me twice as much. I worked my head off on building sites, and he cheated me.' He lifted his glass, slugged back his pálinka. 'He cheated everyone.'

'Kohn is a good man,' said Karcsi.

'A very good man,' Bálint seconded. 'His daughter is an educated woman, and she went to university. She runs a little fruit and vegetable shop, is rich and powerful.'

Absurdity didn't bother him one whit. I glared at Karcsi, but he looked away.

'I've nothing against Jews,' Bálint continued. 'I visit Kohn all the time. His wife died a few months ago, and he's a changed man. I was his apprentice when I was young, and he taught me all about electricity. If you want, we can go see him. Come to my house tomorrow. Meet my wife and my daughter. You'll like them. My wife's a wonderful woman, and my daughter is beautiful and brilliant. She knows how to use computers.'

***

*B*álint had built his own home: 'A modern house, like the ones in Austria and Germany.' It was a white cement block with a double garage although neither Bálint, his wife, nor his daughter owned a car. One concession had been made to tradition: the front door opened onto a kitchen/dining area as in peasant houses.

'The furniture is new.' Bálint waited for my praise of matched sets in varnished agglomerate trimmed with gold plastic. Wife and daughter were also a matching set: under puffed dyed hair, their faces were pinched and mean. My greeting boomed, unanswered, off the cement walls.

Bálint was humiliated. 'They're angry with me,' he explained when, escaping the hostility, we were once again in the snowy street. 'I came home drunk last night. My wife says I drink too much. She's right. But my daughter is brilliant. She can work with computers.'

Kohn had aged considerably. Two men sat with him in his front room. One was tall Béla, husband of the owner of Ildikó's kocsma, the former Jewish bakery.

'He's become quite helpless,' Bálint explained. 'The men here in town take turns caring for him. We take him for walks, bring him food, feed and wash him.'

Bálint and I stood near Kohn. The men chatted quietly, but Kohn didn't participate in the conversation. Was he listening? He had no interest in any of us; he was in his own world. The door opened, and four elderly men entered. They embraced Kohn, asked how he was, but Kohn remained absent. The men also sat, stayed for a long while.

After they left, Bálint reached out, touched Kohn's arm.

Those Absent

'She needs information about the pogrom. Why it happened.'

There was a pause. Had Kohn understood the question? 'I wasn't here. I was out of town on a job. When I got back two days later, all was calm.'

'But what did you hear?' I asked. 'What were people saying?'

'That it was done by people who came from somewhere else.'

We sat for a while longer. Béla suggested we go to the kocsma across the road. He and Bálint helped Kohn stand, supported him as he shuffled along. In the bar, we sat at a corner table. The jukebox pounded out pop tunes; locals slugged back pálinka.

Kohn turned to me. 'There was a *mikva*.'[63] He smiled, as if the memory were a sweet one.

'Where?'

'Behind the synagogue.'

'But there's nothing left?'

'Nothing.'

'Tell me more about Jewish life here in Kunmadaras. About life before the war.'

But Kohn had returned to dreams.

---

63 A bath used for ritual immersion in Judaism.

PART THREE : RETURNING

XX

Like all proud high-spirited races, who allow for other people's dignity as well as their own, the Magyars have excellent natural manners; it has been said of them that they are a nation of gentlemen.

Geraldine Edith Mitton

I was in France when Udo called to tell me that Kohn had died. 'He was buried in the Kunmadaras Jewish cemetery.'

'Perhaps the last Jew to be buried there,' I said

'He had a Jewish funeral. A rabbi came from Szolnok. Karcsi told me that hundreds of people showed up, a huge crowd. Most had never seen a Jewish funeral. They were reverential and considerate. Everyone in town liked Kohn.'

'He never said anything against anyone.'

'That isn't the reason,' said Udo, a man fond of sweet tales and happy endings. 'It was because people wanted to show their respect to the Jews of Kunmadaras.'

Those Absent

PART FOUR:
Tiszaörs

What I knew was that the situation of the peasants...hadn't improved ...You can't imagine the poverty, the exploitation of those people; they worked from sunrise until dark. They shared the harvest with the proprietor, it was called the ninth. I often heard: 'I work for the ninth.' The landowner gave them lodgings; the floor was of beaten earth, always damp; they all had tuberculosis. The mother who milked up to a hundred cows received less than half a litre of milk per day. The schools were sometimes kilometres away and our winters are cold; the children were given a little warm wine to drink in the mornings and they went to school in the snow, drunken and sleepy...

Hélène Elek[64]

---

64   *La Mémoire d'Hélène*. Hélène Elek was the mother of the French/Hungarian resistance fighter, Thomas Elek, murdered by the nazis in 1944.

Those Absent

XXI

On the Great Hungarian Plain, our eye is caught by the peculiar mud-buildings of this treeless landscape, reminding us of the arid countries of the Eastern Continent. Houses are built of sun-dried bricks with beautifully arched porches, all white-washed. The walls of the rooms are also snow-white, white-washed at least twice a year, with a large open fireplace over a square hard-baked clay foundation in the hall...Also the roof is provided by the surrounding fields, consisting, as it does, of thatch which in its construction reflects the love of neatness acquired during a thousand years of practice... At the Eastern and Northern corners of the Plain the art of wood-carving seen in wooden fences, eaves, gable-ends, etc. becomes even more important. The homogeneity of the population of the Hungarian villages, with their indigenous art, is one of the most original, individual and versatile among the European peoples.

Elemér Radisics[65]

I returned to Hungary when wildflowers covered the berms, and winds were sweet, earthy. Udo wanted to buy a house in Kunmadaras. Would I help him find one? A few years earlier, he'd considered purchasing a cement box-like structure near Tarzan's dreary den – it would be a mere holiday hut, a place to store fishing tackle, and only briefly occupied each year.

Since I would also be staying in the house when in Hungary, aesthetics did matter. I dearly loved the traditional houses with their simple beauty and natural construction materials: adobe bricks (mud and straw) whitewashed with lime. Why, I asked Udo, choose a hideous cube? It was important, even necessary, to rehabilitate (not renovate) vernacular architecture, despite local indifference to this aspect of Hungary's cultural heritage.

---

65 *Hungary, Yesterday and Today.* Elemér Radisics, 1884-1972, Hungarian journalist, writer and politician.

The style of traditional houses changed little after the fourteenth century. In the early 1900s, Hungary had the largest unbroken zone of earthen architecture in central Europe, and villages had a cohesive beauty. The layout was simple: a front door opened into the kitchen where social activities took place. On the left was a room used as a pantry; on the right was the large square main room where cottage industries could be carried out, where people slept on trestle beds at night. The houses of local petty nobles, although grander, more complicated, and distinguished by stone-pillared porches, used the same materials in their construction, and they were equally harmonious.

By the middle of the twentieth century, people were destroying traditional houses and replacing them with square villas. The most recent, indistinctive yet expensive, aped those in German and Austrian subdivisions. Cement, breezeblock and plasterboard had ousted adobe and lime; and peculiar local fashion added railing-less upper storey balconies festooned with never-to-be-used barbecues.

There were still beautifully kept traditional houses in Kunmadaras, but they weren't for sale. Those that were, sagged unloved and moribund. Surely, they could surely be purchased for little money and saved from destruction. Having (lovingly) restored houses in Germany and France, I was more than willing to help out. But for negotiation, Udo thought it prudent to apply to his best crony.

These days, it was easy to locate Tarzan. He no longer held court in his dire back street kocsma or any other boozy sleazy establishment. Mariska had put her foot down: all free time was to be spent at home, in front of the television, as in any decent middle-class family.

'She says this is the modern way of life,' he said, abashed, even cowed. Gone the jocular camaraderie, the baggy clothes, the unkempt tangle of hair and drooping walrus moustache. 'Mariska wants me to be clean-shaven. Says it's more modern.' To recover male pride, he forced out a concupiscence snigger, winked: 'Tells me it's more fun in bed without the moustache. The moustache tickled.'

As for Mariska, she was no longer watchful, no longer content to stand in a doorway. Chin high, smile condescending, she snubbed us, ignored our polite greetings. Ostentatiously, on every finger, she sported large gold rings; eight long roped gold necklaces hung from her neck. This booty was the price Tarzan had paid for her return.

'Have to keep a wife happy.'

Udo was dismayed by his chum's meek about-face. Once the archetype of an authentic and eternal rebel, Tarzan was now a large deflated balloon. Yet the previous arrogance appeared briefly when he announced he had, aside from Udo, dropped his friends. 'Their interests, their choices in life, are no longer mine.'

In reality, most had dropped him. To finance Mariska's swag, he had borrowed a considerable amount of money from Karcsi, but never paid it back; he'd borrowed from others in town, too, and no creditor was as indulgent as Udo.

'For property, you've come to the right man,' said Tarzan. 'I have influence. I'll ask around, find out what's for sale, make sure no one jacks up prices because you're foreign.'

Over the next few weeks, we visited many houses – sad traditional houses shoddily renovated with incongruous picture windows, or with adobe walls smothered by a cement coating that, locking in moisture, caused rot and mould. One abandoned house, half-hidden by creepers and a towering pine, stood behind the vanished synagogue. Was I imagining the air of tragedy in its gloomy rooms? I searched for signs showing it had been Jewish-owned. The hostile seller shifted impatiently. No, he knew nothing of its history. He then demanded an exorbitant price.

Finally, on a back street, we found an unmodified house of four rooms with freshly whitewashed mud walls, a good roof, and a vine-shaded terrace. The neighbours seemed friendly – a woman, a gaggle of children and a lounging pack of young men watched from across the road. The woman smiled at me; I smiled back. She waved.

'Perfect,' said Tarzan. 'My son Imre will live here too, and you'll have no worries. He'll move into the room near the end.'

Udo quailed. He had no intention of housing Tarzan's idle and devious son, yet dreaded offending his pal. Beating endlessly around the bush for several days, when he finally drummed up the courage to make that clear, Tarzan was immediately less amenable.

'You'll be sorry. You need Imre to keep away intruders when you're out of the country.'

The next step was to go to the town hall and declare the intention to purchase, but Udo was returning to Vienna, and

Those Absent

Tarzan, churlish and resentful, declared he was too busy for such trivia. Only I was available for the task, and Tarzan was scornful. I was a woman and a foreigner; what did I understand about negotiation, about the Hungarian language, about real estate? I'd soon be pleading for his help, and Udo's door would open wide to Imre.

***

*I*n the town hall, I was directed to a back office. What sort of office? Not understanding much of anything, I was grateful to be directed anywhere. Inside, two women – a dyed brunette, and a bleached blond – were shifting through papers. Neither was friendly nor intrigued. After waving me to a seat, like the good communist bureaucrats they'd irrefutably been, both ignored me. After an exceedingly long while, the brunette looked up.

'An Austrian friend wants to buy this house,' I said in rotten Hungarian, and flapped the scrap of paper with the address.

The brunette took the paper, stared, put it down. Glanced briefly at the blond, and then resumed her paperwork. Confused but patient, I waited. What would I gain by leaving? Eventually, the blond stood, took her handbag and left the room.

The brunette finally spoke. 'House no good. No buy. No buy.'

'Why no good no buy house?' I pidgined back.

'No good. Danger.' Sighing with exasperation, she picked up the phone, dialled a number, had a long conversation, and then handed me the receiver.

'Your friend must not buy that house,' said a woman in perfect German. 'It's in a bad part of town, the Gypsy quarter. If he leaves the house unattended, even for a week, the Gypsies will move in, and he'll never get rid of them. Go to the police, ask them.'

I left the town hall, crossed the road, and went into the police station.

'Do you speak English or German?' I asked the three officers loafing about in the tiny front office. They didn't answer. 'A friend from Austria wants to buy this house,' I said in my ersatz Hungarian, and handed over the scrap of paper.

They began a low, rumbling conversation. Finally, one shook his head. 'No. No good.'

'What's no good?'

'Gypsies. Where now stay?'

'Berekfürdő.'

He scribbled down an address on the scrap. 'German-Hungarian. Berekfürdő. Go.'

Utterly mystified, I left the station, took the next bus back to Berekfürdő, went to the address indicated, a large modern house. A police car was parked in front, and on the terrace stood the same three officers, chatting amicably to a corpulent man who watched as I made my way up the crazy paving.

'Tell your friend not to buy that house,' the big man barked in German. 'If he does, he'll have problems. Gypsies will rob him; he'll have no peace. The police go to that area at least twice a night because of the noise, because of the stolen goods brought to the house across the street. Twenty people are squatting there, and the owner can't get them out unless he tears the place down. And if you, a woman, stay there on your own, you'll be putting yourself in danger.'

'Isn't this a bit excessive?'

He snorted in derision. 'You know nothing. Why do you think the police came here, asking me to warn you? We don't allow Gypsies into this town. I'm part of the neighbourhood watch, and we patrol the streets, keep them out.'

Hating this man and his private militia, I returned to Kunmadaras by bus and pounded down the road to Tarzan's house. Sitting on the fatty cosy-corner, I told him the story. He listened expressionlessly, puffing his lardy cheeks out, sucking them in again.

'Don't you think everyone is exaggerating?' I asked. 'Lying?'

Tarzan puffed and sucked. 'If that's what people say, you should listen. Perhaps they're right.'

'What do you mean, perhaps? You live here. Your wife is Roma. Your two youngest children are part Roma. Doesn't this make you angry?'

But he merely puffed and sucked for a long, silent while. Then his eyes narrowed. 'You can't leave a house empty in Kunmadaras. If you let Imre live there, you'll be safe.'

PART FOUR : TISZAÖRS

XXII

Whoever has once traversed any portion of the Alföld on either side of the Tisza, or has spent but a few days in any one of its villages, may boldly say that he knows the whole of it... When the traveller has been surprised by sleep during his journey across its sandy plains wakes up a few hours after, the only perceptible signs of his progress are afforded by the condition of his horses and the position of the sun... The meadows which extend far and wide, whose undiversified appearance is broken only here and there by the tall wooden crane above some uncovered well, or by a few storks around a half-dried pool; the ill-cultivated fields whose wheat and maize are entrusted to the care of Providence, and the trouble any thief would have in carrying them away... Even the very church-towers which he remembers observing when he last looked about him, standing like pointed columns on the distant horizon, seem to have travelled with him. At any rate he can discern as little difference between those he now sees and those he last saw, as between the village he had then left and the town, which he is now approaching.

Baron József Eötvös[66]

*T*arzan lent me a car, ancient and rattling, probably neither registered nor insured (I didn't dare ask). 'Don't drive at night. Drink no alcohol. Keep to the back roads and drive slowly. Don't attract attention and avoid the police.' It had no brakes to speak of; the tyres were balloon smooth; dashboard lights flashed constantly in dire warning; the back fender dropped off at every pothole or bulge on the road, and there were an extraordinary number of both.

Yet, throughout that sultry summer of violent thunderstorms, the car never let me down, carrying me into quiet villages where abandoned houses dozed in impenetrable gardens and

---

66   *The Village Notary.* József Eötvös was a Hungarian writer, poet, advocate of Jewish emancipation, and a supporter of the 1848 revolution.

Those Absent

were guarded by lonely dogs on short chains. Sometimes rutted lanes petered out in snarled undergrowth or ploughed fields. In one such dead end, far beyond reeds, I found an ancient oak and wooden cross, both ringed by a rotten fence. What was this place? A pagan holy site kept up through the centuries by tradition? The faint memento of a village destroyed by Mongol or Turk ferocity?

There were bygone manors too. Some, smashed by communist fury, had been nibbled to dust by rampant vegetation; others, converted into gaudy fishing lodges, vulgar apartments or clubhouses, were hardly recognizable. One, elegant and glorified by a broad porch with many stout pillars, was abandoned; its empty tithe barn looked discouraged.

And everywhere, footpaths wandered lazily into copses or wound along riverbanks. They conjured up long gone residents: Homo erectus, Neanderthals, Scythians, Illyrians, Celts, Sarmatians, Anartes, Iazyges, Kumans, Lombards, Avars and Bulgars. Who thinks of those vanished people today? Modern life vanquishes ghosts thoroughly, yet these were once their fields. Their villages had stood here. This is where they dreamt.

In deserted cemeteries I found the last totem pole wooden grave markers. Called *fejfa* or *kopjafa*, these wooden markers originated in the sixteenth century when Hungarians were fighting the Turks. The tradition continued during the Reformation to distinguish Protestant graves from those of Roman Catholics who used crosses. Local craftsmen had carved some fejfa; before their demise, elderly men often sculpted their own. All were enmeshed in a riot of trees, bushes, grasses and wildflowers for, according to ancient belief, new vegetation is a dwelling place of the soul. How pleasant these places, far more so than modern cemeteries with gravelled lanes, polished granite and sterile order.

PART FOUR : TISZAÖRS

And outside the fences and walls of Christian cemeteries, were Jewish gravestones, for after Empress Maria Theresa banned Jews from Great Kumania in 1746,[67] they lived in these many villages along its border. Now, there were no Jews left. After the war, survivors of the camps had headed for Israel, or Budapest's greater safety and opportunity.

Once, a pot-holed road petered out in a ghostly town. I parked, then proceeded on foot, passing a former kocsma doubling as a general store – the beer sign hung outside, rusty, faded – with boarded-up windows and doorways. There had been other shops, even a post office; all were dilapidated and abandoned. Veering left, I saw houses, forlorn, collapsing into lakes of mud, but occupied. Scrawny chickens scratched the debris-choked ground, pecked at a dreadful pile of dead and rotting fowl. A few locals appeared, Roma, and they watched my progress with indifference.

'Hello,' I called and hoped friendliness would excuse prying, for I had no intention of abandoning my exploration. One man nodded briefly; a woman mumbled something unintelligible. Two grubby boys playing in puddles said, 'Kiss your hand,' the traditional Hungarian response to an older woman.

What had this place been? A *társközösségeki*, an associate village? In the 1950s, the communist central committee began transferring civic and commercial services out of small settlements and into larger towns. Villages that were once independent became associate villages without municipal services, jobs, transportation or modern sanitation, and residents soon abandoned them. A few Roma were still living in forest clearings and isolated settlements, but under a government-initiated relocation program, the wild encampments were

---

67 In 1746 Jews were also expelled from Buda and banned from other regions in the country.

destroyed, and the Roma were resettled in the newly untenanted associate villages.

Passing another grim hummock of decaying chickens, I arrived at a low, once-yellow building. It had been a manor, albeit a modest one. Partly ravaged, reconstructed as a dismal communist office, it had been devastated once more. On one gable end was a faded, long-obsolete symbol of heraldry: a bear holding a shield. These shattered hints were all that was left of a once-flourishing feudal enterprise.

After Ottoman defeat and withdrawal, their territory was ceded to the Habsburg Monarchy, and a new order of magnates came to power. Allying themselves with the Catholic Church, they fixed their gaze on the Habsburg court, sent their children to Viennese schools, spoke German at home and in public, and condemned Hungarian as a language 'fit for peasants'. Leaving the gloomy feudal defence castles, they gobbled up estates formerly owned by Protestants or others out of royal favour, and built baroque palaces in lush surroundings.

Jesuits crossed through the country, converting Protestants; civil servants were forced to return to Catholicism; Protestant students were forbidden to study abroad; and conversion to Protestantism was banned. Accused of having colluded with the Ottomans, the Roma were pushed out to village edges, and their children were taken away.

Again reduced to serfdom, peasants rebuilt the nobles' villages, manor houses, farms and churches, worked their fields, grew and spun hemp, provided the landowners with eggs, fowl and cattle, financed their weddings and funerals. Women and children laboured in their maize and potato allotments, and one-ninth of the resulting crop was owed to the lords. Nobles and their guests used peasant girls and married women for a night's pleasure, so did estate managers: refusal meant starvation for families.

Not all nobles were magnates, nor did all those with titles possess estates or wield political power. Country squires lived in modest dwellings. Although unable to frequent the upper aristocracy, they aped the behaviour of their betters, fighting duels, brawling, brandishing weapons and demonstrating with haughty arrogance that they were gentlefolk. The peasants, teachers, and members of the clergy all accepted them as undisputed masters:

> *When there is only one person who always talks without being contradicted by anyone, he would finally believe that he had always been talking wisely, and that it was impossible to contradict him. The man who sees the members of his household accepting his words like oracles easily considers them to be oracles indeed.*[68]

Despite their dusting of stature, they had little money. Wearing second-hand clothes, possessing few or no serfs, they worked plots of land like any peasant. Unable to travel far because animals were needed for fieldwork, they hunted, sat

---

68 Jozsef Kármán, 1769-1796. Hungarian romantic writer and Freemason.

Those Absent

in kocsmas and smoked long pipes, drank to excess, played cards and wept to Gypsy music. Those lucky enough to possess a carriage or sleigh rode about the countryside with great ostentation.

Life was even narrower for their women. Banal social events, birthdays, name days, weddings, punctuated country life, and a wife walked in her husband's shadow:

> *She was the daughter rather than the servant of her husband; nor was she his mate in mastership of the house. She sat on his left when travelling in a coach, and when entering the house of someone else, she followed rather than preceded him. She could read but not write, and the real world where she moved was her yard, the kitchen, and the pantry filled with pottery and frying pans.*[69]

But inferior position didn't make women sensitive. As bigoted and affected as their men, they were ruthless to those beneath them.

I came to the sticky wet end of this wrecked village. Here was an wooden cart, long out of commission and containing rotting planks, rags and legless chairs. A soft, despondent sheepdog was bound to this pile of things worthless, and he bared his teeth as I approached, for he was on guard duty. Yet his tail wagged, and he ached for me to pat his head, make his pitiful existence rich for a brief minute or so. He was fettered here for life.

Behind was the Puszta, delectably lonely and latticed by dark marsh.[70]

---

[69] Ferenc Kazinczy, 1759-1831. Hungarian translator, writer, and active in the reform of the Hungarian language. Condemned to death for conspiracy, he was released after seven years imprisonment in Austria.
[70] Incorporating the Hortobágy National Park, this has been a World Heritage Site since 1999.

PART FOUR : TISZAÖRS

XXIII

The inner room is heated by a huge stove of bee-hive shape, two or three metres high, divided into parts by ridges and opening into the hall, whence it is heated, in the absence of wood, by straw. The lowest ridge round the stove, at the level of a chair, is broad and in winter the people sit here to warm themselves.

Elemér Radisics, 1936

*I*n the baths, I heard a group of people speaking German. Unobtrusively (or so I thought), I moved closer to eavesdrop, but they noticed me immediately. One man threw me a look of unconcealed amusement. Was I German? Did I live here? Was I a tourist?

'An Austrian friend wants to buy a house, and I'm trying to find one for him.'

'Then come to Tiszaörs where we live. Many houses are for sale there.'

These people, German, Swiss and Austrian retirees, had arrived in the early 1990s, encouraged by a real estate agent who'd mentioned healing thermal springs, inexpensive houses and the low cost of living. They spent the warmer months in Hungary, wintered in Spain, Greece, Morocco or Croatia.

'But Hungary's not like it used to be,' complained a man named Willi. 'Prices go up every year. Who do they think they are, the Hungarians? This isn't Germany.'

'They cheat you if you give them a chance. They don't have the faintest idea what it means to do a job properly,' added Beate, his wife. 'Letting them join the EU will ruin everything.'

'Do you all speak Hungarian?'

'It's too difficult. And why bother? Hungarians speak German.'

Those Absent

'Germans and Austrians have always lived here,' said a woman named Helga. 'We came long ago. We were invited here by Empress Maria Theresa.'

Did she really think owning a holiday home was comparable to an eighteenth-century colonisation programme?

***

Destroyed during the Ottoman conquest, the village of Tiszaörs was rebuilt in a grid pattern. Low long whitewashed houses, one side to the road, crouched behind wrought iron fences, and gardens were lush with fruit trees and vegetables. Most surprising in this perfectly flat landscape was the high tumulus near the village centre. This towering earth castle, possibly an ancient Scythian or Sarmatian burial mound, had again become a cemetery in recent centuries, and the usual tangle of vegetation snagged the totem-pole markers along its broad flank.

I found the perfect house one street away from the earth mound. Solid although well over a century old, its beauty wasn't immediately apparent for the front yard had been stripped bare of plant life; inexplicably, villagers ripped out flowers, vines and shrubs when putting a property up for sale.

Under sweating linoleum, the beaten earth floor had gone mouldy, and layers of brown lacquer smothered beams and broad windowsills. Furniture filled the rooms, not traditional handcrafted pieces – those had long since been burnt – but communist-era pressboard beds, dressing tables, and armoires painted to resemble walnut. Happily, the traditional *búbos kemence*,[71] a ceiling-high voluminous clay oven, was still in place,

---

71 The Yiddish equivalent is the *pripechik*. Cone shaped in Hungary, made of clay bricks and lined with mud, these effective ovens were used for heating houses as well as for slow cooking.

although jammed with plastic, tin cans and waste paper. Such ovens can keep the heat for days. In traditional Jewish homes, food was placed inside on Friday afternoon and the door was sealed. On Saturday evening, at Sabbath's end, a warm meal was ready to eat.

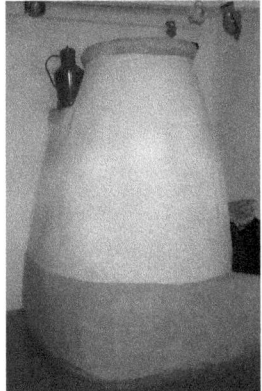

When Udo arrived, he stared at the iron stove rusting in the entry, at the worm-eaten beds with reeking straw mattresses, at the spongy, patched spots on walls, the collapsing barn roof and the outhouse slumping dangerously to the left. But cherry, plum and walnut trees flourished in the back garden, and tiny bright green tree frogs yapped. The idea of possessing such wealth convinced him, for he had always lived in cramped apartments.

The sellers, two sisters and two brothers, were happy to get rid of this house built by their great-grandfather. They were modern folk, they insisted. The apartments they lived in near Budapest were recent. They found it incomprehensible that foreigners would choose such a primitive place. Suspicious of Udo, of me, of the notary, of each other, each separate family member and spouse counted and re-counted the purchase money eight times.

We began work immediately. Udo sanded away the lacquer

on beams and window ledges, revealed the golden acacia underneath. Karcsi and I visited sites where traditional houses were being demolished, and we salvaged used but healthy adobe bricks. Digging out wet spots faultily patched with cement, I filled them with the bricks, painted all with lime wash, and replanted grapevines along the terrace. Karcsi restored the kemence oven with mud and straw; he and his crony József covered the dirt floor with wooden planks, repaired the rotted roof, lengthened the terrace, and rebuilt walls of an end room that would be mine.

Since Udo was in Hungary only every second weekend, I supervised the restoration, and this led to conflict. Karcsi and József resented working for a woman, and they insisted on using cement for construction. To that end, they had many sacks delivered. 'Hungarians are modern. Building with straw and mud is Gypsy work,' although, Karcsi admitted, he had spent part of his apprenticeship using such traditional materials.

As obdurate as they, I sat on the stacked sacks of cement and hindered their employ: the two men went on an angry three-day strike, drinking at the kocsma around the corner, idling drunkenly in the garden. To my relief, a truck arrived on the fourth day and carried the cement back to the builder's yard. Work with lime, mud, straw and rescued bricks resumed.

Villagers came to the gate and stared. Although I had been certain that restoration of a traditional house would be appreciated, no one was admiring. Karcsi and József – they still spent much work time knocking back pálinka in the kocsma – never failed to tell me that my middle-class 're-peasantisation' was viewed with a jaded eye.

'No one understands why a foreigner from Canada, a modern country, wants an old house. Only the poorest people live in such places. People are saying you must be crazy.'[72]

Once, the couple living in the green cement villa on the left inched hesitantly into the yard. 'This is how houses were when we were children,' said the wife. 'It looks nice.' But she and her husband were determined to expunge any trace of peasant life.

My neighbour on the right, Gizi, also lived in a traditional house. A tiny woman with curling brown hair and overly large glasses, she was an English teacher in the city, several hours away. She'd grown up here and returned on weekends with her elderly mother.

'When I was a child, flowers and mulberry trees lined the main road. There was also a village green with a sweep-well, and beside a lovely leafy copse, there was a row of thatch-roofed houses. Because the village was so beautiful, film studios came out and made two movies here, one in the 1950s, and one in the 1960s. After that, the green and well were cemented over for a parking lot, the copse was chopped down, and the thatched cottages were destroyed to make way for the new housing development.'

'Didn't anyone protest?'

'Why would they? Everyone has to show how modern they've become. They want their neighbours to see they've reached a higher social level, that they have money and can afford new villas. Of course, some things have improved. Full electrification didn't arrive until the early 1960s, and these back streets were unpaved until the mid-1990s. In the rainy season, the mud mixed with the filthy water and manure leaking out of everyone's stables. When I went to school, I had to wear rubber

---

[72] Much later, when I complained about the destruction of the country's architecture to a young Hungarian parliamentary representative, he said he hoped it would stop before it was too late. He then added, rather cynically, that it was good to see that I, a foreigner, was leading the way.

boots and carry my shoes under one arm, but as soon as I got to the main street, I'd hide the boots under a bush. Wearing them meant you lived on a back road and were of lower status.' She paused. 'Still, everything is changing too quickly. In my English conversation courses, my students only talk about reality TV.'

Hungarian village circa 1944[73]

Laden with many bottles of frankly awful homemade wine, Karcsi, Ildikó, Bálint, Kata and Enikö came to see the house. They also brought baking tins heaped with raw pumpkin, others with sliced potatoes topped by pork fat, foods that would be roasted in the búbos kemence. That bulky clay oven charmed them: what an exotic throwback! They'd all destroyed their own years before, but waxed on about how good meats, stews and vegetables had tasted when cooked slowly inside, how warm rooms had been, and how, as children, they'd slept, curled against the rounded clay cones.

Hungarian style, the guests removed their shoes at the door, pulled on felt slippers. Udo and I ushered everyone into the main room where we'd set up a long table, but all said it was quite lovely, however they preferred to remain in the kitchen. No argument could sway them. For these descendants of peasants,

---

73 Photo courtesy of Attila Szabo

the kitchen was the room for social events. Dragging in chairs, side tables, wooden crates, anything they could find, they made themselves comfortable around a minuscule kitchen table that could only accommodate three with comfort.

Karcsi goaded dry corn stalks into a roaring fire in the kemence's belly. Then, pushing embers against its walls, he placed the tin trays on the oven floor and shoved the clay door into place. An hour later, the potatoes and pumpkin were faintly smoky, meltingly delicious. And, elbows banging, knees bumping, glasses tipping over and plates hanging perilously, we feasted.

Those Absent

XXIV

A little cobbler, I,
A little cobbler, I,
Living life from day to day,
Happily, gaily, and well.
Tell me, little cobbler,
Do you have any food?
Are you in need?
Can you borrow from anyone?
No one lends me anything,
No one makes me loans,
A little cobbler, I,
And go about barefoot.

Yiddish Folksong

Samu, the mayor's husband, came to read the water meter set into a deep hole in the garden. He alone was responsible for the purity of village drinking water, dosing it with chemicals and keeping it free of contaminants. Its erratic quality – it was often too vile to swallow – was due to Samu's fluctuating state of inebriation. Fluent in German, he wooed foreign residents with writhing sycophancy, convinced that international contact elevated his status. His, alas, was a fickle loyalty: those who entrusted him with house keys discovered that, during absences, their residences, now filthy and disordered, had been clandestinely let to strangers.

This morning, I trailed after Samu as he crossed the yard. 'You were born in this village. Can you tell me about the Jews who lived here?'

Instantly ill at ease, Samu ignored my question.

'Jews lived in all the villages in this area,' I insisted.

'Not here,' he muttered. 'In Tiszaigar, the next village, there were Jews, never here.'

'There must have been a few here, too.'

Samu again chose silence and pretended meter reading needed the utmost concentration. Then, avoiding my eyes, he tucked his clipboard under one arm, crossed back over the yard and passed through the gate. I followed. Grabbing his bicycle, Samu slipped his clipboard into a little sack and prepared to skedaddle. But there I was, standing right in front of him.

'In Hungary, there was never a problem with the Jews,' he said. 'Hungarians protected Jews, but the rich ones left and took their money with them.' He backed up the bike, wheeled it onto the lumpy tarmac.

I was unwilling to accept the outright lie. 'Hungarians protected Jews? In 1944, too? You really believe that?'

He stared down the empty road as if something fascinating were taking place just out of sight. Then muttered, 'Deutsch.'

'Deutsch?'

'Jewish family. A long time ago. The Deutsch family.'

'How long ago? Before the war?'

'I heard the name, that's all.'

'Tell me more.'

'Another man, too. An administrator for the nobles. He lived out there somewhere.' One hand waved toward distant fields.

'When?' Was he referring to Sándor Klein? In 1909, Klein, a wealthy man, considered himself part of the gentry and invited guests to hunting parties on his extensive lands.

But Samu, pedalling away, called over his shoulder: 'Never Jews in this village. Never.'

He had to be wrong. Since nearby Great Kumania had

Those Absent

remained closed to Jewish settlement until 1867, Jews had lived in every one of these surrounding villages, entering Kumania to peddle during the day, returning home at nightfall. Because Christians frowned upon trade – no respectable Magyar would stand at a shop counter, serve customers or go from door to door – petty trade had also been carried out by Armenians, Serbs, Macedonians and Greeks, spice and coffee merchants of Balkan origin, who benefited from family connections in the Ottoman Empire. In the eighteenth century, however, Empress Maria Theresa forced them to choose between exile and cutting Levant connections. Most opted for the latter, and Jews replaced them.

Although educated and permitted to practice medicine, Jews were excluded from guilds, forbidden to own or farm land, study and practice law, enter the civil service, teach, occupy any position of authority over Christians. Yet dispersal throughout Europe, when coupled with long experience in money lending, gave them a great advantage in commerce. Invited by landowners to live on manorial estates, they administered finances, negotiated agricultural produce, transported salt and timber. Aware of prices, needs and quantities, in constant contact with their peasant neighbours, they knew the best time to buy up grains, store them until prices were right. With the profits they made, they extended loans.

Such negotiators and administrators were an elite. Living in fine houses at the main crossroads, they kept the nobles wealthy enough to maintain exorbitant, often ruinous, lifestyles. Yet even the most brilliant were viewed with contempt: all they acquired became the lords' property.

Many village Jews were *arendars*, brewers, leaseholders of the nobles' inns or mills, but most were rabbis, wheelwrights, smiths, shoemakers, tailors, bookbinders, butchers, and cobblers.[74] Countless Jewish peddlers, *Pinkeljuden*, wandered the roads, walking stick in hand, long pipes sending a stream of smoke into the air. Some carried weather-resistant tarred bundles on their backs, others, wicker baskets for glass and ceramics, or cabinets filled with books, sewing articles, dice, drapes, remedies, matches, salt, ribbons, embroidered purses, watches, handkerchiefs, belts, scarves – items precious to women who might never venture further than the next village a few kilometres away.

Going from farm to farm, one village to the next, and never missing a back street, a peddler blew a whistle to attract attention, made every dog howl, and called out his wares. Alerted by the din, a crowd gathered. Haggling, snatching up minuscule amounts of fruit, mushrooms, cabbages, fowls and honey (peasants rarely had a surplus of anything), collecting rags, bones, hides, flax, wax, wormwood and wool, buying horsetails, manes and the hair of indebted women, profits were often reduced to a pittance. Sometimes no money was exchanged: eggs were traded for bristles, bristles for woollens, woollens for tatters.

Business concluded, peddlers fulfilled their second function. Settled comfortably in the local kocsma, they passed on messages from distant relatives, gave news of the ruler's health, of recent crimes, the fates of unfaithful spouses, and detailed the latest manifestations of the evil eye. Glib and charming, they easily garnered displeasure. Jealous husbands hated them, and resentful local shop owners labelled them liars, tellers of tall tales, thieves. But most peddlers dreamt of amassing enough money to buy a nag and wagon under which to sleep at night – a modicum of comfort in the rainy season – and others hoped

---

74   Cobblers were often hard up, for both peasants and Jews went barefoot to save shoe leather.

Those Absent

to leave the road and set up shop.

At the bottom of the social heap were homeless Jewish vagabonds. Wealthier Jews, forbidden to employ Christians, engaged a few as servants, but between 1740 and 1840, the countryside abounded with such wretches.

Village Christians and Jews lived no differently from each other. They shared proverbs, fairy tales and stories of hope: a poor tailor who dreamt of treasure and found coins in his oven, a starving cobbler who discovered, in the crook of a tree, enough gold to save his family. With the exception of pork, Jews and Christians ate the same foods prepared in the same way, grew vegetables and fruits to survive and were equally frugal. Taxes to vineyard guardians, lamplighters, bell ringers and the nobles pinched the purses of all, but only Jews paid the tolerance tax imposed by Empress Maria Theresa in 1746.[75]

One major difference was study. The Church limited the education of Christians, for only priests needed to be literate; Jews emphasized literacy, a necessity for religious study, and a means of advancement and comfort. 'Shrewd like a Jew,' was as popular a saying as, 'Out of the way, Jew, when the peasant comes'.

After 1783, Emperor Joseph II's edict for the Betterment of the Jewish Nation permitted residence in royal free towns, apprenticeship to Christian guild masters and attendance at some universities. Jews could henceforth carry swords, rent land, hire Christians, join the liberal professions and the military, be ennobled or become part of the peasantry. All were to adopt German surnames, and, because time was short, they were hastily selected. Some were based on occupations –

---

75 The tax of 20,000 guldens was steadily increased until it reached 160,000 guldens in 1813. To survive, Jewish moneylenders raised interest rates, which incurred more hatred.

Schuster (shoemaker), Fiedler (fiddler); others were descriptive – Klein (little), Gross (big), Schwarz (black). Those higher on the social scale preferred names reflecting natural phenomena: Birnbaum (pear tree), Grunwald (green wood) or Bach (stream). But so many were given the same name by the authorities, only nicknames distinguished them: one local man, Schwartz, was dubbed *Gatyátlan* (no underwear) possibly because he couldn't afford any.[76]

In 1867, full emancipation was granted, and this could result in amusing situations:

> *In an assembly of voters gathered for communal elections, a pastor proposed admitting Jews to the voting area. A tailor... with the intention of ending the discussion underway, gave his vote, and justified it in this way: 'We don't need the Jews.'*
>
> *A Jew amongst those in the assembly, looked at the tailor with a tragicomic air, then announced that this enemy of his religion was wearing, at this very moment, the pair of pants that he, the Jew, had brought to him for repairs. 'And this man,' he cried, 'who is wearing my trousers, claims one doesn't need the Jews!'*[77]

***

'I never heard of Jews living in this village,' said my neighbour Gizi as we chatted over the garden fence.

'Before the war,' I prompted. 'Why not ask your mother? She might know something.'

'My mother isn't from here. She grew up near the Transylvanian border. Anyway, she isn't interested in talking about the past.' Nervously, Gizi glanced over her shoulder, for that tyrannical woman was ever ready with reproach: 'What a lazy girl you are. Wasting time talking when the hedge needs

---

76 *A Brief History of the Jews in Heves County, Hungary.* Dr Ágnes Szegö Orbánné.
77 Bulletin de l'Alliance Israélite, 1867-68.

trimming, and the trees want pruning.' Or leaves needed raking, the house cleaned from top to bottom, and outside walls had to be scrubbed and painted.

Never rebellious, Gizi was apologetic. 'My father took care of things when he was alive. Now it's up to me.'

'You could refuse.' She was at least forty years old.

'No. We Hungarians obey our parents… well, perhaps not so much these days. My daughter doesn't obey me. But my mother never learnt to do chores. Her father was rich, and she grew up in a fine house with many servants. When the communists came to power, her family lost everything, so she married my father. He was from a peasant family.'

'Did she love him?'

'She needed a husband, and he was acceptable because had a good job at the post office in Kunmadaras. But he was transferred back here, to this small village where he'd grown up, and they began living in this house built by my paternal grandfather. My mother never forgave my father for the loss in status. He fixed up the house, decorated the windows with woodcarving, added rooms, put in plank floors, created this lovely garden, but he could never please her. No one can – except my brother, because he's a doctor.'

'What's going on here!' Unnoticed, that elderly woman had come up to the fence. Rapping her cane on the hard ground, she castigated her daughter: 'I'm ashamed of you. I'm always ashamed of you. Wasting time. It's disgraceful.'

Gizi's eyes sparkled briefly. 'She's angry because we're speaking English, and she can't understand what we're saying.'

'You haven't done half the hedge yet!'

Dutifully, Gizi picked up the trimmer.

'You said your father lived in Kunmadaras,' I said before she could leave. 'Did he ever mention the pogrom?'

'Pogrom?'

'The Kunmadaras pogrom of May 1946. Locals attacked Jewish Holocaust survivors.'

But her face hardened. 'That's impossible. There couldn't have been a pogrom in Kunmadaras. My father was interested in history, and if there'd been a pogrom, he'd have mentioned it.' With a little wave, she vanished behind the boxwood.

***

Several times a day, a belching tractor rumbled out of a yard across the road and passed the house. Perched on the seat were old András and his wife. She was shrunken, silent, ailing; he, fat-bellied and jovial, grinned constantly, exposing the only two teeth in his possession – long yellow incisors. The couple had a tiny allotment between village edge, walnut trees and Puszta. Once laboured by serfs, ownership of these parcels is unclear today, and locals use them for their beehives, their rows of grapevines.

When not out in his plot, András tended the fruit trees around his house and worked his vegetable patch. Slow, tubby – his stomach was of a mighty size, and his legs were stumpy – he was ever eager to pause, come chat over his garden fence. Although patient with my splintered Hungarian, he, distressingly, insisted on speaking to me in pidgin Hungarian mixed with pidgin German, thinking this truncated mishmash would be more comprehensible to a foreigner. Yet I was grateful for his cheery near-edentate smile, his open friendliness.

'Kunmadaras,' he said to me one morning. 'Very bad. Bad for Jews.'

Those Absent

I was dumbfounded. 'You heard I was asking about the Kunmadaras pogrom?' I had forgotten how quickly gossip travels in small places. Had Samu or Gizi said something to him?

'Family, Kunmadaras.'

'You?'

'No me,' he replied. 'Me, child. Me, Tiszaörs. Hear story. Pogrom story. Terrible. Jews kind people.' He shook his head sadly. 'Terrible, terrible.'

'Jews lived in this village, too?' Perhaps I would finally learn something.

'No Jews. Kunmadaras Jews, Tiszaigar Jews, Tiszaigar cemetery. Me, child. Remember Jewish butcher, *shochet*.'[78]

His use of the Yiddish word astounded me. 'You know the word shochet?'

'Everyone call man shochet. Live Tiszaigar, bicycle Kunmadaras, kill chickens. Pass here, main road. Black hat, long hair. Good man. Mud roads. No cars. Horses. Wagons. Bicycles.'

'And Kunmadaras? The pogrom? Tell me more.'

'Me child.' He shook his head. 'Me child.'

And so the conversation ended. Perhaps András had no information to share.

Village Shochet[79]

---
78 Ritual slaughterer.
79 Photo courtesy of the Museum of Hungarian Speaking Jewry, Safed, Israel.

PART FOUR : TISZAÖRS

XXV

I have met Hungarians of intelligence and culture, who were personally acquainted with non-Austrian Germany, very much struck with the difference between that country and their own. All the Austrian populations spend so large a proportion of their incomes on animal gratification and ostentatious display that they have necessarily less to spend on the productions of literature and art.

Arthur John Patterson

*E*dit and László kept goats and made their own cheese, which they sold from their house. The two local shops sold only individually wrapped industrial squares, but this couple's herb-flavoured cheese tasted like a more fragrant feta. It was much in evidence; solid, yellow rounds hung from rods near the kitchen stove and filled a back larder. Although they spoke no German, both were descendants of ethnic Germans who had come in the eighteenth century.

'Now, of course, we're Hungarians,' said Edit. 'Our ancestors arrived when this village was taken over by the Catholic Church – it had been Protestant, but the Catholics forced them out. We ethnic Germans built the houses, set out the streets and planted the mulberry trees. They're gone now, those lovely trees. The communists cut them down and sold the wood.'

Fetching an atlas from a back room, László pointed to the Moravian villages of ancestors. 'We weren't treated like Hungarians in Maria Theresa's time. We were never serfs, and no one could take our freedom away from us. There were two separate societies, German and Hungarian.'

'Rather like today,' I said.

Both smiled uncomfortably. If I had made a joke, they thought it rather unfunny.

Those Absent

'I suppose you're right and...' Edit stopped. Had she been about to say something not entirely flattering about the modern Germans, then realised I, too, was foreign?

***

After Ottoman withdrawal, to rebuild villages that were little more than charred beams and mud, to transform wasteland into productive fields and to increase the Catholic population, Empress Maria Theresa and the Austrian Imperial Council launched a great colonization scheme in Hungary. Tax exemption, free land, livestock and building materials were offered as incentives to German settlers from Slovakia, Moravia, Swabia and Silesia.

Many accepted: landless younger sons; those toiling for feudal lords; famine victims whose crops had fed invading armies. Not all new arrivals were voluntary: Protestants and others considered 'socially undesirable' were either forcibly relocated or encouraged to do so.

Arriving in horse-drawn wagons, or on barges floated down the Danube then dismantled for house rafters, the German-speaking incomers eventually became the country's largest minority after the Roma, and although they hailed from different regions, Hungarians dubbed them all 'Swabians'. Few learnt Hungarian, but great patriots, they called themselves German Hungarians, not Hungarian Germans.

Thrifty, orderly, they built traditional Hungarian-style houses in a grid pattern around churches, lined the roads with mulberry trees for the silkworm trade. With no dislike of commerce, through hard work, discipline and sacrifice, they succeeded as traders, shopkeepers, market gardeners, bakers, shoemakers and butchers: German bratwurst became, after the addition of paprika, traditional Hungarian sausage.

The most successful Swabians aped the Magyar nobility, buying immense properties and reigning over their Hungarian peasants like titled lords. Others moved to the cities, took Hungarian names, joined the army and bureaucracy where the protection of the Christian Brotherhood helped them climb career and social ladders.

Self-imposed isolation incurred the hostility of Hungarian neighbours: weren't all Swabians wealthy? Deeply conservative, averse to the struggles of other minorities and resentful of their business rivals, the Jews, Swabian merchants endorsed anti-Semitic politics. In 1829, they produced a memorandum complaining of the increase of Jews in the country and recommending Jewish 'peddling' be limited. There was nothing new in this: along with Greek businessmen, the powerful merchant class of German origin, present before the Ottoman conquest, had agitated to prevent Jewish residence in towns and cities.

But Jewish migration to Hungary was always constant, particularly after Karl III, archduke of Austria and king of Hungary, introduced the 1726 Familiants Law in Bohemia, Moravia and Silesia. To limit the Jewish population, only the eldest son in a family had the right to marry, and only after his father's death; a younger son could marry when the older brother died. If there were daughters but no sons, a family was considered extinct.

***

*E*asy to see which houses belonged to the recent German, Austrian and Swiss expatriates. Some had purchased the newer square villas, but those with traditional buildings 'improved' them with white floor tiles, cement, Spanish-style grillwork, PVC windows with roll-down shutters brought in from Germany

Those Absent

and Austria. There was statuary – cement Venuses, cherubs and barbecues resembling picturesque wells. A few, Helga and Erwin, Peter and Monika, claiming a love of Hungarian tradition, tore down their adobe houses and replaced them with identical structures in industrial materials.

Gardens classically divided into a back orchard, a vegetable garden and a front yard for grapevines and flowers, were transformed into perfect lawns punctuated by regimented walkways and surrounded by high chain-link fences. Behind Peter's swanky house – a few cattily referred to it as 'Peter's Palace' – a waterfall and arched Japanese bridge ornamented two kidney-shaped fishponds, a jab at sophistication slightly marred by the neighbour's grunting pigs in a low dark hut, three meters away from the dividing fence.

Meeting in the baths each morning and each evening, these expatriates marked out days with visits to one another and afternoons of coffee and cake. Never frequenting the kocmas, rarely showing up for local events, they made occasional forays to restaurants with bilingual waiters and menus in German. Their contact with Hungarians was restricted to hiring them for work, or asking for their help when translations were needed, yet they celebrated birthdays and anniversaries with backyard parties and prepared 'typical' Hungarian dishes, *gulyás* and *pörkölt*, in the modern peasant way: in big pots over gas fires. Other than the Hungarian husbands of two German women, no local Hungarians were invited.

'What language would we speak with them?' said Hannelore. 'Anyway, they'd feel uncomfortable with us.'

'It's not worth learning Hungarian,' said Heinz, a florid man. 'Tried. Gave up. Too hard. And when you do make an effort, they pretend they don't understand.'

PART FOUR : TISZAÖRS

'They aren't like us, no matter what you say.'

Did they stay in this country simply because houses were cheap and the thermal baths close? Didn't they, like me, appreciate the slower way of life, the wealth of birds, the lazy dirt lanes, all the beauty of a rough, bleak plain?

'Even if you can't communicate, the locals are friendly,' I said. 'They appreciate any effort we make to be part of village life.' I was wasting my breath. Having but a superficial knowledge of history and mores, these older people believed their nationality made them superior.

Octogenarian Sophie stared pointedly at me. 'People don't understand how manipulative Hungarians are. Thinking we can all be friends!' She, viper-tongued, became aggressive whenever time her ancient and creaking husband Walter dared chat with me. 'You see what happened with that Dieter from Dortmund, the one who owns the campsite in Tiszafüred with his wife Rosie? They had this Hungarian woman, Csilla, working in the office and living in the room reserved for staff. They needed her there all the time because they don't speak Hungarian and they aren't going to learn it either – after all, Dieter is sixty-five, and Rosie is sixty-three. That Csilla? Thirty. Blond and ambitious. What happens next? One day, she moves downstairs, begins living with Dieter, and Rosie is forced to go back to Germany. Worse, I've heard Csilla is pregnant.'

'I asked Dieter how good his Hungarian is these days.' Walter's lecherous eyes gleamed.

Each time the expatriates returned from visits to Germany or Austria, they hauled with them freezers, stoves, refrigerators, garden tools, washing machines, bread and cake mixes, biscuits, butter, vats of German drinking water, tires, nails, screws, meat and motor oil. They trusted nothing made in Hungary; they tuned their televisions to German stations.

'How much do you pay that Csaba who works for you?'

'Three hundred forint an hour,[80] but at least he doesn't drink and comes on time. He doesn't whistle or sing either, thank goodness. Not like the last man who came to work for us. But you can't trust them. You always have to be after them, telling them what to do. You know what Csaba did yesterday?' Beate leaned forward, indignant. 'He asked for butter with his lunch. Can you imagine? Margarine isn't good enough for him? You think he eats butter in his own house? That he has money to pay for it? I doubt that.'

'Hungarians don't want to work, that's the problem. You can't find anyone to water your roses, cut your grapevines or mow your lawn. They don't want to shovel the snow for you when you're away. They've all become lazy.'

'Look how they treat their animals. We take care of our dogs and cats, have them neutered. Hungarians keep theirs on short chains, never take them for walks, let them breed, then dump the puppies or kittens into the roadside and let them die. Or they beat them to death with iron rods like our neighbour does.'

Hungarians did treat animals appallingly, and the Germans and Austrians often adopted the pathetic cats, the stray dogs otherwise shot, beaten or run down. But if anyone dared mention that Monika's huge, destructive Rottweiler roamed the streets alone, threatening villagers and killing fowl, she was contemptuous. She wasn't a Hungarian; therefore, the new injunction to keep dogs on a leash didn't apply to her.

'It's up to Hungarians to adapt to us. So what if my dog kills a chicken or a goose? They should keep their birds locked up. We spend our money here. They profit from us.'

---

80   Approximately one dollar.

'They think they can get away with everything,' added Marlis, an angry, bitter woman married to Imre, a self-hating Hungarian. 'They'll see what happens when they're forced to conform to European Community standards. They'll see.'

'But they love us,' said Willi. 'They love our being here.'

Helga turned to me. Smiled. 'Empress Maria Theresa invited Germans to come settle here.'

***

'The Germans and Austrians who came out here in the 1990s and bought houses, they're all miserable,' said Götz, the restaurant owner from Köln. His clients were melancholy exiles who killed the day's long hours at his bar, mourning cities they'd abandoned, pals left back home, and the once-familiar corners of a life that, with rose-tinted hindsight, seemed ideal. Some had been drawn to Hungary by concupiscent promise, others by the dream of owning a house and garden in some homey village.

'They're miserable with each other, miserable with themselves. They couldn't afford life in Germany or Austria, so they came here. Believe me, they don't understand what's going on. They think Hungarians are innocent peasants, grateful for their money and presence. What changes have expatriates brought to this country? That bar on the main road in Tiszafüred is a mafia-run whorehouse, and the beds have plastic coverings that can be hosed down. Same with the tanning studio and those so-called luxury apartments at the other end of town. All mafia-run, all geared towards foreign tourists. As for the girls, you never see the same one twice: like slaves, they're sent around the country, so there's always someone new for the customers, and no one can get emotionally attached.

'Back when I lived in Germany, I'd come here on holiday.

Those Absent

In the communist days, Hungarians were warm and friendly. I loved hearing the old Gypsy music, and it was being played everywhere. It was part of the country's charm. It was authentic. Now, everyone wants pop, techno and other commercial junk. The poor brainwashed clods think it shows how modern they are. That they're ideal capitalists.

'I used to hang around with Gypsy musicians, and when my daughter decided to get married, I told her I'd get a group to come to Germany and perform at her wedding. She really liked the idea, but my wife went crazy. She hated Gypsies, said I couldn't force dirty Gypsies on our friends. I didn't listen to her. I sent the band train fare, and they showed up in Köln and played. My wife, she took one look at the lead violinist, he's a dark handsome guy, and she fell in love. Then she divorced me, married him. They're still together.'

Götz, short, handsome, with a lion's mane of white hair, made the best of his life here in no-man's-land. His relationship with the attractive but thieving Hungarian Ili was an on-again, off-again proposition, ending each time she pocketed a customer's change, charged double, or marked up items never ordered. Like his clients, he can never go home.

'I made a bad decision, sold everything I had. Now, I'm stuck.'

PART FOUR : TISZAÖRS

XXVI

Behind a small table, at the end near a counter protected by a wooden barrier, sat a great jovial-looking man, with a large red face and fat flabby cheeks, drinking, a bottle opposite to him, and in company of a woman equally repulsive-looking; with half-shut eyes he was leering at her, and holding her round the waist to bring her nearer to him. She with her bare arm held a glass of red wine to her lips, and smacked them with all the grimaces of a cat. A barrel-organ fastened upon low wheels, with its mahogany case partly covered with red cotton, was placed against the wall. The musician, dead-tired, was fast asleep on the ground, his wrists closed in front of his instrument; the innkeeper, leaning over a slate, and furnished with a piece of chalk, was adding up with an absorbed air the receipts of the evening.

Victor Tissot

Once, villagers worked together, tilling, fishing, herding. At the day's end, they gathered to chitchat on the wooden benches lining the roads, and in the kocsmas. Now, evenings were spent in front of televisions. In one kocsma, a television was placed on the counter at dusk, and steady drinkers watched silently, snagged by the non-drama of reality shows. And at six each morning, here they were again, shuffling impatiently in the pale light, waiting for kocsma doors to open.

There were five such places in town, and I frequented all, seeking a view into local life, a chance to test vocabulary, a social entry... of sorts. The kocsma at the crossroads had once been the centre of village life, but was now sleepy and dull. Heavy metal whined drearily from a tinny radio, and two slot machines protested with electronic screams when no coins were chucked into their greedy mouths. Decorations from some long-forgotten feast hung – faded cut-outs and wilted shreds –

Those Absent

from the nicotine stained ceiling, and daylight slipped weakly through sagging nylon curtains.

Habitués of this locale were solitary inebriates: a limping little man with blank eyes ever fixed on some interior dream; a hostile male with shaved head, trimmed beard and toothbrush moustache; an antiquated crock who held seamless conversations with no one; a beautiful but incoherent woman in her forties – gossip said she had been an airline stewardess but had decided, like her father, grandfather and uncle, to drink herself to death. There was a young couple – she, with much pierced flesh and little energy, ever drowsed on the boyfriend's shoulder; he, with multi-pierced nose and brow, leafed through magazines detailing the antics of television stars and sports heroes.

No shifty, crafty, sly characters of yore made an appearance, nor was there any lively action – drunken peasants hacking tables to shards, a crash of glasses hitting a wall, a wailing Gypsy violin or puffing accordion. There was no throat-clutching smoke from a cracked stove, no pong of drying sausages, sour cabbage or beets. I was several generations too late.

'The weather's turning cold,' I said in Hungarian to the moon-faced barmaid.

She stared, shook her head uncomprehendingly. 'Me speak Hungarian,' she said in pidgin Hungarian.

'I'm speaking to you in Hungarian,' I insisted. 'And the air is cold despite the sun.'

But she responded with mute gestures, refused to acknowledge my effort. I was foreign and foreigners speak no Hungarian. She stubbed out her cigarette, lit another.

Further along the road was a modern kocsma, upmarket because of the shiny white plastic and plasterboard. Here was the best coffee in town, but I was one of the few who ordered it. Elderly female customers were equally pertinacious breakfast drinkers. One elegant lady with snowy hair preferred vodka; Anci, with bottle-thick glasses and heavily veined legs, and raggedy Irénka, who lived in a wooden shed hugging the earth mound and cemetery, both partook of a mysterious red mix. Men – all were named Misi, Béla, Karcsi, Gyula, József, László or Sándor[81] – preferred pálinka for breakfast.

Between bouts of whitewashing houses, sitting beside mountains of onions and bagging them to sell to passing motorists, canning vegetables, slaughtering and plucking chickens, slaughtering cows and pigs, doing fieldwork, building houses, repairing roofs, digging trenches by hand, the habitués wandered in and out of the kocsmas, spent all they earned on drink or the slot machines. Some, realising I was capable of basic Hungarian, told me their stories; Sándor's health had deteriorated in communist coalmines. 'Puszta boys didn't know how hard life would be in the mines and factories.'

Black József, the Roma who worked at the reeking open rubbish dump said, 'I should have spent my life reading, doing something with myself, but I didn't. As for you, you spend all your time writing. It's a lonely job, and you need company.' This he supplied in the rejected stuffed animals he found – a rocking horse, many teddy bears, legless dogs, a greyish rabbit, an indefinable creature rubbed colourless, handmade cotton dolls – which he left at my gate. Sincerely touched, I washed and sewed together these shredded once-cherished playthings

---

81 Given names are chosen from an officially approved list of several thousand. If not on the list, parents must apply to get the name approved. Chosen names must not be derogatory, must be easily recognisable as either male or female. Foreign names must follow Hungarian spelling: Jennifer becomes Dzsenifer, Joe is Dzsó. Those from officially recognized minorities are allowed to choose names from their own culture.

Those Absent

and swore I would never abandon them.

Misi, short, nervous, never spoke but shouted. He was a chronic complainer: his jealous lady friend was making his life miserable, his handmade slipper business was going badly – 'People don't appreciate craftsmanship, they all want something for nothing'. He and his wife had fled communist Hungary by crashing through a Yugoslavian border barrier on a motorbike, then had spent twenty-five years in Canada. 'Until I got stupid and came back. I thought, communism is over, things will be different. What a mistake. What a big stupid mistake. I had everything I wanted over there.'

But didn't he need this Hungarian setting? This kocsma next door to his house was his stage. Seven, eight, fifteen times a day, he'd roar in, fingers snapping, arms flapping, a ham actor in full declamatory swing. The lost Canadian paradise he hankered after was a fairy tale. In Hungary, comrades popped by day and night to chew the fat with him; in Canada there had been no such camaraderie and no cheery kocsmas.

Slant-eyed Endre shaved his head and tattooed every bit of skin like a Hun of yore. He had come home to this village after a few years in a Budapest prison and went from one foreigner to the next, begging employment of any sort: grass cutting, plastering, painting. He applied himself to the tasks until wheedling out an 'emergency' advance (there was no food in his house, his baby was ill and needed medication, his wife had been taken to the hospital in Szolnok). And once the cash was safely in his pocket, he never returned to work. Here he'd be, in the kocsma, hail-fellow-well-met, buying drinks for all, displaying a new tattoo. At his side was his beautiful young wife, her waist length blond hair newly streaked.

Recent thefts were attributed to Endre – bicycles, a canoe, several power lawnmowers – but the objects had belonged to Swiss, Germans and Austrians. Who would defend those foreigners? Hadn't Europeans always exploited Hungary? Local loyalty remained with the departed Soviet soldiers. Not considered the flunkies of socialist repression, Russians were sadly missed partners of black market opportunity.

'In the old days, you could do business with the Russians,' said Endre. 'Give them a load of wood for vodka or caviar, and life was good. But the Germans, the ones here, they count every penny. Every time you work for them, they stand over you, watching, making sure you're doing the job correctly. They don't trust us.'

'Because they think they're superior to us,' said Márton, a teacher. 'They can't be bothered learning Hungarian.[82] How would they feel if we lived in their country and didn't speak German? If we never mixed? They'd complain, say Hungarians can't integrate. I lived in Germany, and when people discovered I was Hungarian, they lost interest in me. Now they're here in our country, but they don't like us. They know nothing about our history.'

'They think we should be grateful because we're being admitted into the European Union,' added Vilmos, an aggressive ropy man ever clad in pseudo military gear. 'But the Europeans only want us as a cheap workforce. Slaves, that's what we'll be.'

'*Sieg Heil,*' said Endre.

From the far corner, ever-drunk Gyula sniggered. 'Slave? Not me.' When the German whose house he was repairing had refused him yet another advance, he'd loaded his employer's cement into his flashy German wheelbarrow, carried both off and sold them.

---

82 This was true of an older German or Austrian generation, but not those who have recently come to the country.

Those Absent

Sándor, with great drooping moustaches and formless wool cap, was rarely sober. One morning, barely able to open the kocsma door, he headed across the main road, a battlefield of hurtling cars and rumbling trucks.

'Shouldn't we go help him?' I asked nervously.

Misi who was stuffing a load of cash into the slot machine (he hoped to win enough for a plane ticket back to Canada) didn't look up. 'He doesn't want help.'

The others moved to the window and, roaring with laughter, watched Sándor's staggering and dangerous journey. He reached safety on the road's far side, and then lost his bearings. Round and round he turned, until clumsiness caused his cap to slip. Grabbing for it, he flailed vainly for a minute or two. Then, feet failing him, he collapsed into the deep ditch. Inside the kocsma, knees were slapped in glorious mirth. What a performance!

I was not diverted. 'Shouldn't we do something?'

'Let him lie there,' said Misi, not lifting his gaze from whirring cherries, grapes and oranges. 'He'll sober up, go home. Drunks in ditches? That's normal here. You'll see.'

Jenci, a square lumberjack of a man with vibrant red beard and moustache, stood out from the others. He lived in a large new house set in the middle of a lumberyard. I would often see him in his battered truck, roaring over the roads, delivering cut wood for household fires. His exhausted-looking wife was always beside him, one of those long lanky women whose every movement is unconsciously graceful. Their six children, the youngest, a boy of eight, the eldest daughter who would soon be off to university, all worked in the yard, manipulating electric saws with ease, loading logs, seemingly unaware that such toil set them apart in modern society.

PART FOUR : TISZAÖRS

One evening, Jenci came over to me in the kocsma and, on discovering I could hold some conversation in Hungarian, offered to buy me a drink. Well-spoken, extremely loquacious and mercifully spiking his story with German words, he told me of his aristocratic ancestors, once-famous statesmen, landowners of deep forests to the north.

'Our family didn't suffer under the Germans, but under the communists.' He talked of the 14,000 people who, between 1950 and 1953, were deported to labour camps on the Puszta, to mines, quarries, steelworks and carpenter's yards where they were fed pigswill, tortured and executed. Why?

'All you needed was an aristocratic title, or you owned a successful farm or a big apartment. Or you had an enemy with influence, or you were a member of the Social Democratic Party. My father was an educated, cultivated man fluent in many languages, but he was imprisoned and murdered. I had uncles and cousins who were arrested. But we survived. We led a double life, secretly keeping up the time-honoured rituals and our culture.' Continuing the traditions of a lost world.

He drank heavily, became more effusive and less coherent, launched into complicated histories I was unable to follow. He saw only my polite interest. And I knew I would never fully understand, that I was condemned to glean what I could on the surface.

Those Absent

XXVII

A legendary figure is the 'garabonciás,' a lean and hungry lad who is said to pass unseen through the country. If he finds food in the house, he blesses the family, but if he goes away starving, all sorts of misfortune may follow, so that when a peasant's cow falls ill or dries up, or his hayrick catches fire or when hailstone's ruin his crop, they say that the garabonciás has taken revenge for not finding any food left out for him.

Charlotte Lederer[83]

Csaba, the dark-haired bartender, showed me an Austro-Hungarian coin he'd found when an ancient graveyard had been dug up to make way for the new housing development. Dating from 1807, rubbed almost illegible, a deep cut on its rim had been inflicted by graveyard pick or shovel. Villagers once slipped coins under shrouds hoping the newly deceased would contact dead relatives and invoke their aid. I mentioned the custom, but no one in the kocsma knew of it.

'People don't believe superstitious crap anymore,' scoffed Misi who was, as ever, working the slot machine at the back wall. 'Hungary is a modern country.'

In the face of modernity, the fantastic creatures of earlier generations have slunk away. Gone, the phantoms that hid in clumped trees, haunted walls or sacred wells; vanquished are the vampires, devil's dogs, the myriad supernatural creatures that roamed through the night unchecked. Vanished, the trolls who caused travellers to fall from bridges, the eerie ringing bells that lured the unwary outside village boundaries to die of exposure, the poltergeists that made daily life a misery. Where are those

---

83   *Made in Hungary*. Charlotte Lederer, 1840-1898, Bohemia (now Czech Republic) a Jewish writer of children's books.

evil spirits that, disguised as seductive women, hideous crones, tattered peasants or wandering Jews, lurked in wild marshland or fields of corn? If they spoke and you responded, death would soon follow. Absent, are witches who could steal milk from a neighbour's cow by magic, invisible hands that beat cows to death and phantom horsemen who rode horses to exhaustion. These days, if you leave cinders around your bed, you'll no longer see the devil's imprints at dawn.

Back when ritual allayed malevolence, suspected vampires were exhumed and burnt; all saw how the bodies writhed in evil agony as the fire consumed them! At the death of an unmarried girl, her effigy, dressed as a bride, led mourners in a death dance; drops of well water were returned to the spirit within; food thrown onto the hearth kept fire spirits calm. In houses of the dying, mirrors were covered lest they reflected evil, and open windows encouraged the soul to depart. House floors remained unswept and fires unlit until burial, for if a soul found home life too comfortable, it would stay and haunt the family. One peasant heard his avaricious dead wife in the kitchen at night 'lapping up freshly made pork pies like a pig.' A *lantekh* took up residence in a Jewish inn, strewed food, spilt milk and forced the innkeepers to sell out.

In 1873, a young Jewish girl's clothes caught fire, and she raced into the street, calling for help. Peasants, seeing Julie's hair ablaze, thought she was the devil, and making the sign of the cross, most fled. One fearless soul fetched his gun and tried to shoot her. Missed. And as Julie lay dying, all realised they were not looking at a devil, but a village girl.[84]

'If you want to buy this coin, I'll sell it for one euro,' said Csaba. He was collecting euros for the day when they would

---

84   *L'Hongrie*, Univers Israélite, 1874.

Those Absent

replace Hungarian currency.[85]

Vilmos, clad in his hunting gear and as belligerent as ever, muttered something I didn't catch. There were assenting grunts from a few others.

'What did he say?' I asked Misi.

'He said that we don't need euros. We have our forints, our roots and our traditions. We Hungarians have a unique history. Europe can't give us anything we need.'

Did the others also think that the semi-mythical Magyar narrative would claim a respected place in the twenty-first century?

'Europe doesn't give. It takes,' said Misi. 'Look at our history. The entire Carpathian Basin belonged to us, the Magyars. Then what happens? First the Turks invade, then the Austrians take over. Then the Europeans create Trianon to take away Transylvania and give it to Romania. And now they want to tell us how to run our own country?'

I hoped someone would say more. None dared, certainly not pro-European Csaba.

'If you're looking for customs, they've disappeared. Every time I come back to this village, I see things have changed,' said Dénes, a bow-legged, twitchy man nicknamed the 'Englishman', for he had slipped out of Hungary during the 1956 revolution. Living in the north of England, his accent was a colourful mix of Hungarian and heavy Yorkshire. 'Look at pig killing. A few years ago, it was a traditional day. It was a wife's duty to fatten the animal, and when it was ready for slaughter, it was brought in front of the house in the early morning, its throat was cut and

---

[85] Hungary had planned to adopt the euro in 2007 or 2008, but because of debt and inflation the date was changed to 2010, then changed again. In 2015, Viktor Orbán declared the government would not replace the forint, and that it would remain a stable currency in the coming decades.

the blood was collected in a big pan. When the pig was dead, its hair was singed off, it was cut up, white and blood sausage were prepared, everything else was salted and the stomach was filled with brawn. We worked together, all the neighbours. We drank a lot of brandy, had fun, ate soup with noodles, stuffed cabbage, sausages and roasts, washed it all down with homemade wine. That's how it was done.'

'People still kill pigs in their front yards,' I said, for on many mornings, I had been woken by the screams of terrified animals being butchered.

'It's not the same. It's only a family job. These days there's no feasting, no sharing, no conviviality. And how much longer will people be allowed to kill their own animals? European Community rules will stop that custom. Some people here don't understand that. They just think the EU will make them rich.'

I glanced at Misi, but he was concentrating on losing money. I stood, prepared to leave the kocsma and fetch the euro for Csaba, but as I reached the door, the owner, a stout older woman, shouted: 'You can't go out! The church bells are tolling.'

Everyone looked embarrassed. Only Dénes sniggered. 'She's telling you it's unlucky to pass through a doorway when church bells are ringing, that you're putting yourself in danger. It's superstition. Don't pay any attention.'

'They ring a lot,' I said, elated to find this throwback.

'Every time a person dies, and five times a day until burial.'

'To keep evil away?'

Dénes was still grinning. 'To make money. Each time they ring, the deceased's family has to pay the church. Since it takes a week before someone's buried, bell ringing brings in a tidy sum. Death is expensive in Hungary.'

Those Absent

'Let me tell you about the church.' Misi abandoned his slot machine, for he loved having a tale meant to shock. 'When I was a kid, I was always in trouble, and the priest kept telling me to ask for forgiveness. He scared me, because, back then, everyone believed a priest had special powers. One day, he said he wanted to talk to me, that I had to come to his house. Because I was frightened, I took my time, and when I finally got up the nerve to go see him, I was too shit scared to knock on the door. So I snuck around the back and peeked in the window, just to know what he was up to. And what do I see? A naked woman running through the living room, laughing. I knew who she was, too, a married woman from this village. After that, I wasn't afraid of the priest. He was like the rest of us. No extra powers.'

'For centuries, the church kept people ignorant so it could stay rich. Toil, church and fear, that's all people knew,' said Dénes. 'Today, everyone gets the so-called truth from television. Tell me, is that any better?'

***

*Y*et, it was still here, the charm of slow-moving places. Horses clip-clopped down the road, pulling the few remaining carts back from the fields. Door-to-door peddlers passed. One oldster, a huge sack of grain tied to his bicycle, sang out a melodious stanza to attract buyers; bell ringing knife sharpeners came on foot, dragging their heavy grinding wheels; Roma men and women called at gates, aggressively sold sheets, pillows and covers of lamb's wool, or they collected feathers. Slightly more up-to-date was the non-refrigerated wooden ice cream cart pushed by a bicycle.

Although families imprisoned at least one grunting pig and several sheep in narrow, tragically dark, back sheds, chickens, geese and ducks could wander where they chose, peck worms and plants. Family cows, collected each morning by the cowherd and urged on by snapping, tail-wagging mutts, headed onto the Puszta for a day's grazing. And when the evening sun turned deep orange, all returned, the cows puffing softly, nibbling decorative shrubbery. Then, abandoning cowherd and mutts, they turned left or right, arrived home on their own steam. Shortly after, villagers, milk cans suspended from bicycle handlebars, gathered at the dairy, a tiny concrete building beside an unkempt field. And there, under a tall tangle of acacias, they gossiped away the waning light.

I'd watch from the cinder block terrace of the kocsma directly over the lane. How I wished I had enough language to join them, or to eavesdrop (how much more interesting conversations seem when we can't understand them). I wanted details of homegrown drama, to be privy to village secrets. I ached to understand the frowns, tsks and snickers. But a foreigner possessing no cow, no peasant background and no local references, I would always be excluded.

Those Absent

XXVIII

We entered a dirty, most odoriferous enclosure, where were dunghills polluting the atmosphere, ragged clothes hanging on the hedges to dry, stretches of stagnant water in which geese were wallowing with all the pleasure of pigs, surrounding a well that was out of order, and whose beam, raised like a solitary arm to the skies, seemed to implore help. In sheds, half-hidden by nettles and weeds, in the midst of which, like monstrous spiders, some pumpkins climbed with twisted spirals, were heard the eager gruntings of hungry pigs. Thin dogs with haggard eyes and sharp teeth growled with a ferocious air round the thresholds of the doors, waiting in vain for the long-expected bone.

Victor Tissot

A dirt track crossed a little footbridge, meandered out of the village in a lazy, undecided way. Accompanied by Dog, the lame stray I had adopted, I wandered between high banks of brown and frozen flowers and leafless tangles of wild grape. In the far distance were half-savage-looking herders with their tepee-like huts of long twigs covered by skins and odd rags. I didn't approach, for their snarling mutts kept me at bay, and this was a desolate and lonely place.

Such a largely-forgotten road had once been a major throughway for many: swine, goose, and horse herders, tin smiths, knife sharpeners, leather, metal or wood workers, musicians with their instruments, Jewish peddlers, itinerant labourers, escaped soldiers or serfs, wandering monks, beggars, drifters, déclassé nobles, the bankrupted and those ruined by alcohol or politics. Many carried nothing heavier than tales; most sought food, company or a barn with a bit of dry straw for the night.

A few kilometres later, the track halted at the zipping main highway before changing character and continuing on the far side. No longer ambling or casual, but a steady avenue lined with stalwart acacia and chestnut trees, it led to the manor of Bano.

Home to the Széky family from the sixteenth century until the arrival of communism, this estate once took in all the surrounding plain. It had been the Székys who had invited Jews to live in their many villages straddling the Tisza River: Tiszabö, Tiszafüred, Tiszaszentimre, Tiszaigar, Nádudvar and Dévaványa. Today, the elegant lane comes to an abrupt end at the prefabricated buildings of a former collective farm.

There was no one around. Did I, a snoop, an intruder, have the right to poke about? As usual, curiosity prohibited retreat, and I veered right onto a path, one reclaimed by weeds, puddles, shattered branches, and clawing shrubs. Just where the ruined trail stopped, was the manor. Once painted ochre yellow, *Kaiser Gelb*, a wooden double door must have stood under the high-arched pane-less window of the porch. Outside walls had crumbled, or had been destroyed in a frenzy of hate. Pillars, high-ceilinged upper floors and the roof had all buckled, and over shattered plaster and brick, the conquering vines triumphed.

Sixth sense warned I wasn't alone. I turned, perceived a man half-hidden in the underbrush. 'Was this the manor house?' I called out, judging it best to make friendly tea-party chitchat.

Those Absent

But the man stared, silently backed further into the vegetation: an inauspicious beginning. 'The paths are terrible,' I said brightly. 'So much mud.' This conversational offer also fell flat.

Turning, he shuffled away, disappeared into a confusion of leafless elder. Warily, looking over my shoulder, I rounded the manor, but there was no information to be had. Twenty metres away, other pre-fabricated, communist-era buildings with corrugated roofs stood in a line. To the right, half-hidden by low scrub, was a row of small, whitewashed houses. Bare beams showed some to be abandoned whilst outside others - remodelled, upgraded - washing hung.

In these cottages, serfs, servants or estate workers once lived. Primitive huts back then, dug one meter deep into the ground, their adobe walls had risen no higher than a meter and a half on the outside. There had been little furniture: built-in shelves served as beds; mattresses were straw-stuffed sacks; winter's bitter cold was staved off by burning dried thistles, weeds, manure and straw. In the worst situations, two-room dwellings housed eight families, often twenty-five people, with each family claiming one corner as private space.

I again came upon the strange and mute man when I returned to the collective farm buildings. Beside him, a woman was busy sweeping a miry patch of earth – a useless sort of enterprise. I went over, asked where I could find the ancient track to the village of Tiszaigar.

'The main road is down that way.' The woman pointed to the tree-lined alley.

'Not the main road. The old road.'

'There is no other road,' she said, perplexed.

'The road villagers took when they came to work the land.'

'The village of Tiszaigar is too far.'

'Only two or three kilometres.'

She frowned. 'Why would you attempt such a distance on foot?' But she and the man (no longer mute) began discussing landscape and directions.

'There's a muddy back lane that no one uses anymore. I'll show you where it starts.' She led the way, crossing the yard, negotiating murky pools and liquid sludge. 'Your boots will be filthy.'

They were already hopelessly so, and Dog's coat was in a similar mucky state. 'Is this a nice place to live?'

'Wonderful. My children love it. Quiet.'

I asked about the ruined manor house. How long had it been like that? But she shrugged. Certainly, she didn't care. Instead, she chatted about her eldest son who was studying engineering.

'Beautiful, this landscape,' I said. The Puszta lay before us, as gauzy as a cobweb, its pale horizon only occasionally interrupted by a doodle of bare branches.

'Tourists always think places are beautiful because they're not used to them,' she said truthfully. 'I was born here, in Bano. I've seen this every day of my life.'

'Your parents were born here too?'

She nodded. 'And my grandparents and great-grandparents, and before that, too. Like my husband's family.' Serfs and their descendants.

Where our lane crossed a misery of stinking slurry oozing from a metal barn, she stopped, pointed. 'It's out there somewhere. I've never taken it. Good luck.'

I passed the barn. In the adjacent stableyard were remarkable and ancient creatures, descendants of Kuman cattle: slender, gnu-like, their horns reached high, perhaps a meter or more in length.

Those Absent

A man roared up on a smoke-belching tractor. Stopped, got down, opened a gate. 'Where are you going?' he asked in a friendly way.

'To Tiszaigar. On the old road.'

'Perhaps it doesn't go there anymore. It's far, anyway.'

'What do you know about the Székys?'

He shrugged. 'My father told me about them. They were rich. When the workers had nothing, the Székys had a collection of expensive cars. They drove around the country, but those who worked for them couldn't buy winter fuel. When the Székys had flush toilets in their house, the workers had no running water. That's how things were back then.' He swung back up onto the tractor, slammed it into gear and chugged away.

The dirt road was easy to find, running steadily between waterlogged fields. The deep ruts of wagon wheels were still visible, baked into place by summers of relentless sun and hardened by the ever-present wind. In the rainy season, horses and oxen must have sunk to their withers in mire. I trudged on in the footsteps of those who'd banded together in bleak places, people erased by time. And soon enough, Tiszaigar's red roofs appeared. The air filled with the cackle of fowl, the barking of shackled dogs, the dull thud of wood being chopped.

In 1854, 500 Jews lived in Tiszaigar. There had been a

ritual-bath, a synagogue, and the rabbi had been the famous Talmudic scholar, Menachem Bleier. But, by 1900, most had left to go live in busier, livelier, less religious Tiszafüred, twelve kilometres north. Other than the little cemetery near the main road, was there any sign of their earlier presence? The streets were empty. There was no one to question.

I hung around. Eventually, opportunity presented itself in the form of a sag-faced tipsy man draped over an ancient cycle. I went over to him. 'Once, there were Jews living here.'

Suspiciously, perhaps wondering what I really wanted, he nodded, muttered, 'Cemetery.'

'I know the cemetery. And the synagogue?' Elderly, he certainly had information.

He nodded again, continued to do so for a full minute. Then gesturing for me to follow, he began wheeling his antique contraption down the road. Where houses petered out, he pointed to a field of weeds and a rotted wooden barn.

'This is where the synagogue was?'

'And Jewish bath.'

No trace of either. We stared at the field for a few minutes before returning to village streets. He pointed to a modest house. 'Jewish family, once. Next house Jewish too.' A minuscule corner house, the sort that had a shop in the front and one back room for family life. 'Jewish grocery. Simple people.' Further along, he paused before impressive gateposts in red brick. 'Here too, Jews.' The original, no doubt imposing, building had vanished, was replaced by a modern structure with railing-less suspended balcony and a huge garage.

'Jews, all gone. War. Grocer, tailor, women, children. Nice people.' He indicated a bar perhaps built in the 1980s. 'Old Jewish kocsma here before.' At the back of this building in yellow cement were barns. Places once used for storing grain?

He stopped before his green metal gate, fumbled with a key.

'Tell me more about the Jews,' I said, hoping to delay him. 'Do you remember any stories?'

He was silent for a minute or two, his jaw working sideways, his tongue probing a bad back tooth. 'No one hated Jews. Jews, Hungarians, no problem. Never.' Opening the gate, shoving the bicycle before him, he entered. Leaving me on the gritty road with all my unanswered questions.

PART FOUR : TISZAÖRS

XXIX

Thirty years ago, the bodies of those who were hanged remained on the gallows until they literally fell to pieces. The superstitious people used to come in the night to cut off a shred of the dress, or, what they valued more, the little finger. If anyone had in his pocket a little finger of a man who had been hanged, he imagined he could steal without being found out, or even without being seen by anyone. Over the countryside, it was not rare to come across gibbets where the bodies of the betyárs were left – a warning to all who might be tempted to follow their example in a life of adventure, but also a life of crime with its inevitable consequence.

A traveller one day seeing several children playing merrily under a tree from whence hung a skeleton, stopped his carriage and said to them, 'Children, are you not afraid of that horrid skeleton?'

'But why should we be afraid of him?' they answered. 'He was our father'.

Victor Tissot

Village protocol dictated that, unless on intimate terms, women didn't venture into a man's lair – certainly not a bachelor's. Instead, men and women chatted to each other over garden gates. But I was foreign, not local, and I had begun going to Misi's house for conversation, coffee, a glass of wine.

In his tiny kitchen, an outsize table, six massive wooden chairs and a hefty sideboard ate up all available space. To circulate, one had to squeeze sideways past refrigerator, enamel sink and stove. There were many other rooms in the modern, two-story house he rented. Cumbersome modern furniture filled a large lounge, a smaller study, an open central dining area and an impressive upstairs landing, but those spaces were for show only. Despite Misi's twenty-five years in Canada, his peasant background dictated that social activity must take place in a kitchen.

Those Absent

He was again single. His long-time girlfriend had abandoned him and, broken-hearted, he had begun searching for her replacement. He needed someone to do his laundry, iron his shirts; he enjoyed cooking but hated washing pots, mopping up, sweeping and dusting. A woman with money was also a requisite, for his sheepskin slipper business didn't do well. Although an excellent craftsman, he was no salesman, and all he earned disappeared into slot machines or went for beer and cigarettes.

This evening, clad in a natty suit from his life in Canada, his soft paunch was hidden under a grey silk shirt topped by a flashy tie. Clean-shaven, his grey hair trimmed, combed and elegantly puffed, he looked quite the prosperous dandy of sixty. Soon he would drive to Kunmadaras, meet his blind date, a well-off widow of sixty-three.

'You look good,' I said with absolute sincerity.

Chuffed, he pulled back his shoulders, stood straighter. 'But I'm not sure about this woman. People are different in Kunmadaras. It's twelve kilometres away, but they have a different mentality. They're Kumans. They're not like people in this village or up the road in Nagyiván. When we were young, we never dated people from Kunmadaras or Kunhegyes.'

A few days earlier, he'd gone to meet another Kuman, a fifty-year-old blonde. Caught in a messy divorce, she couldn't be seen with him in public. Another Kuman woman was too old, and a non-Kuman divorcee with a big house was too fat.

'The real problem with women around my age is they all have their own lives, their own homes. They don't want to come and take care of my house. And younger women? All they want is a man with money, a steady income. If you don't have that, they give you trouble. That's what I told Gábor. I warned him. Not that he listened to me.'

Gábor was the village policeman. A week before, his wife had committed suicide after Gábor had taken their three children and gone to live with a nineteen-year-old barmaid.

'Gábor's son is the same age as the barmaid,' I said.

Misi flicked his hand. 'Who cares about that? Gossips. Gábor's a good man, a good cop, that's what counts. There used to be a Gypsy here, and he was always stealing things. He went into the garden of an old woman at night, stole all her chickens. Imagine stealing chickens from a poor old woman. Gábor knew the Gypsy did it, so he takes him into custody, slaps him around a little and tells him to clean up his act. What happens? The Gypsy does it again. Of course. What do you expect? That's what Gypsies do. Gábor hauls him in again, only instead of wasting time talking, he bashes the Gypsy around, breaks his legs. Then he takes him out and leaves him in a ditch.' Misi roared with laughter. 'After that, he didn't steal any chickens.'

What was funny? I was appalled by this story and by Misi who claimed to have the values of any democratic Canadian. 'How about arresting the man and charging him with theft?'

'What good would that do? Gábor would have to fill out reports, investigate, wait for the results. All that takes time, a year, maybe two years. The Gypsy? He'd get off. They don't have money, Gypsies. He wouldn't have paid compensation. He'd just go out and steal again.'

'And this makes Gábor a good man in your eyes?'

Misi was irritated by my 'sentimental' attitude. 'Look, you're a foreigner. You don't understand how things work here. This is how we handle crime. You slap people around. There's too much theft, and there aren't enough police officers, so we do things the easy way. Don't forget there's a Gypsy mafia, too. You don't mess with those guys.'

Those Absent

'The police are corrupt, I said. 'They stop you along the road, invent infractions, demand a cash fine and pocket the money.'

'That's what I'm trying to say. Things are like that here. Official theft and unofficial theft, it's not the same. The police are badly paid, so nobody argues if they demand a little extra. It's normal, almost official. As for those guys on top, the inspectors, the police chiefs, they do what they're told. As soon as an investigation gets touchy – it doesn't matter if it's murder, or a financial scandal, or arson, or if a big shot gets caught with his pants down – one word from someone important and the case is closed.'

'No one complains?'

'Who's going to complain? You get your hands on extra money, so you shut your mouth.'

Nothing new in this. Once, the most ruthless outlaws, the betyárs, were greatly admired by peasants who, crushed by toil and poverty, could only dream of adventure. Transformed in songs and romantic novels into an utterly charming desperado, a Robin Hood figure desperately loved by an innkeeper's wife, all claimed that, if given respect and hospitality, a betyár would never resort to murder. Downtrodden peasants willingly took a betyár's side against the noble's hated instruments, the gendarmes.

In reality, betyárs were violent bullies. Deserters from the hated Austrian army,[86] or serfs and indebted peasants, betyárs took refuge in forests, marshes or on the open Puszta. Invading kocsmas, they feasted royally, forced guests to strip and dance all night; visiting lonely farms and villages, they victimized the peasants. Those refusing demands for food, wine, tobacco, money or objecting when betyárs 'flirted' with wives and

---

86 A high percentage of Puszta lads, forced into the military but incapable of accepting discipline, became bandits.

girlfriends, knew their revenge: pillaged houses, burnt barns, destroyed crops and stolen animals.

Especial entertainment was afforded by tormenting Jewish peddlers or itinerant priests – weren't both worthy and wealthy targets? Beating their victims, attaching them to crosses, tying them by their feet to trees, shoeing them like horses, or burying them up to the neck, one much-admired betyár, Patkó, captured a Jewish honey-seller, stripped him, smeared him with honey and rolled him in feathers. Resembling some fantastic animal, the poor peddler was led to town gates where shrieking women and children raced away, and dogs snapped at his heels. Only a few kilometres from this village, out where souvenir sellers wait for tourist buses near the modern Patkó (Horseshoe) Inn, the Jewish innkeeper, Zsigmond 'Patkoci' Schwarcz died in a shootout between betyár and *pandúr* in 1900.

The word betyár is ever present. There are fanciful betyár songs, idealistic betyár folktales and the 'betyár specialty' is offered on most restaurant menus. But devoid of its former meaning, the appellation is mere nostalgia for a fabricated past.

'You can't do anything in this country these days,' said Misi. 'Normal people have no rights anymore. Not like in America. In America, when someone tries to steal your chickens or your possessions, you pick up a gun and POW! But in Hungary, you aren't allowed to defend yourself. When I was in Canada living the good life, I forgot how fucked up the mentality is over here. How the communists fucked it up. Back then, we were told, "Everything belongs to you, to the people." So everyone got one idea: "If everything belongs to me, I can help myself. It's my right." You needed a can of paint? You went to some guy painting a building and said, "Look, I need paint to touch up my living room," and he'd show up with ten, twenty cans. And chemical fertilizer. Everyone had hundreds of sacks stored in their barns, because you can only cover your fields with so much of the stuff. On the cooperatives, bosses bartered with it, gave it to friends. Or if you drove a tractor filled with sacks of animal feed, you'd stop at home and take off a few sacks to sell or to feed to your own animals. And pigs: a worker in the cooperative would take a few of them home and raise them.

'Then, in 1989, when communism ended, people went into the factories and took what was left, the machinery, the electrical wires, everything, and sold it all for nothing. A few years later, when people wanted to get the factories going, keep everyone employed, make the economy work, nothing was left. And that's because Hungarians are so fucking stupid.

'Look at the Jews. I have nothing against Jews as a people. I respect them, although I went bankrupt in Canada because of a dishonest Jewish businessman. But Jews, they're tough. They take land that isn't theirs and build houses on it. They fight for themselves. Hungarians give in and no one else fights for them. Hungarians are always victims.

'I'll tell you about a Jewish doctor who lived in this village. There was never any problem with Jews, just with this doctor. There was a cleaning lady, she used to come to him. One day she's washing the floor, and the doctor takes her. Like this. Like a dog.' Half crouching, Misi pumped his hips a few times. 'And from that, she had a baby boy. And the boy grows up, becomes a big shot, a powerful man, just like the Jews always do.' Misi laughed, a lubricious sound. Then sobered. 'All Hungary is a backwater. I'm going back to Canada. As soon as I get some money together, I'm gone.'

PART FOUR : TISZAÖRS

XXX

In matters of civilization they [the Gypsies] have remained absolutely stationary, the only alteration being in their dress, which now consists of cast-off Magyar clothes and rags. There are, however, degrees among them, the lowest type...live in mud huts, holes in the ground, or hollows in the rocks on the outskirts of villages, and supplement a livelihood of theft by tinkering and primitive odds and ends of industry. This type of Gypsy is a half-naked picturesque rogue, and hardly a blessing to the village he selects as his temporary residence. The rest...are of purer race, and are never stationary. They wander continually over the wilds, pitching rude tents and canopies, or sleeping under the stars, and living on what they can steal or obtain by begging. In order to obviate the demoralising effect of having gipsy visitors for too long in a village, laws have been framed compelling them to move forward every two or three days... for long experience has taught the Magyars that a lengthy sojourn never develops instincts for civilisation in the gipsy. The birth of a child is looked upon as a fine opportunity for acquiring presents, and a cunning father will carry his baby to perhaps twenty magistrates in succession, inducing them all to stand godfather and play the benefactor.

Margaret Fletcher

A round little Roma woman, hair bound in a scarf, stood at my front gate. Holding out one hand, she rubbed her stomach with the other and frowned pitifully. She was begging, but Dog barked ferociously. Unoffended, the woman waved gaily and moved down the road.

I saw her a few weeks later, standing in her garden, surrounded by sacks of cement, a new toilet, sink, bathtub, a mountain of soggy ripped cartons, bundles, ancient suitcases, furniture and discarded clothes. She waved as though we were the best of chums.

Those Absent

'Bathroom put in house soon,' she shouted in pidgin. 'Modern, modern.' Coming to her front gate, she opened it, took my arm and pulled me into the house where the same chaos reigned: clothes in tumbled heaps, destroyed cartons shoved into corners.

Had she received an improvement grant? Extensive work had been done: there was a modern kitchen and the beginnings of a bathroom in a corner of what had been the square, traditional main room. Unfortunately, the adobe walls had been cemented over, and already the pervasive smell of mould hung on the damp air.

'All new. Tell your friends in Germany.' Her smile was sly. 'They come and buy my house.' She would sell this modernized building then happily move to another dank ruin.

'I'm Canadian, not German. Canadians don't buy holiday homes in Hungary. It's too far.'

'Yes,' she agreed with easy humour. 'But I sell cheap. My name, Dóra.'

***

*T*aped to a lamppost, a paper announced a Roma ball. There was a primitive sort of drawing – one darkish hand held a whitish one. Did this mean the ball would be a meeting place for Roma and non-Roma? Would there be 'Gypsy' music, *cigányzene*? Surely the Roma would never content themselves with the usual chewed-over elevator pap!

In the baths, I mentioned the ball to the Germans. Willi sneered, Beate ignored me, Helga and Erwin were dismissive. 'Gypsies don't mix with us. Why mix with them?'

Only Brigitte, the unconventional widow once married to a Hungarian, was apologetic. 'You see? We all stopped thinking years ago, and it's too late to begin again.'

I would go to the ball. If people thought it odd seeing an unescorted woman, I didn't much care. Foreigners can't be expected to know all the rules.

***

A cluster of Roma men smoked cigarettes on the steps of the cement cultural centre. They stared at me. At the door, one man blocked my way, said something I didn't catch.

'Can't I come inside?'

Noting I understood little, and no doubt classifying me a dull tool, he smirked and moved aside. People gaped as I crossed the lobby and went to stand by the open double doors of the ballroom. There, tables had been set out along the walls, and nicely dressed people – I had seen many of them in the village – sat in family groups. Aside from one elderly elegant man escorting a beautiful, mature, genteel Roma woman, and a young married woman with long golden hair, all were Roma. And up on the stage, a musician churned out Sinatra, Mantovani and pop songs on his synthesizer. It was an ordinary, middle-class scene.

I watched for a while, then bravado deserted me. I wasn't part of this group, but a complete outsider. I knew no one; I didn't know the correct behaviour. Why linger?

Suddenly, I heard a wild shriek, and rushing towards me was round little Dóra. Throwing her arms around me, she dragged me across the ballroom to her family table, presented me to all, then pushed me onto a chair. A plate loaded with food appeared in front of me. I protested, but to no avail. 'Eat!' Covertly, Dóra filled my glass from a bottle hidden under the table: coca cola mixed with homemade pálinka, and heavily laced with rum. It was vile.

Those Absent

The others in the room stared unashamedly for a half hour or so. Then I became a predictable part of the scenery. Dóra's daughter dragged me onto the dance floor where a gaggle of other women joined us. Once, a delightfully rakish-looking man came to our table and asked me for a dance, but before I could gleefully scrabble to my feet and throw myself into his waiting arms, Dóra had sharply and shrilly shooed him away. She was my chaperone, my guardian. I was her possession.

When it was time to leave, it was clear we would do so as a united family. In the dark street in front of my house, all bid me goodnight, hugged me affectionately. It had been an agreeable evening.

***

'How was your Gypsy ball?' Willi asked when I next saw him.

'Great fun.' I mentioned Dóra and her hospitality.

'Oh, that fat little Gypsy woman.' His mouth was a humourless rictus. 'She goes around begging.' Beside him, his wife, Beate, tittered.

Later, meeting József, a local teacher, and his fiancée Ilonka, I mentioned the Roma ball.

'Well, the good thing about this village is that no Gypsies live here,' he said. 'That's why Germans and Austrians come and buy houses. They don't want problems.'

'My parents live in Kunmadaras,' said Ilonka. 'They can't go on holiday because if they leave their house, the Gypsies will break in.'

'But there are Roma living in this village,' I said. 'I know where their houses are. Most of the Roma here are perfectly respectable citizens with jobs.'

'No,' József insisted. 'The Gypsies you saw at the ball come from somewhere else. From Nagyiván, not from here. No Gypsies live in this village, I can guarantee that.'

***

*U*do arrived with two eggs rolled in paper. He had picked up a hitchhiker, a youngish man. 'I knew no one would stop because it was dark, and he was a Gypsy. He'd just been released from the Karcag hospital and missed the last bus – he'd already walked fifteen kilometres. He lives in Nagyiván, but he said he'd be more than happy if I dropped him off in this village. That way, he'd only have eight kilometres more. At the turnoff, he got out and thanked me profusely. There I was, in a warm car. He had a two-hour walk in the cold. So, I told him to get back in. He couldn't believe his luck. He kept shaking his head, saying how lucky he was.

'He lived in a hovel. The roof was caving in, and a pile of junk filled the whole yard, but he wanted me to come in, meet his family. He wanted to thank me for my kindness.

'Inside, there were dirt floors, a little coal oven, one table, a few chairs in the kitchen, nothing else, but everywhere you looked, there were men, women and children. His mother showed me the other room, a bedroom with no furniture, just a few single beds. In one, two men were sleeping, one with his feet at the top and head at the bottom, the other with feet at the bottom and head at the top. I never saw anything like it. It was like being back in another century. But everyone was smiling, telling me I was their guest, asking what I wanted to eat. I had money in my pocket, and these people with nothing wanted to feed me. Finally, I accepted a coffee, but that wasn't enough. They wanted to give me more. The mother found these two eggs, rolled them up like presents. I tried to refuse, but she let me know that was an insult. And these are the Gypsies everyone hates?'

Those Absent

XXXI

...if we liberate the serfs, am I expected to use a hoe myself, me and my five daughters? If I had been born a peasant, I would certainly never wish to be anything but a peasant. It is a real pleasure to be one. Why take this pleasure away from them?... and as for this idea of national education! What is it good for? The people raise themselves without our having to raise them... And now the peasants have to learn to read also? But if they do, they'll never believe what their priest tells them. For the moment, women, and those parasites, the Jews, all of them can read, and that gives them ideas... If we want the people to have freedom, we mustn't give it to them because if we don't give it they'll have it, but if we give it to them, they'll certainly lose it.

Mór Jókai[87]

On the last street in Kunmadaras, a graceful whitewashed house with a broad terrace once must have belonged to a noble or important person. Today it's a museum where a fire burns merrily in the bulb-shaped oven, and discarded furniture of an earlier time lines the walls: handmade carved wooden trunks, benches with moon/sun circles. In the larder is a framed etching: The Imperial Austrian Army Hangs the Thirteen Hungarian Generals of the 1848 Revolution.

Puzzled, Udo stared at the picture for a long while. 'What's all this about?' With no knowledge of his country's history, that pan-European revolution with its ideals of liberty and constitutionalism meant nothing to him. Hadn't Hungary's union with Austria been one of mutual respect and deep loyalty? What was this unpalatable whiff of discord? 'I can't believe my country did something so unjust.'

***

---

[87] *The Stonehearted Man's Sons.* Mór Jókai, 1825-1904, Hungarian novelist.

PART FOUR : TISZAÖRS

On the eve of the 1848 revolution, Budapest was a fashionable city, yet two out of ten inhabitants were destitute, one out of three rented airless back rooms or a mattress for the night, and exhausted workers were controlled with an iron hand. In the rural world, the large impoverished[88], population of indentured peasants and serfs had no recourse to justice. They could – and did – engage in go-slow tactics that hindered agricultural production, but to compete in the modern world, reform was necessary. Serfdom had to be replaced by wage labour, new roads, canals, bridges and rail lines were needed, but only the most innovative members of the gentry considered modernization.

Struggling with agricultural tariffs and lack of capital, many nobles abandoned their estates, headed for towns and cities where they monopolised newly created posts in the military, the bureaucracy and law enforcement. Boisterous and corrupt, insensitive to the suffering of the poor, they resented any reform that threatened the feudal system, and continued to hold dear the illusion of aristocratic power and privilege.

To hide corruption and catastrophic incompetence, a nationalist movement, Magyarisation, or the return to a 'true' Magyar identity, was born. Embroidered variants of national costume were resurrected, a Hungarian folk dance, the csárdás, was created, so was pseudo-traditional music. Hungarian, spoken in obscure pockets of the country and scorned as 'peasant's prattle', began replacing Latin and German, although its vocabulary pertained to rural life. Before its use in administration, medicine, technology or commerce, it needed to be upgraded. For that, a new literature flourished, with books and poems vaunting the true Hungarian soul.

---

88 The average peasant wore shoes or boots at one period in his life – during his military service.

Those Absent

Magyarisation and nationalism triggered hatred toward all that was 'foreign' in the 'Kingdom of Hungary', the de facto province of a vast Habsburg Empire whose borders took in Transylvania, Bukovina, and parts of Slovenia, Slovakia, Croatia, Serbia and Ukraine. Comprising well over half the population, non-Hungarians created their own national revivals, and began demanding (often violently) self-rule.[89]

Lajos Kossuth, son of a landless noble, became a popular revolutionary leader with his demands for freedom of the press, parliamentary democracy, minority rights, separation from Austria and an end to the feudal economy. In March 1848, inspired by the Viennese worker's uprising, a group of revolutionaries stormed the Buda fortress to release political prisoners, an act as pointless as the storming of the Bastille:[90] the fortress contained only one unpopular socialist. But the revolution gained ground. The Habsburg monarchy was deposed; the Hungarian Revolutionary Army miraculously won several battles against the Austrian Army.

In December, 1848, Austrian Kaiser Franz Joseph replaced the epileptic Ferdinand. He applied to the Russian tsar for military aid, and by August 1849, the Hungarian revolution had been quashed. The army surrendered, the government was outlawed, and the new constitution was revoked. Kossuth escaped to the Ottoman Empire; Prime Minister Lajos Batthyány, thirteen generals, and one hundred rebel patriots were put to death. One thousand Hungarians were sentenced to twenty years imprisonment or forced labour, another 50,000 were forced into the Austrian Imperial Army, and several society women were publicly whipped. Public gatherings, including theatrical performances, were outlawed.

---

[89] According to a 1910 census, there were so many minorities in the country that only half of the population spoke Hungarian.
[90] The Bastille had held six petty criminals and one sex offender.

Hating Habsburg repression, many Jews had joined the Revolutionary Army, had established, equipped and staffed hospitals. When the revolution failed, Jewish loyalty was forgotten – someone had to be blamed. Synagogues were attacked and pogroms spread. Singled out for punishment, Jews were inducted into the Austrian army, and the community was forced to provide thousands of uniforms and to pay for the army's horses and tackle.

***

*A*lthough serfdom ended in 1848, peasant life barely changed. Seventy to eighty percent of former serfs came into possession of land. When added to acreage already held by free peasants, this was less than two and a half percent of the country's farmland. With no concept of wage labour, no access to credit, most found their holdings too tiny to sustain them. They continued working for the estates and were paid a pittance.

To limit family size, women and children slept on trestle beds inside the house; men slept on planks covered with rushes or straw out in the barns. Waking before dawn to clean stables and pigsties, fill carts with manure, milk cows, workers laboured in the fields until night. At noon, wives brought lunch baskets containing bowls, a hunk of bread, perhaps an onion, a pickle, a pepper, but there was often no soup to fill the bowls, and men only pretended to eat: one couldn't lose face in front of neighbours: 'When you go to someone's house, don't peek into the pot to see what's cooking. And when it's time to eat, don't stay. Don't look into the lives of others'

Brutality was ever present, the tool of teachers, drill-sergeants, the police, overseers and husbands. Workers could be hanged or flogged, although new 'liberal' laws stated that farmhands between the ages of twelve and eighteen could be beaten in

Those Absent

such a way 'as not to cause a wound which does not heal within eight days.' Older men were whipped. Toiling without pay, women rewarded employers with gifts of appreciation, and girls still earned a hunk of bread and extra lard by providing favours. Some nobles, angry they no longer possessed their serfs, destroyed the houses on their lands. In 1880, restrained by gendarmes, peasants watched helplessly as homes and gardens in hundreds of villages were obliterated.

Unable to participate in elections – the right to vote depended upon property ownership and educational qualifications – the peasants were trapped in a narrow life: as the saying went: *a paraszt nem ember*, a peasant is not human. The infant mortality rate was extremely high; and because caring for the aged was a financial burden, many an elderly man took his own life. Yet, life expectancy did increase.

The sons of impoverished country nobles began working as estate administrators, bailiffs, notaries, schoolteachers, military officers and churchmen, and they formed a new middle class. Bricks, not mud, were used for new houses; roof tiles replaced reeds. Hand-carved trunks and benches gave way to manufactured furniture, and front bedrooms were converted into 'clean rooms' with curtains, clocks, mirrors and lamps, where men drank beer, played cards and skittles. Women, locked into domesticity, became dedicated readers, and the best-loved novels were romances in which lower-class females met the high-status males who introduced them to passion and opulence.

At first, peasants didn't dare join in flashy displays: wasn't flamboyance reserved for those of higher birth? Soon enough, a younger generation sported large pocket watches and built sizeable homes.[91] Eager to indulge in the new conspicuous

---

91   Architecture continued to underline difference: well-off nobility had two story mansions whereas poorer noble's houses had stone columns on the street side of the building where they could be seen. Those lower on the social scale had pillars

PART FOUR : TISZAÖRS

consumption, shop girls paraded through the streets in gaudy clothing and bright jewellery, and domestics aped the fashions of their employers or donned their castaways until new laws forbade them to wear clothes suitable to burgers.

***

'But the serf mentality remained for a long time,' said Attila. He had been a musician in Budapest before slipping out of communist Hungary and marrying German Paula. When communism ended, he returned and purchased a holiday home here in the village. What did the finicky Germans, Austrians and Swiss make of him? He cared nothing for their opinion. Straining suspenders held in place torn trousers, emphasized a nicely rounded gut. His mane and beard were wild and white; his wit was sharp and his conversation a delight. Paula, equally sharp-witted, frequented the Germans; Attila stuck with Hungarians. The house interior was Paula's undisputed territory; the untended garden was Attila's.

Even on the dullest days, here he was, propped against a whitewashed house wall, enjoying bird battles in the peach and mulberry trees, listening to the wind in the long grasses. Beside him was a gas cooker, and in a black greasy pot, he boiled meat into pâté or fried thick slices of aubergine. A steady stream of visitors came to pay him homage and listen to his stories, and I joined the fan club. Our friendship grew, and I soon became a privileged guest, one with the right to partake of the oily hot fried vegetable.

'My father was a dental technician in Budapest,' said Attila. 'He knew a Dr Gábor Baty, an important aristocrat. After the last war, Baty had to work as a dentist because the communists had taken away all his land. He was the last of his line, a morphine

of wood.

addict because he'd been shot and was in constant pain, but he was an excellent dentist. His clients were aristocrats who'd hidden away a little money. Baty told my father he'd give him work if they made a deal: each would declare just ten percent of what they earned. The hardest part of the job was getting your hands on gold, but my father had some left over, a heavy ball of it, so he could work without attracting attention.

'One night, someone knocked on our door. My mother went to answer and came running back into the kitchen. She said there was a strange man outside, and she was frightened. I went to the door with her, and saw a man who looked like a beggar, like someone who lived in the streets. He wore a shabby coat, trousers that had been mended a thousand times, and his shoes were torn open. There was one incongruous thing: he was clean and freshly shaven. I asked him what he wanted – my mother thought he was there to beg.

"I am Jóska," he said. "I come from Dr Baty."

'So we called my father. He came to the door and said: "Oh yes, Jóska. Please come in."

Jóska inched into the apartment, pulled out a shredded rag he'd tucked into his clothes. Inside was all money Dr Baty owed my father. A huge sum. This Jóska was Baty's lackey. His parents, his grandparents, his ancestors had been serfs for hundreds of years on the Baty estates, on the land that had been taken away, but he remained completely loyal to the Baty family.

'After that, Jóska came regularly with the money from Baty. He was always ragged, but there was never a single forint missing. Each time he came, my mother asked him if he wanted to eat something, and he'd shake his head. Then she'd ask if he wanted soup – that was probably all he'd ever eaten in his life – and he'd nod, mutter, "thank you," sit down at the table, slurp a bowl of soup loudly in the peasant way, mumble, "thank you" again, get up and leave. He'd never talk. We couldn't get him to say another word. For years, Jóska travelled from the country with the money and took all the risks. Then Baty died, and Jóska vanished.'

Those Absent

XXXII

The pain cuts deep into our heart to observe that in most of our synagogues not the Hungarian language but German or Judeo-German is spoken. The reason for this is not a religious one, but a superficial attachment to accustomed ways. What right do the Orthodox congregations have to spread God's commandment in a foreign tongue? No one can give a real answer to this. We do not know when our brethren will come to the realisation that this blind and slavish reverence for Yiddish is absurd... Do they want to wait, particularly our Orthodox brethren, until this weakness of our religious service is placed before the House of Representatives?

Jakob Steinherz[92]

In 1867, with the creation of the dual Austro-Hungarian Monarchy, Budapest became one of Europe's most brilliant cities. Scientists, industrialists, poets, painters and philosophers enjoyed the beauty of elegant cupolas, balconies and bronze doorways. Fully emancipated, Hungarian Jews had the same political and civil rights as their Christian compatriots, and were playing an active role in the country's cultural life, in finance and commerce.

By 1900, although comprising a mere six percent of the population, forty-two percent of journalists, forty-five of lawyers, thirteen of craftsmen, twenty-six of those in the arts, and forty-nine percent of doctors were Jewish. Jewish writers, scholars and musicians[93] were active in creating the new Hungarian culture; Jews were present in the civil service, trade unions, radical party politics, the freemasons and progressive clubs. Half of the city's merchants, industrialists and bankers

---
92   *A Magyar Nyelv a Zsinagogaban.* Dr Jakob Steinherz, in 1905, elected leader of the progressive Jewish community in Székesfehérvár, Hungary.
93   Béla Bartók, annoyed that much of his audience was Jewish, responded with outright anti-Semitism, and Vienna's anti-Semitic mayor, Karl Lueger, dubbed the city 'Judapest'.

were Jewish, and their business acumen so benefited this country, that Emperor Franz Josef honoured twenty-five families with baronial rank and ennobled another three hundred.

To prove they were loyal Magyars, the Jewish Magyarisation Society was created. Coreligionists were instructed to use Hungarian in daily life, not German, and certainly not Yiddish, that embarrassing gibberish.[94] Forty thousand adopted Magyar names, usually Hungarian translations of the German names given to their ancestors a century earlier. Wearing modern Magyar dress, they attended synagogues where the raised central reading table, the bimah, now stood in front like any church altar. Rabbis and cantors wore ecclesiastical garments; men and women sat together and, as in churches, there were choirs and organs.

Jewish Magyarisation soothed Christians. It made Jews seem less foreign, and impoverished nobles were less reticent to sell their estates to wealthy Jews wishing to emulate the aristocracy. When indebted and no wealthy Christian suitor was available, fathers welcomed well-off Jews as marriage partners for sons and daughters, although the Jewish spouse would be excluded from social invitations, a rejection accepted with resignation.

Alongside assimilation came self-hatred. There were no Yiddish newspapers, and Jewish writers claimed they were Hungarians, not Jews. Many chose baptism, identified with reactionary regimes, distanced themselves from the oppressed, and from the minorities demanding autonomy.

---

94 According to Yudel Mark in *Never Say Die: The Yiddish Language: Its Cultural Impact*, the Dictionary of the Yiddish Language has 200,000 words, all used in all countries at all times. Spanish has approximately 250,000 words, Russian, 125,000. One reason for this large vocabulary is that Jews were amongst the most cultured people in Europe; in the sixteenth century, when many rulers were unable to write their own names, almost the entire Jewish male population and a considerable number of the female, could read. Thirteen million people spoke Yiddish before WWII.

Those Absent

Incoming Jews from Galicia, Romania and Russia, attracted by the country's relative freedom and financial opportunities, were not welcomed by the urbane Hungarian Jews who took measures to hinder their arrival and residency. The newcomers, poor country bumpkins, were an embarrassment. Many used the hated Yiddish language; some still dressed in sixteenth-century traditional garb, mumbled in the synagogue, made wild gestures when speaking, and spoke far too loudly. Christian neighbours were bound to react negatively and consider all Jews 'foreign'.

***

*I*n the town of Tiszafüred, fifteen kilometres away, communist-era buildings are interspersed with modern structures, and campgrounds, hunting lodges, restaurants, tourist hotels and pensions. Some recent homes resemble colourful concrete cupcakes topped by PVC icing; their gardens are ornamented with burbling fountains, cement goddesses, gnomes, curlicue wrought iron, fake wagon wheels, plastic baskets and decorative wheelbarrows.

Some elegance has, nonetheless, survived. One official building in the town's centre was a former manor; its aristocratic owner had been an amateur archaeologist. Imbued with nineteenth-century destructive zeal, he conducted wild excavations in this area, unearthed countless Neolithic artefacts. He bequeathed his finds and extensive library to his townspeople. Today, aside from a few volumes in a museum basement, nothing is left. At the end of WWII, vengeance was wrought on any representation of the aristocracy: the artefacts were crushed underfoot, and the books were burnt in one grand *auto-da-fé*.

It was Karcsi who introduced me to blonde blue-eyed Ágnes

Szegö, the last Jew of Tiszafüred. A writer, researcher and Holocaust historian, she ran the charity that maintained the Jewish cemetery, brought Jewish cultural events to town and kept alive the memory of the vanished community.

Walking through the streets together, she brought to life those absent: Jewish merchants Gáspár Ernst; Jozsef Grün, and Lörinc Róth who died in the 1848 revolution; the rabbis Mozes Schönfeld and Herman Rosenberg Gerzson; Drs Ignác Menczer and Lajos Rosinger; the lawyer, Dr Henrik Soltész. In 1877, one third of those in the Fire Brigade Association were Jewish. The Jewish Women's Association, created in 1883 and still in existence in 1941, organised balls, theatrical and musical productions, used the profits to help the sick, supply underprivileged children with winter clothing and school equipment, and collect dowries for girls from impoverished families.

Any trace of Jewish businesses – the tailor's, the shoemaker's, the grocery, the watchmaker, the bank and the inns – is gone. Only the large synagogue building remains: it had become an electrical appliance outlet.

'They tried to destroy it,' said Ágnes, 'but it's so solid it couldn't be pulled down.'

After Ágnes returned to work, it started raining. I took refuge in a nearby kocsma with an old-fashioned display window filled with potted plants. The barmaid was hostile, the room was unattractive and chilly, but I had an hour to wait until the bus left. Ordering a coffee, I pulled out a book.

The owner, a thin man with a toothbrush moustache, came out from the back and threw open the front door. The few customers, serious male drinkers, protested. The room was cold enough, someone said.

Those Absent

The owner sniggered. 'It's because of the smell. The smell in the room.' Smoke from his smouldering cigar drifted into the air, and he launched into a droning monologue. Used to not understanding longwinded (and often dull) conversations in Hungarian, I blocked out his voice – it was only noxious background noise – but the words began untangling themselves.

'Hitler can come back anytime he wants. He didn't finish the job. Got rid of most of the Jews but left too many. Too many Gypsies, too, he can come back, finish them all off. Jews never learnt their lesson, charging twice as much as anyone else, exploiting us.'

The men on the benches grunted.

I looked up. The owner was watching me, smirking. He knew who I was, and I was the smell he was referring to.

So, my Hungarian had improved after all.

***

*R*eturning to the village, I went to see Attila. The rain had let up and, despite the chilly air, he was at his post, propped against the garden wall. I told him what had happened, but he merely humoured me with a story, perhaps the best, and only, solution.

'Say what you want, Jews are different,' he said. 'Jews are businessmen. But Hungarians? No. Hungarians are stupid, and you can't bargain with them either, because they never learned to do business. I'm Hungarian, so I know what I'm talking about.

'You go to a flea market, see something you want, but the price is too high, and you say to the seller, "Why not take a hundred forint less?" Right away, he says, "no." Later you come back because you need the thing he's selling, even though it's nothing special, simply a piece of junk. This time the seller gets angry when you ask him to bring the price down a little. The third time, he won't talk to you or he'll insult you. One hundred forint is no loss to him – it's a few cents, and it would make the buyer feel a little better – but the seller won't do it.

'My father could have made a lot of money as a dental technician, but because he was a Hungarian, he couldn't bargain. He worked for one Jewish dentist, a guy who smelled of garlic, the wave hit you as soon as you saw him, but he was a perfectionist. If he didn't think something was exactly right, he'd send it back. He drove my father crazy because he was also a perfectionist. One night, after my father had worked fifteen hours straight, the dentist sent something back. Again. By now, my father was fed up. He said, "I won't do this anymore. That's it." He called the dentist, told him that.

'But the dentist was a Jew, and he knew how to deal with Hungarians. The next day he called my father, said: "Okay, I'll pay you a hundred forint more." And my father accepted because he was a Hungarian and couldn't bargain. He would be paid a tiny bit more – a few cents – and for that, the dentist could continue to make his life miserable.'

Those Absent

XXXIII

She sweeps the kitchen floor.
Under her blouse something still says
She loves him – and sweeps some more.
Again, she does the dishes,
And scours the copper pan.
How like the smoke from a chimney
Is the love of any man.

Anonymous Folk Poem

*G*izi was in love, a joyless state. She grew thin, and behind the heavy frames of her glasses, her eyes were wretched. It had begun one afternoon. Hearing she was single, Misi had come to her gate and invited her out to dinner.

'I looked at Misi… and something magic happened. It was strange, because I've known him all my life. He was the village bad boy. But seeing him there, suddenly everything changed. Of course, my mother stood beside me the whole time, listening to the conversation, and as soon as Misi left, she began nagging, telling me I couldn't go out with him, he'd always been in trouble, and his family was of lower status than ours. My mother wants everything to revolve around her, so I didn't listen. I wanted to be with Misi.'

After an excellent restaurant dinner, Misi suggested they go to the baths. 'I said I couldn't because my mother was waiting up, and he made fun of me: "You're forty-four years old. Why do you have to go home to your mother?"'

From that time on, each weekend Gizi stayed with Misi at his house. She was in seventh heaven; she had been rescued from the single state. Finally. Yet, it was a short-lived ecstasy. Misi's girlfriend had returned, and Gizi was no longer welcome.

PART FOUR : TISZAÖRS

'Misi won't even say "hello" to me when he sees me on the street.'

Years before, Gizi had divorced a dull husband – divorce had been easy in communist times. She had begun leaving Hungary, officially to perfect her language skills as a teacher. In reality, travel enabled her to meet with foreign pen pals. In England, she'd cohabited with an alcoholic Irish poet who ran after other women, 'but always came back to me.' Then there was a man who ran a bed-and-breakfast and needed a cook. In Amsterdam, she'd lived with a miserly Dutchman, but unable to work and earn her own money, she obeyed her mother's injunction to return home and care for her ailing father. There had been others, too: a married diplomat, a vague and shiftless American, but those dalliances had evoked no passion in her. It was the avaricious Dutchman who, in broken-hearted hindsight, now seemed ideal.

'If I'd stayed with him, I'd be married and have a new car and a big house. Instead, I have nothing. Misi told me he loved me, but now I'm alone and I can't go anywhere. Everything in Hungary is for families. A single woman is isolated.'

'You live in the city, and you can join clubs, meet new people.'

She was horrified. Go somewhere on her own? Never. That would underline humiliation. No: Isolation was proper punishment for those in the inferior single state.

I brought Gizi to meet Kata in Ildikó's bar. 'You see? Kata is single, and she has fun.'

But Gizi was scathing. 'Decent women don't spend their time in bars. Kata isn't like me; she has a peasant background. You're a foreigner, so you can do things like that. I can't.'

***

Those Absent

*S*everal weeks later, the girlfriend left, and Misi called Gizi. 'He told me he'd made a terrible mistake. He was fed up with his girlfriend's moods, her temper and her jealousy, and he wanted me to come back. I love him and things are wonderful.'

Short-lived bliss once more: the girlfriend was back in town. 'I'll never fall in love again,' Gizi declared. She was getting older; chances were slim of finding a suitable mate. 'Hungary's a terrible country for single women. Look at the lonely-hearts columns. Men want the same thing: young women who are slender, attractive, well dressed, financially independent, and they have to be able to clean and cook well. Men aren't ashamed to write that down. That's why I've always had foreign boyfriends.'

'But Misi is also Hungarian.'

Stoutly, she defended her recalcitrant lover. 'Misi's not the same. He's almost Canadian.'

'What about Hungarian women? What do they want?'

'A rich foreigner. You should hear the teachers at the school where I work. They don't care about love. Only money.'

***

*A*s soon as she arrived on Saturdays, Gizi headed for Robi's house. He, a roly-poly devious man, an insurance broker known to pocket his clients' payments, was a frequent visitor at Misi's. He was, for Gizi, an excellent source of information: Were Misi and the girlfriend still together? Did he look happy? Who did the cooking?

Robi fed Gizi the painful data she craved: yes, Misi loved his girlfriend; they would be getting married; they would soon leave for Canada. Any hint of conflict had Gizi reporting to me with schadenfreude: 'Robi said they had a huge fight on

Thursday because Misi went to the kocsma. She's forbidden him to drink. He can't talk to other women either.'

Although Gizi suffered horribly, at least they were talking about Misi. In exchange, Robi propositioned Gizi shamelessly, peeking into her windows and hoping to catch her in a state of undress. Finding Robi physically and morally repulsive – his regular girlfriend, a kindergarten teacher from Kunmadaras, was pregnant with his child – Gizi tolerated some sweaty advances as the price to pay for vicarious domestic bliss.

Hoping to run into Misi, Gizi began accompanying me on long afternoon walks. Passing the rows of whitewashed earthenware houses, the earthy-sweet gardens with their pale new cabbages and flowering potatoes, we only turned back at the newer streets lined by cement villas. As we negotiated weed-ruined sidewalks, Gizi pointed to houses where village characters had lived out forgotten love stories. All were calamitous: the beautiful young girl who had loved a married man. 'He loved her too, but he had a fragile wife and two young children. Her family carted her off to Budapest, and no one ever saw her again. Her married lover killed himself shortly after.

'And, beside those trees, that's where the veterinarian lived with his wife, a slender Polish beauty with golden hair to her waist. All the men, even schoolboys, were in love with her, but she passed along this road every morning, basket over one arm, head high, never looking left or right. One day, she and the veterinarian defected and went to Canada. A few years later, when he came back, she stayed over there. She was working as a waitress in a golf club restaurant. To her, that was better than life in this village.

'You see that house with the porch facing the road? Two sisters lived there, and one was beautiful. The priest used to

Those Absent

come to visit all the time, and we soon discovered he was in love with the beautiful sister, and that she loved him too. Of course, he could never marry her, never give her children because he was a Catholic priest, but they could go to Szolnok where no one knew them, live together there. She would be his housekeeper. And, because she loved him, she did it. They were together for many years until one day he decided to retire to a monastery. She'd sacrificed everything for him, her home, her hopes of marriage and a family, and now she would be all alone.'

Many knew of Gizi's failed romance. Even pot-bellied András who lived across the road did his best to comfort her, handing her a clutch of flowering sprigs, telling her she would find someone else to love, someone worthy. Hadn't Misi been the village bad boy? People never change. *'Kutyából nem lez szalonna,'* said András – you can't make bacon out of a dog. Even Gizi giggled and, for the moment, forgot to speak up for her lost paramour.

Only Gizi's mother was gleeful that the romance had failed. 'I told you his family's social level is beneath ours.' Once more, her daughter would cater to her. Perhaps to foil that exigent woman, Gizi began bringing Traute with her each time she returned to the village. Tall, bony and in her early sixties, Traute was a German exchange teacher.

'She took the job to get away from her unfaithful husband,' Gizi confided. 'But she's so rigid, the other teachers hate her. I'm the only one who feels sorry for her.'

Joining us on our strolls, Traute spewed out her anger. She hated her husband! How she suffered. He had bought a luxury apartment in Konigsberg for his mistress. 'A bitch. A manipulator. My husband is putty in her hands. She had terrible debts, and he paid them all off. How could he do this to me? I dressed elegantly. I gave the dinner parties. I charmed the contacts he needed in order to be successful. I was the perfect wife. And now he wants to throw me over. I can't lose my life style or my big beautiful house. I worked for that house. I put all my energy into it, because, believe me, I've known suffering.

'This might sound harsh to you, a Jew, but you can't imagine how we Germans suffered during the war. Horrible things happened when the Russians came. We had to leave our homes and hide in the woods. Girls, women were raped by Russian soldiers. You Jews… you all think you were the only ones who had a difficult time.'

A few weeks later, after Traute returned to Germany, she telephoned Gizi: she and her husband had had a terrible argument. She'd pushed him, he'd fallen, hit his head on the edge of the refrigerator. She'd left him lying on the floor. An hour later, he was dead. An accident.

'She murdered him,' said Gizi with undisguised envy. 'You see? She got everything she wanted – the big lovely house, and all that money.'

***

'I heard your girlfriend came back,' I said to Misi when I saw him on the street.

'You bet she did.' He was triumphant. 'When she showed up at my workshop, I told her to get over to the house, take out the broom, the mop, the bucket and begin cleaning. I said, "You've been gone for too long. There's a whole house to keep you busy."'

'And what did she say to that?'

Misi laughed. 'She shut her mouth. She does what I tell her to do.' And he strutted off down the cracked sidewalk, a pudgy cockalorum.

Those Absent

XXXIV

The roof was supported by heavy projecting beams, black and smoky; the glazed mud walls were cracked, threatening destruction; rickety chairs stood in front of lame tables, shining with grease; in one corner on the ground were a pail of water and a basket of rubbish and a broom; and on a miserable fire a saucepan was trying to boil; ragged clothes, torn cloaks, and trousers of an indescribable colour hung on wooden horses, recalling those wretched garments taken from the victims of suicide or murder that are to be seen hanging up in the Morgue.

Victor Tissot, 1881

Despite freshly painted walls and the booming jukebox, Ildikó's kocsma was not up to the new European Community standards. Inspectors had returned, and noting the tattered linoleum and peeling plastic bar, the dreadful toilet and lack of hot water, they condemned the lot.

Ildikó had no money for bribes ('that's the way you get things to work in this country,' said Karcsi), but perhaps her landlady, that loyal (non-paying) drinker would take things in hand, consent to either a generous pay-off or to substantial renovation. However, under pressure from a thriftless daughter in Budapest, the woman decided to sell.

We all took the news badly. How could this kocsma vanish? Where would shepherds with long moustaches and floppy hats sing sad songs of the Puszta? Where would Kata read palms? Where would everyone feast and jump about to silly music? Those unmatched uneven-legged tables, the fake Grecian urns with their flower arrangements, the cheap plastic 'woodcuts,' the Christmas-light heart and Borsodi beer clock, how we would miss all. Kunmadaras was unthinkable without this haven.

PART FOUR : TISZAÖRS

Before closing, there would be one important feast: Tarzan's daughter Zsuzsa was engaged to a rich young man. 'Very successful,' said Tarzan. He, proud father, was hosting the engagement celebration in Ildikó's kocsma. Fiancée and fiancé would arrive from Budapest along with the future in-laws, and Udo and I were invited. Tarzan had other news too: he and Mariska were about to buy a beautiful new house, and he wanted to show it to us.

As we clambered into Tarzan's car, he waved a cassette. 'Listen to this. It's the traditional Gypsy music I told you about. You see? I didn't forget. You'll like it.' He slid the tape into the player, and the thud of cheap rock, the wah-wah of echo chamber filled the air.

Tarzan parked on a calm street of modern middle-class homes. 'That's it.' He pointed to a substantial bourgeois dwelling with a golf-course-perfect lawn and splendid rose-bed. 'We'll take possession as soon as the money arrives. Mariska and I will be starting a business in the back garden, raising chickens, maybe a thousand, and fattening them for the slaughterhouse.'

Appalled, I stared at him. 'In a residential area? How did you get permission to do that?'

'I have influence with important people.'

'You're getting a government grant?'

His answering chuckle was foxy, self-satisfied.

What would the neighbours think of the scheme? Little did they suspect that emerald grass and bobbing blooms would disappear under a swamp of mud; that, over by the trim mixed hedge, the bitter Rottweiler would continue his half-life on an arm's-length chain; that this rarefied middle-class air would soon reek of intensive animal production. What about the clustered junk, rotted clothes and shattered toys in Tarzan's

Those Absent

yard? Would all make the journey here?

'Yes, this is where we'll be after the event. My daughter is marrying a rich man. That's to be expected. She's highly educated. Works in a bank, speaks seven or eight languages.'

***

*T*he paper taped onto the door of Ildikó's kocsma read: Closed for Private Party. Tarzan's guests, a crowd of future in-laws, gathered outside. They were middle-class people, fresh from Budapest, the country's newest well-to-do. Prim, clearly unhappy, they stood on the ragged street, no doubt wondering what dreadful deed they'd committed to have landed in such a dreary place. To the left, cows grazed peacefully between a mud-walled barn and long-armed sweep-well. To the right was the jumble of this provincial town with its pot-holed roads and punctured sidewalks: Kunmadaras was punishment from the gods.

Catching sight of Udo and me coming down the road – two foreigners would raise the social tone of this get-together – Tarzan was visibly relieved. So were the future in-laws. Pumping our hands with vigour, gushing, they rejected my offer of bad Hungarian and insisted on bad English. All made it clear that this trip to the backwoods was quite an adventure, an ordeal never to be repeated.

Perhaps to make certain we would correctly gauge his social status, one future brother-in-law had come armed with photos, and he pushed them into our hands: shots of his house in a Budapest suburb. That large, new, pristine dwelling had today's senseless plethora of roofs and gables, an azure swimming pool and an over-size garage. Idly, I wondered if these people openly identified with Western Europe and the EU, or also praised the purity of Magyarness.

I didn't recognise the fiancée. Zsuzsa had changed greatly

since our meeting a few years back. Gone, the elastic togs, heavy make-up and dyed black hair. Demure, reasonable-looking, her brown hair was cut short and her clothes were sophisticated. Did she look like a happy, engaged woman? On the contrary. Visibly bored, indifferent, she had no affectionate glances for her paramour, a handsome, lean-faced man. He, besotted, was a good boy. Her indifference seemed to fan his passion.

Dust-filled gusts brought spatters of rain from a louring sky. Now there was no choice but to take shelter in the kocsma's back room where the pushed-together tables had been covered in white cloth, and the bogus Grecian urns were filled with real flowers. Tarzan had provided for the best, but no mistaking, for these city slickers, the absolute best was all wrong.

The kocsma was shabby, not modern. The small back room lacked pretension, glossy plastic 'woodwork', white tiled floors and straight plasterboard walls. Where was the expected commercial rural bric-à-brac: nicely lacquered wagon wheels, shiny sabres and sickles, crocheted cloths, picturesque parts of ploughs, a sleek whip or two? Far from pretending to rusticity, this was the real un-bargained-for thing: torn linoleum, blazing neon lights, grey afternoon light seeping through torn, fake net plastic curtains.

Also present was the fiancée's mother, Tarzan's ex-wife, ghastly pale, wire-thin but sober for once. An odd-looking rubbery man kept her standing upright, but when she raised her glass, her hand shook violently. Here, too, was Mariska, father-of-the-bride's woman, a village Gypsy. Never would she be socially acceptable. Well aware of her inferior status, wounded by snubs, Mariska in a frilly dress and pretty shoes, her beautiful hair flowing to her waist, cowered in the darkness of a corner. She knew no one would speak to her or acknowledge her. Even Tarzan, in his role as the fiancé's boisterous and proud father,

Those Absent

had marooned her: he was doing his sycophantic best to impress the Budapest guests.

Although I had no reason to like Mariska, the situation was inacceptable. Going over to her, I took her arm, told her how lovely she was, and said she would be sitting with Udo and me during dinner. Thus, the assembled company gratefully separated: the chic Budapest relatives, the fiancée and fiancé, sat at one table; ex-wife, rubbery man and two locals made themselves comfortable at an adjoining one. Udo, Mariska and I were at a third table, quite removed from the others. Soon enough, an uncomfortable Tarzan joined us. Certainly he was the host, the self-important father-of-the-future-bride, but this coterie considered him a lowly rural embarrassment, and they were letting him know it.

Kata and Ildikó, not elegant waiters in white, brought out delicious food that was consumed silently and without praise. The indifferent fiancée opened her mountain of gifts expressionlessly and thanked no one. Then the affair was over.

No one tarried, but climbing into new expensive cars, they roared back to Budapest, two hundred kilometres away. They'd done their duty. What an adventure! A voyage to the foreign part of their own country.

PART FOUR : TISZAÖRS

XXXV

People laughed at Austria in those days, they called it the 'rag and bone Empire' and its multi-tribal army a 'gypsy camp'. Our first impression of it was of a collection of swarthy, emaciated men in blue greatcoats and faded forage caps on which the metal discs bore the Emperor Franz Joseph's cypher in perforated letters.

Konstantin Paustovsky[95]

'*E*very day is a gift from God,' said Rózsa *néni*[96] as she opened her gate and led me into a garden of tumbling grape vines. 'So many died young.'

She, a handsome slender peasant, was almost a hundred years old. Patting thick white hair pulled into a neat bun, she made certain all was in place, for I was here to take her photo at the request of her great nephew, Miklós, the pharmacist. He, a nervous man, was already present. 'I will translate for you,' he said in German.

'I can manage in Hungarian,' I answered in Hungarian, proud of this hard-won (albeit horribly imperfect) accomplishment.

'I will translate,' Miklós repeated

'Perhaps the foreigner would like to see my house,' said Rózsa néni to her great nephew.

'You can speak to me in Hungarian,' I said, certain I would impress her.

'What is she saying?' Rózsa néni asked Miklós. 'I can't understand foreign languages.'

'I'm speaking to you in Hungarian,' I insisted.

'Tell the foreigner to come into the house,' said Rózsa néni.

---
95 *Story of a Life*. Konstantin Paustovsky, 1892-1965.
96 Women over a certain age are referred to as *néni* or aunt; men are *bácsi* or uncle. Both are deferential ways of addressing those unrelated by blood.

Those Absent

'She'll find it interesting.'

'My great-aunt says to come into the house,' said Miklós in German.

'Please, speak to me in Hungarian,' I begged, but any protest was useless. I was a foreigner, I spoke with an accent, therefore I could not understand or speak Hungarian.

The house, larger, roomier and more solid than most, was the dwelling of well-off peasants. Its front terrace was broad with many thick, sculpted pillars. In the main room's half-gloom, walls were decorated in the traditional way, with coloured religious pictures, family photos and wooden crucifixes. In an adjoining bedroom, two beds were heaped with hand-embroidered cushions. The lower, more modest bed, was her own; the larger, more pretentious was her husband's. It was made up for his use, although he had died forty years earlier.

Rózsa néni pointed to a photo high on the wall of the main room. 'My grandfather. He died during the First World War when I was a girl. To the left, you can see our church. He helped pay for the church bell, but it was taken out soon after, melted down for ammunition. He never knew because he was already dead, killed in Serbia. No one thought we would lose the war.'

A quick war, an easy victory, that's what all expected. A few treasonous pessimists dared mention that Hungary's industry was ill suited to a war economy, that debonair army officers were frittering away days and nights playing baccarat and indulging in flirtations, that soldiers were insufficiently trained and their weapons were obsolete: what chance did decorated prancing horses stand against new machine guns? What about a soldiery comprised of oppressed and disillusioned minorities, Czechs, Slovaks, Slovenes, Serbs and Croats? Wouldn't there be division within the ranks? But who listened to wet blankets?

PART FOUR : TISZAÖRS

Austro-Hungary was a great power; its disappearance was inconceivable.

The summer of August 1914 was beautiful, hazy. To the exhilarating pom-pom-pom of military bands, soldiers marched to train stations where blushing young women handed out flowers, and the crowds cheered. Arriving in Serbia and Russian Poland, they beheld bucolic scenes: harvests had been brought in and the earth smelled of warm straw. Sweet fruit hung ripe from overladen boughs, cows grazed amongst bobbing wildflowers, and chickens pecked in tidy farmyards. The soldiers helped themselves, luxuriated, set barns and houses on fire in heady ebullience. Certain victory was a thrilling idea, and these young men were on a grand adventure.

None were prepared for constant artillery fire, poison gas, barbed wire, hand grenades, gangrene, dysentery, typhus, cholera, parasitic infections, trench mouth, trench foot or death by exposure. Antibiotics did not exist, and minor injuries were often fatal. Surrounded by bloated corpses, harried by rats, the soldiers lay in mud, blood, offal and died. As did local populations. Fields were destroyed, forests, wildlife, villages, homes, cultures, an entire way of life. In 1917 the front collapsed, yet fighting dragged on. Until a new enemy appeared: Spanish flu.

Hungary lost 1,200,000 soldiers; another 3,500,000 were mutilated. Survivors straggled home, discovered little had changed: their families were dying of starvation, and the nobility controlled the land. Soldiers imprisoned in Russian camps were uncompensated; ethnic minorities were unrepresented in government.

Desperate, men took to the roads, robbing and murdering. The Red Watch, formed by those exposed to communism in Russian camps, ate all they could find, pillaged and destroyed manor houses, churches and Jewish shops. One band broke into the home of former Prime Minister István Tisza and, declaring him responsible for the war, beat him to death.[97]

Parliament was dissolved, and Hungary was proclaimed an independent republic with universal suffrage, freedom of the press and assembly. Mihály Károlyi, leader of the Independence Party, was appointed prime minister, and shouting their approval, chrysanthemum-waving citizens poured into the streets.

Four and a half months later, after being handed a note delineating the country's new borders under the Trianon Treaty, Károlyi resigned. Hungary had lost two-thirds of its pre-war territory, eighty-four percent of its timber, forty-three percent of its arable land, and eighty-three percent of its iron ore. This amputation quashed the (unrealistic) dream of re-establishing Hungary's pre-sixteenth-century historic borders, and removed large sections of today's Vojvodina, Croatia, Ruthenia (Ukraine), the Burgenland, Romania and Slovakia: it is still a bone of contention one hundred years later.[98] Finding themselves residing outside their homeland, three million ethnic Hungarian refugees poured into the country.

The Hungarian Communist Party, founded in a Moscow hotel, soon attracted thirty to forty thousand members, many of them unemployed ex-soldiers, young intellectuals and Jews who had abandoned Judaism and despised those who hadn't.

The party leader, Béla Kún (Kohn before he changed it) was the son of a non-practicing Jewish father and a Jewish mother whose family had converted to Protestantism. Kún had fought on the Russian Front until captured in 1916; he

---

97   Having granted titles to wealthy Jews and appointing some to his cabinet, Tisza had long been a target for anti-Semites.
98   To keep the issue alive, Viktor Orbán has posted, on Facebook, maps of Historical Hungary.

became a communist while in a prison camp in the Urals. The new coalition of Social Democrats and Communists under Kún promised that, with Soviet Russia's help, Hungary would reclaim its borders. A temporary constitution guaranteed free education, cultural rights to minorities, suffrage to all over eighteen except clergy, exploiters and 'certain others.'

Two months later, a dictatorship of the proletariat was proclaimed. Private property and land holdings over 40.5 hectares were to be liquidated, as were banks, privately owned commercial and industrial establishments, of which a large proportion were in Jewish hands. In a wave of Red Terror, tribunals ordered 590 executions for crimes against the revolution: one tenth of the victims were Jews. To discourage counter-revolutionary reaction, civilian hostages were taken, many of them leading Jewish capitalists.

For the peasants, little changed. If they had believed Kún's government would come to their aid, they discovered it intended to create collective farms, expropriate their grain and send it to feed those in the cities. The regime's hostility towards religion also alienated this population still guided by the clergy.

The Romanian army occupied the country, looted Budapest, led off all the horses. Peasants, already living in extreme deprivation, were forced to supply Romanian soldiers with food, animals and fuel. After a mere 133 days in power, the Hungarian Soviet Republic collapsed and Kún retreated to Soviet Russia. He was later responsible for the death of 60,000 Crimeans before being executed in the 1930s, a victim of Stalin's purges. The government of Hungary shifted to the right.

'After WWI, do you remember that time?' I asked Rózsa néni. 'Life must have been difficult.'

Ignoring my question, she pointed to other framed photos

hanging alongside the crucifixes. 'My cousins, uncles and aunts.' Rigid-looking men in white shirts, women in stiff dresses and aprons, their hair hidden under scarves, all stared straight into the camera. Behind them, stretched endless dark fields.

Post-war society was much as it had been before: some participated in modern life while others were caught in a semi-feudal world. The Catholic Church, one hundred important families and eleven thousand large landowners possessed forty-eight percent of cultivated land. Their ill-paid manorial labourers and servants dressed in rags and went barefoot. School was a luxury, for children were needed for harvesting and planting. The servants of peasant farmers slept in kitchen corners, or in a tiny hut – a doghouse of sorts – in the courtyard, but their lot was better than that of landless labourers. Harshly treated, hired for spring planting and autumn harvest, most dug holes in the fields and passed nights there.

'It's not like today,' said Miklós. 'Life was different. Rules were obeyed, roles adhered to. Men could never show weakness. They rarely spoke or smiled, and their word was law.'

'Women and children had to comply,' agreed Rózsa néni. 'I was married twice. My father picked my first husband. I didn't want him, but I had no choice. My marriage lasted two months. I married again, but I couldn't have children. God punished me for divorcing.'

'What happened if you refused to do as you were told?'

'You were disowned. That was terrible. Many committed suicide when that happened, because the family gives you your identity. If an unmarried girl got pregnant, the family threw her out. Few took her side. Some went to the city and gave their babies away. Others killed themselves.' Rózsa néni didn't look as though she disapproved; unseemly behaviour was unacceptable.

'So life *could* be hard.'

'Not at all. We had our fields, and the soil was good. We had fruit and vegetable gardens. Families were small, two or three children, never more than you could afford. Each day, when work was done, we would sit together. Women would weave, and there was always music. We had a cimbalom player in the family, a violinist, too, but both died in the 1950s. After that, people forgot the old music. There was never enough money, but life wasn't bad.'

Those Absent

XXXVI

The csikós will share his last bite with his dog, who will wait in respectful distance until his master has finished his meal and takes off his hat, which by poking in the top of the crown, is made into a bowl into which the remains of the soup or rich red gravied gulyás are poured. At a wink from his master, the dog rushes to the improvised bowl and gobbles up the tantalising food to the last drop. The csikós claims that this treatment is also good for the hat, making it watertight.

Charlotte Lederer

One sunny afternoon, villagers saw Misi's girlfriend climb into a flashy red car driven by an unknown man. When Misi came home from his workshop, he found not a hot dinner, but a cold hob. For the next week, his face sagging in disconsolate folds, he slumped in a white plastic chair in front of the kocsma, smoked steadily and felt sorry for himself. 'If I'd stayed in Canada, I'd be rich, without worries, doing what I want, living the good life.' Then, once more, he called Gizi.

She was happy to return to his arms: no more weeping into cups of chilling tea in her garden; no more asking Robi, the insurance broker, for news. Despite her devotion, Misi treated her poorly, ignoring her in public, borrowing money from her and never paying it back, complaining she cooked too many vegetables but didn't use enough fat, and bragging of his sexual prowess: 'She can't get enough. When we're in bed, I tell her, "Turn over, go to sleep, I'm not a young man," but she can't stop.'

Frequently, he pointed out how temporary their arrangement was: 'She has to accept I'm leaving Hungary, perhaps next month, perhaps next summer. I'm going back to Canada. I'll walk into my house, tell my ex-wife, "Okay, that's enough of this funny business. I'm your husband. Time you settled down, did your job.'"

Each time he mentioned Canada, Gizi panicked. But Misi wasn't going anywhere; his version of Canada was an unreachable Shangri-La. Gizi didn't mind staying home and cleaning his house while he regaled his kocsma audience with tall tales; one weekday afternoon, when Misi showed up at her apartment with a bouquet of red roses, she was in heaven. What a declaration of love! Until Robi told her that the flowers had first been brought to the ex-girlfriend in Debrecen who'd thrown them back in his face.

The long-standing friendship between Udo and Tarzan had dribbled to an uncomfortable end. The new, socially ambitious, clean and tidy television-watching Tarzan who obeyed Mariska, was a disappointment. Udo missed the times spent drinking together in seedy kocsmas, the easy, droll camaraderie. Paying Tarzan's bills had been a small price for access to a wild, woolly and imperfect Hungary. This sterilized version was too similar to what he'd always known in Austria.

Tarzan and Mariska didn't move to the new house or start preparing chickens for the slaughterhouse. They stayed on the back street where the fettered Rottweiler continued to moan his agony of boredom in the disused oil drum, and the yard remained a muddy bog with rotting heaps of once-luxurious clothes. But Mariska, taking her two boys to school, was chic and fashionable, and the boys were clean.

Ildikó's kocsma, that Jewish bakery, was sold, and the new owner gutted the building. When it reopened, Karcsi, Udo and I went to have a look. The wall separating bar and back room had been ripped out; the floor, cemented over, was covered in white tile. New plasterboard walls were white; the ceiling was smothered by white polystyrene; the bar counter was a modern

Those Absent

affair in miracle material. The sign above the door had been changed; this was no longer a kocsma but a bistro. The owner was cool, unfriendly – perhaps she felt this was the modern way. Regulars scattered, and most, I never saw again. Without Ildikó's kocsma, Kata spent days watching dubbed sitcom passion. 'Me romantic. Love, love, love.'

Ildikó became the manager and cook at a restaurant attached to a quaint, branch line train station in the swampland. In the summer, trainloads of shrill tourists photographed themselves in front of a disused locomotive and ordered fatty local foods. On Saturday evenings, well-dressed middle-class locals filled the large glassed-in terrace, ate gulyás stew and listened to Józsi play World Music. It was a respectable, polite crowd.

Perhaps to show that the good times were certainly not over, Ildikó threw the occasional private soiree for the privileged inner circle: Karcsi, Kata, Ibolya, István, a few other locals and the five or six pals from Püspokladány. But I found the bar, with its shiny railway gewgaws and varnished memorabilia, strangely barren: it could be anywhere. The old gang, although willing to drink and dance, had become more reserved. They wanted to fit into a changing society, one that disqualified shaggy singing shepherds, men in shapeless hats, and women in faded dresses and rubber boots. I began avoiding the parties.

One afternoon, Kata and I bicycled out to the restaurant. Five heavy-set local men sat at an outdoor table downing pálinka and waiting for a meal. Ildikó, in a cooking hut not far away, stood over a pot of boiling lard in which bloated sausages, oily chunks of meat, and things long, whitish – perhaps intestines – bobbed. From time to time, she pierced all with a sharp knife: 'So the fat seeps into the meat. The men said they want it especially fatty.'

PART FOUR : TISZAÖRS

She and Kata chatted like long-lost friends who hadn't seen each other for a whole week; I, choked by the odour of hot grease and offal, stayed a certain distance away. Sagging strips of flypaper spanned the room, hung over preparation tables and cutting boards, and thousands of dead flies were stuck hopelessly to their glue. No surprise. Here in the swampland, insects filled the air. To my left was another deep fryer filled with oil; here other flying creatures had met their doom and were floating, a solid black mass, on the surface. Fascinated, I noted hillocks of dead bugs on the floor along all the walls, pushed into forgetfulness by a broom.

'Don't health inspectors object to so many corpses in a kitchen?' I asked.

Ildikó was annoyed by my question. 'The owner has an "in" with the right people, so the inspectors don't look around. With contacts and money, you can do what you want.'

Abandoning the dreadful scullery, I went outside to join two dogs. One, a poor ratty creature with an open wound, spent life on a pitifully short rope. The other, free but terrified, skulked away at my approach. I rubbed the tethered dog's rough fur, and he was grateful. Other than beating them, no one touched dogs here.

I returned to the kitchen, fetched scraps, a few bits of bread, anything I could find. 'Why is one dog tied up and not the other?' I asked.

'One is a stray, and the other is the guard dog.'

'Doesn't anyone ever let him off the rope?'

'Of course not,' said Ildikó with the usual Hungarian indifference towards animals. 'They'll shoot the stray. The other stays until the restaurant closes for winter, then he'll be shot, too.'

Like the dogs guarding the melon fields outside town:

adopted for a season, then done away with. Why spend good money feeding them?

'That's quite unacceptable.' I told Ildikó I would come back with a car, take both dogs to Tiszaörs, find homes for them or keep them.

Ildikó shrugged.

But when I returned with leashes two days later, both animals were gone.

PART FIVE:
The Jews

Jewish Family[99]

Close to the cemetery, we could hear the angry rumble of an over-excited crowd punctuated by cries of anger: 'Bastards, Jews, pigs, lice-ridden murderers.' I trembled with the fear from this hatred. When we approached, I saw that tombstones had been knocked over and that some were broken. There were boys and girls jumping on the tombs, red and sweating, laughing wildly. In another part of the cemetery, a laughing crowd was watching, with great hilarity, a group of young people who had lowered their pants and who were dirtying our tombs with their filth. But what shocked me even more was to see those girls with their eyes shining brazenly, looking at the repugnant act of these men with admiration.

David Tulman,[100] 1973

---

99   Photo courtesy of the Museum of Hungarian Speaking Jewry, Safed, Israel.
100   *Va-t'en*. David Tulman, 1901-1987, rabbi, member of the Jewish division of the International Brigade during the Spanish civil war.

Those Absent

XXXVII

When the light is crooked, the shadow is crooked.

Yiddish Proverb

'I heard something quite interesting this week,' said Gizi. 'Because you mentioned a pogrom in Kunmadaras, I wanted to learn more, so I went to the school library. And the librarian said, "Oh, the Jews. I can tell you all about them. My mother was a maid, and she worked for a Jewish family. Each time a baby was born, my mother was forced to cut her finger and give her blood for the baby to suck."' Gizi was triumphant. 'Isn't that the sort of thing you told me about?'

'Absolutely. Blood libels were often started by uneducated, superstitious servants who either invented stories, or passed around rumours they'd heard.'

Despite the Jewish prohibition of the consumption of blood, early church fathers, later the Jesuits, encouraged the flock to believe that Jews needed Christian blood. So deeply ingrained was this doctrine, poor Christians were known to offer their children to Jews for sacrifice in exchange for money.

According to popular belief, Jewish women used Christian blood to ease labour pains; Jewish babies, born blind with their fingers covering their eyes, needed Christian blood to see; Jews smeared themselves with it at wedding feasts; and rabbis bathed their hands in it before blessing congregations. Jews profaned the host, piercing it with nails, beating and grinding it in mortars to obtain Christ's blood, which they then scattered on Christian fields to kill crops and cattle. As late as the 1940s, Hungarian peasants were convinced that Jews used their phylacteries to strangle Christian children and spread their blood on the genitalia of their own sons to increase their fertility.

Reported in newspapers, corroborated by the church and anti-Semitic propaganda, blood accusations were never retracted: thus myth was reality.

'The librarian swears her mother is telling the truth, so I said you might want to talk to her. She said she'd be happy to do that. Are you interested?'

Of course I was. 'I'd also like to speak to her mother, if possible.' Would she stick to her story when confronted by a Jew?

Gizi promised to arrange a meeting then call me. 'It's so strange hearing this sort of thing. I thought everyone lived in peace, the Jews and everyone else. We helped each other.'

What did she know? Born in the 1960s, there were no village Jews left to tell tales.

***

*I*n 1849, a young servant, Christine Leckawaetz, raced out of Levi Hirsch's butcher shop screaming for help; in her hand was a large knife. When a crowd gathered, the girl claimed that Hirsch had tried to cut her throat because he needed Christian blood to mix into the matzo he was preparing for Pesach. Luckily, she'd managed to grab the knife and escape. Shouting imprecations, throwing stones, the mob smashed Hirsch's windows. The violence would have escalated, but the local priest appealed for restraint. 'Let justice be done.'

Townspeople hooted and cheered as Hirsch, his wife, daughter, and two sons were arrested and led through the streets. All were questioned separately, as was Christine Leckawaetz. When finally confronted by Hirsch, Leckawaetz admitted the accusation was false. She'd made it at the instigation of a rival butcher, István Voelktz, who'd promised to marry her and give her fifty florins if she could induce villagers to rise up against

Those Absent

Hirsch. Voelktz and Leckawaetz were imprisoned for several months and fined.[101]

In 1882, another blood libel had far-reaching consequences. In the village of Tiszaeszlár, Eszter Solymosi, a fourteen-year-old Catholic servant, was sent by her mistress to make purchases in town. She was never seen alive again.

Passover was approaching, and word spread that Jews had murdered Eszter. Sámuel Scharf, the five-year-old son of the *shammash* (beadle) was held for questioning. Encouraged by money and sweets, he claimed his father had lured Solymosi into the synagogue where the ritual slaughterer had cut her neck; that his brother, Móric, had held a cup to receive her blood. Later, under torture, Móric Scharf confessed that butchers Ábrahám Buxbaum, Leopold Braun and Salamon Schwarz had undressed the girl and cut her throat.

Twelve men were arrested. The notary, József Bary, was examining judge, and he tortured the accused, conducted his interrogation without witnesses, and stated publically:

> *The majority of the Tiszaeszlár Jews emerged from the Khazar scum... They don't study, don't cultivate themselves, they don't wash; they only do business and make children. They perjure themselves. They often commit arson. They mutilate their enemy's livestock. They accuse others without any grounds. They bribe people wherever they can... They pray loudly and cheat silently. They scalp the wealth off the soil and the skin off people. They are as fecund as bugs. They are as resourceful as sparrows. They ravage like rats.* [102]

When the body of a drowned girl was found in the Tisza River and identified as Eszter Solymosi, her mother insisted it was not her daughter but someone dressed in her clothes. Anti-

---
101 *Hungary.* The American Jewish Yearbook, 1849-50.
102 *A Blood Libel History from Miép, in Anti-Semitic discourse in Hungary, 2003-2004,* cited by János Dési.

Semitic agitators, amongst them the town's Catholic priest, claimed Jews had smuggled in the corpse to conceal the ritual murder. Several raftsmen were arrested and mistreated until they swore that a Jewish woman had ordered them to put the body in the river.

Throughout the country, terrified Christian servants fled their Jewish employers. Jewish houses were plundered, and Jews were attacked. Győző Istóczy, judge, founder of the Anti-Semitic Party of Hungary, advocated the establishment of a Jewish State in Palestine and the deportation of all Hungarian Jews thither since, 'in modern times, the mass execution of Jews can no longer be carried out.' Insisting the accusation was a falsehood, Prime Minister Kálmán Tisza appealed for peace; the exiled Lajos Kossuth said a charge of ritual killing was a dishonour to the country and not worthy of modern civilization.

At the trial one year later, it was pointed out that Solymosi had died by drowning. Her neck hadn't been cut; no bloodstained knife or piece of her clothing had been found in the synagogue. Although the accused were acquitted, they were insulted and threatened by spectators, as were witnesses and lawyers for the defence. Pogroms broke out; a state of emergency was declared.

Eszter Solymosi remains a symbol for Hungarian anti-Semites and neo-Nazis. In 2003, the Hungarian Justice and Life Party (MIÉP) led by István Csurka[103] placed a wreath on Solymosi's grave in Tiszaeszlár. The ritual is continued each year by demonstrators carrying Árpád-stripe flags[104] and protesting against Jewish cruelty, inhumanity and 'difference.'

---

103 Csurka was a Member of Parliament from 1990 to 1994 and from 1998 to 2002. In the fall of 2011, he was named intendant of Budapest's New Theatre, and he promised to do away with 'oppressive' liberal productions.
104 Flags with four red and four white stripes originated during the Árpád Dynasty. The Hungarian Nazi Party – the Arrow Cross – used the striped flag with an arrow and cross symbol in the middle.

Those Absent

That the accusation of ritual murder was unfounded bothers no one.

***

Gizi didn't telephone that week. When she returned on Friday evening, she had disappointing news. 'The librarian changed her mind. She doesn't want to meet you or talk about that story. Her mother won't talk to you either. She claims the experience was too traumatic.'

I told her I wasn't surprised.

'But are you certain the story isn't true?' Gizi asked.

'That she had to give her blood to each newborn baby? Of course, I'm certain.'

Gizi looked confused, even embarrassed. 'But tell me, why do Jews need Christian blood?'

PART FIVE : THE JEWS

XXXVIII

Amongst the poor of the city, are many Jews...In the area around the Keleti train station...we found many families who, other than the clothes they wore, possessed neither towel nor shirt, nor bed sheet. In several families, all members wear the same pair of shoes. Around thirty-five per cent of the children were ill...in the home of a Jewish peddler the rats had eaten the left arm of a baby during the night. In many apartments, there is no electricity and no money for petrol or candles, so the inhabitants must spend the long winter nights in darkness. In one room of an apartment, the father of six children with tuberculosis lay unconscious from a self-induced overdose of morphine after having buried his last child...The greatest number amongst the needy and suffering is overwhelmingly high amongst Jewish children.
Report from the Children's Protection League, 1921[105]

*I*n August 1919, the National Army, under Vice Admiral Miklós Horthy, swept through the country in a wave of violence known as the White Terror. Seventy thousand socialists, intellectuals, workers and peasants suspected of communist sympathies were tortured and imprisoned. Of the 5,000 who were subsequently executed, more than 3,000 were Jewish. Weren't Jews responsible for the war, for the defeat and collapse of the Habsburg Alliance? Hadn't Jewish factories delivered war material of inferior quality? Hadn't Jewish communists lynched innocent Hungarians?

Anti-Semitic newspapers, many issued by the Catholic Church, claimed Jews sought world domination, and a false document, purportedly written by a member of Kún's regime, was published in *Studies of the Companions of Jesus:*

People of Israel, with the help of our allies we have brought

---
105 *Ungarish-Judisches Elend*, Kinderschutzverein, AIU Archives.

> *revolution. We will no longer consider ourselves Hungarian Jews... Do everything in your power to put all available means in the hands of your co-religionists. Do not magyarise your names. Woe to anyone who allows himself to be baptised. Jehovah is with us. Our thousand-year exile is at an end. Our new country will be in the lands between the Tisza and the Danube.*

How easy to forget that Jews had paid for arms during the war, had been overrepresented in the military and honoured with medals of distinction. An impressive number of field doctors had been Jewish; the Jewish hospital, funded by Jewish charity, was still giving ninety percent of its consultations to non-Jews. Anti-Bolshevik committees had been funded and manned by Jewish citizens; Jewish soldiers and officers had served in units disarming Red Army contingents; Jews had been massacred as monarchists and capitalists during Kún's regime.

In Budapest, Jews were rounded up in the streets, on trains, in homes, and even those who 'looked' Jewish were beaten. Eight hundred disappeared without trace, and the prisons were filled with those doomed to die of starvation. Few cared. Jews were finally getting what they deserved.

On October 15, 1920, the National Assembly voted in favour of the numerus clausus: Jews were now a separate nationality, and their admittance to institutions of higher learning was restricted.[106] The Catholic bishop, Ottokár Prohászka, was triumphant:

> *Jewish tenacity and intelligence has pushed younger generations of Hungarians into the background... What is called anti-Semitism is only our determination not to let the Jews take a superior position to us. It is better that Hungary perishes, than become prosperous through Jews.*

Political prisoners were amnestied, but Jews remained in

---
[106] Under international pressure, the *numerus clausus* was modified in 1928.

prison. Pressure groups forced merchants to give their stores to Christians; Jewish judges and magistrates were removed from their posts; Jewish innkeepers saw their licences revoked; war widows and invalids were expelled from town markets; the telephone exchange refused to connect calls made by Jews; and Jews were evicted from polling booths.

One hundred thousand left the country, shifting business and culture to Vienna. This, finally, caused some concern: Western loans were needed for industrial development and markets had to be found. How could this be accomplished without Jewish help?

In March 1938, the First Jewish Law limited the number of Jews in the press, theatre, film and commerce. When Hungarian artists and writers protested, the Church chastised the Jews for not mending their ways.

Three years later, the Second Jewish Law prohibited intermarriage and gave Judaism a racial definition. Newly converted Christians were again Jews. Finally, the Church protested. This additional measure decreased the fold, thereby reducing monetary support.

***

'The church was so powerful,' said Panni, the Tiszafüred librarian. 'Every family had to give a part of everything we produced to the priest. If you had ten kilos of wheat, you gave him one. You killed a pig, you gave the priest some meat, and he always showed up at exactly the right moment. The priest had fields given to him as an honorarium, and all the villagers had to work in them a few days of every week, to clean and repair the church. No one minded. That's what was done, and we never asked questions. The priest was number one man because he was the most educated in the village. He read letters, filled out forms, organised everything, came into everyone's house, ate meals with us all. He was always there.

'Once, when I was a little girl, it rained for such a long time that it was impossible to leave the house. Because of all the mud, my mother couldn't send us to church. A few days later, she received word that she had to pay a fine, or go sit on a bench in the town hall for four days as a penalty – all because we'd missed church on that one Sunday! It was so unfair. She dressed us up warmly, my sister, me, my brother, herself, cut up some bread, made sandwiches, put them in a bag, and we went to the town hall. When we got there, she said, "I'm too poor to pay a fine, and I can't sit here for four days because I have much work to do, and three young children to care for. But the four of us will sit for one day." So we sat there the entire day. They didn't know what to do with us. After that, they let us go home.'

PART FIVE : THE JEWS

XXXIX

Night. A tavern in Wedding
In bow tie and jacket
Four thin silhouettes
Sit on the oaken benches
'Comrades' – Harold is speaking
'Man is always good.
He has shed
And he will shed blood.
What is left is – drinking.
Softly be it said,
Man begins his stinking
Even before he's dead.'

Moyshe Kulbak[107]

Out at the baths, steam rose from reedy ditches, blanketed the row of derelict private huts where high-ranking communist officials had lazed away concupiscent afternoons with lush ladies. I sat with Dénes, the bow-legged 'Englishman', at a wobbling Formica table in the communist-style restaurant where lacquered walls sweated and the aroma of hot bean soup hung heavy on the soggy air.

'You were living in the village in the 1940s,' I said.

'Of course I was. I was born there in 1936.'

'Then you must have known the Jews.'

He was silent for a long minute. Beneath a wispy white fringe, his smeary eyeglasses were as crooked as usual, but he didn't look uncomfortable. Perhaps fifty years spent in England had given him distance from the more infamous incidents in contemporary Hungarian history. 'What is it you want to know?'

---

107 Moyshe Kulbak, 1896-1937, poet, novelist and dramatist, born in Russia (now Lithuania), murdered in Stalin's purge of Yiddish writers.

Those Absent

'What you remember.'

'What I remember is that our local Jews were like those in most villages. They were kocsma owners and shopkeepers, not farmers or peasants. They were good business people, and they educated their children. That made people jealous. I went to school with a Jewish girl, Judit Deutsch. We were in the same class. Her family lived a few houses away from that new superette on the main road. They were grocers, and their shop was in the front room. That was typical, back then. One tiny little shop, very simple, but people were still jealous.'

Jewish kocsma[108]

'And then?'

'Okay, did I see Hitler? Of course, I did. When he came to Hungary, all the school kids were taken to Szolnok to see him. They lined us up along the train tracks and told us to wait. So that's what we did, standing for hours, watching trains go by. Finally, one came through and we were told Hitler was on it, and we all had to wave. We couldn't see him. We didn't know if he was really there, but we did what we were told. We waved to show our respect, our loyalty. That's what was expected of us.'

'Judit, too?'

'Who knows? I suppose it's possible. What I remember is

---

108   Photo courtesy of the Museum of Hungarian Speaking Jewry, Safed, Israel.

when Judit and everyone in her family had to wear the yellow star, no one in the village protested, no one at all. We were part of the machine. It's always the same: most people are followers, the others are leaders. The leaders call all the shots. There was no court back then, there was no law. Just leaders calling the shots.

'In 1944, the Deutsch family was ordered out of their house, and with the other Jews, they were marched away to the ghetto in Tiszafüred. As soon as they were gone, the villagers broke into Jewish houses and began plundering. I was young, eight years old, but I was there in the Deutsch house, and I saw everything. They had big glass-fronted cupboards filled with books, and people smashed the cupboards and ripped up the books. They tore the whole place apart, and they were laughing the whole time. They were like crazy, wild people. Okay, maybe not everyone in the village was the same. There's a story about people hidden under a haystack, but who knows if it's true? No one talked about ghettos or death camps. Everyone in the Deutsch family died in Auschwitz, and their house was given away.'

'Every time I ask about village Jews, people deny there were any.'

'There's still a lot of jealousy in a village, even now. Don't forget that.' His gaze was as steady as his voice. A warning? 'Believe me, it's still dangerous for Jews in this country. People don't kill them now because they'll be punished, but the hatred is here.'

Those Absent

XL

And he opened his large, square mouth
And blew on my glow
And put me out.

Malka Heifetz Tussman[109]

*T*hanks to Ágnes, my photographic exhibition of the vanished Jewish villages would open in the Kiss Pál Museum of Tiszafüred before travelling on to Eger and Budapest. It would include a section on the Hungarian Holocaust, and Ágnes took me to meet her uncle Sándor.

He, a psychiatrist, lived in Miskolc, in a building of friable grey cement just past shabby discount emporia offering cell phones, televisions and sex aids. To reach the dangerously rusted exterior stairway leading to his apartment, we passed through a courtyard of overflowing bins. But dilapidation ended there.

Fine-boned, elegant, Sándor ushered us through a dark vestibule and into in an airy room, with soaring ceilings and tall windows. Covering every wall were paintings, sketches and etchings. Most startling was the honey-coloured furniture with its exquisite marquetry.

'After the Holocaust, I had nothing – no family, no house, not a stick of furniture. My wife was another camp survivor who had lost all. We had little money, but we had to make a home, and new furniture was expensive to buy. All we could afford was second-hand, so we acquired these pieces. No one wanted them, and they were cheap.'

'Where did they come from? Were they pillaged from a manor?'

'Probably.'

---

109   Malka Heifetz Tussman, 1893-1987, Ukraine, Yiddish teacher, poet.

In the adjoining room were more pieces, equally magnificent. Above them were framed photographs: moustachioed men, half-smiling women. All wore the more elaborate fashions of a vanished era. 'My relatives and my wife's relatives. They all died in Auschwitz.'

Sándor pulled out a wooden box. Still more photos: a smiling woman in a rowboat on the Tisza River, babies in woolly clothing, a laughing couple with three children, people sitting under a leafy oak, waiting out the summer heat.

'Auschwitz?'

'Auschwitz.'

Here was a house with whitewashed walls: 'Our family home in the village of Tiszaroff. You see? Jews lived like the other villagers. Peasants had fruit trees? So did we. We grew vegetables. We kept a pig like our Christian neighbours.'

'A Jewish family with a pig?'

Sándor laughed. 'We were integrated. If we went to the synagogue, it was only for the high holidays. Everyone was friendly with everyone else. We were all part of the same society. Sure, Zionist groups all over Hungary were encouraging Jews to get out of the country and head for Eretz Israel, but they didn't have much success. Why go to Israel? We were loyal Hungarian citizens. Nothing would happen to us.'

More photos: weddings, portraits, school classes, merchants

Those Absent

in front of their shops, people seated in parks surrounded by shrubs and flowers, a couple with bicycles, babies in prams.

'Here are my parents with my sister. This woman was my cousin, a teacher. She died in Auschwitz. My uncle was a doctor on the front during the First World War, but he perished in a forced labour battalion on the Russian front in 1942.' Along with thousands of Jews who, forced to go naked in winter, were starved, beaten and sent over minefields.

In one photo, a soft-faced, smiling woman wore a dark dress.

'What about her?'

'Auschwitz.'

Another box, more photos, always the same answer. Yet I kept on asking, for I was hoping for an exception: the person with a future.

***

*T*iszaroff, set in reed and marsh, is a crossing point on the Tisza River. A flat wooden raft carries the few car and foot passengers to the far bank where a rutted lane leads on to more exuberant swampland and drowsier villages.

'Do you know where the synagogue used to be?' I asked in the village kocsma, in the grocery, the restaurant, and in a workshop. No one seemed to have heard of such a thing.

PART FIVE : THE JEWS

I walked along unpaved roads, passed well-kept houses with roofs of beautifully patterned thatch, stopped at a wooden bench. Here, three ancient folk perched, propped upright by their canes.

'There was once a synagogue here in Tiszaroff,' I said.

They nodded in perfect unison. 'Next street, turn right.'

'Across from the new kocsma.'

'It's an empty field. Nothing left.'

'Nice people, the Jews.'

'Nice people.'

'They had a good life in this village. No problem. No problem at all.'

'We never heard anything bad about Jews. Never.'

'Nothing bad. Never. Nice people.'

'Very nice people.'

How time tidies up memory and rearranges history.

I went to the field. They hadn't exaggerated, for there was no sign of the synagogue. In the distance, a sagging barn and crumpled house, both smothered by creepers.

Near the street named after György Dózsa, leader of the failed fifteenth-century Peasant Revolt, I found the eighteenth-century manor house. In its park, were three two-hundred-year-old oaks, the sole survivors of modern renovation. The edifice, completely modified, has become a luxury hotel.

Those Absent

XLI

The provincial ghettos have the character of sanatoriums. At last, the Jews have taken up an open-air life and exchanged their former mode of living for a healthy one.

Adolph Eichmann, 1944

Travelling through Hungary, I searched for improvised ghettoes – those temporary prisons in fields, factories, barracks and community buildings where Jews were interned before their transfer to work or death camps. Outside Tiszafüred, at the no-longer Jewish-owned brick factory, no plaque shows that, in 1944, this was an over-crowded holding place, lacking in clean water but furnished with open-air latrines meant to humiliate and dehumanise. Here, midwives subjected women to humiliating body searches for jewellery; police and civilian personnel used torture to obtain information about hidden valuables. There were deaths, many suicides.

On June 8, the Jews were marched along the river from the ghetto to the Tiszafüred train station. Packed, eighty-to-one-hundred, in freight compartments only large enough for forty-five, they were sent to Auschwitz. Before their departure, Dr Pál Polgary, the district's chief administrator, made a speech: 'When you return,' he said, 'it will be as fertiliser.'

In Jászberény, the ghetto has become a pleasant garden near the public library; in Mezőcsát, it is an empty field near the ruined synagogue in the town centre. The Gyöngyös ghetto is now a supermarket parking lot; in Szolnok, the sugar factory, once a ghetto, still functions behind high grey walls. In other towns – Kisújszállás, Törökszentmiklós – former ghettoes are calm residential streets; in Füzesabony, the field is part of a new housing estate; elsewhere ghettos have been turned into junkyards, copses and car repair workshops. Nowhere, do memorial stones or plaques designate these as hellholes, the anterooms of death.

I searched for synagogues. In Abony, it was a windowless ruin in a field of rubble and used, in post-war years, for something else – an office? A factory? A skinhead observed my exploration, then followed as, leery, I returned to the train station. An older woman refused to answer when, in Püspokladány, I asked where the synagogue had been. Pinched face irate, she scuttled down the street. Inhabitants of this town eagerly persecuted local Jews, denouncing with fervour those refusing the yellow star.

There was still one Jew living in Hadjúdorog, but on the day I passed, he was absent. In one local synagogue, now an overstuffed furniture emporium, I made my way between bedsteads and mattresses, admiring painted birds, flowers, vines and grapes on the high ceiling. The shop's owner followed on my heels, resentful and suspicious. Was she worried I would claim her wood-look tables and wardrobes as war compensation?

I returned to Kunhegyes, to the derelict synagogue I had seen when first arriving in the country. It was gone. No trace of the beam-propped wall, unhinged doors or wooden seats. A woman in a housecoat watched from an apartment block across a shaggy, junk-strewn field.

'The synagogue? It was destroyed recently,' she called out. Slapping her bedroom-slippered way over rubble, she approached. 'People claimed it was unsafe. Once Jews lived in houses all around here, but they were taken to the ghetto in the Gypsy quarter, then sent to the camps. I was only little, but I remember. Most were shopkeepers, but there were four doctors and a lawyer. A few came back after the war, but they didn't want to stay.'

Those Absent

In Egyek, a history teacher met me in the school courtyard. 'Here's where the synagogue was, right here.' Marching furiously along vanished walls, he marked out a rectangle on the tarmac. 'They tore it down, then covered everything over so there was no trace left.'

'Why?'

'So no one would remember what they'd done.'

PART FIVE : THE JEWS

XLII

Shall I never see you, my dear home, again?
And how many rise through the chimney in flame?
Greetings to you, loved ones, in your place unknown
Sometimes think of me, for I must be gone.

Unknown Author, Auschwitz

*I*mpossible to miss the changes to the Karcag synagogue. When I'd first seen it, the building, with boarded-up windows and crumbled façade, had appeared to be abandoned. Now, the yellow stucco was new, and windows were of stained glass. It was a handsome building, but the main gate was always locked tight whenever I passed.

Given permission to live in this city in 1852, Jews arrived from the surrounding villages. By the 1940s, many businesses around the leafy main square were Jewish owned, as were the granaries poking their noses up on the near horizon. Of 778 Jews who lived here, 461 died in work or concentration camps. Was there still an active Jewish community today?

Feig (a Jewish name) the clockmaker lived on a back street in Karcag, in a house surrounded by discarded furniture, planks, metal, and scraps of uncertain provenance or use – an inauspicious setting. In my arms was a cumbersome wood case wall clock in need of repair, and I rang the bell at the gate. Feig came outside, stared at me.

'You're Jewish,' he said.

'How do you know?'

'I know.' Then, throwing open his gate, he clinched both me and the sharp-edged clock in a painful and over-enthusiastic bear hug.

Inside the house, he shoved me into an armchair, fetched

Those Absent

cups, plates, and cutlery. He had finished baking, and we would feast on cookies and cakes. Jumpy, excitable, incapable of remaining still, Feig pranced from one room corner to the other, fiddled with picture frames, tools and knickknacks, fired unrelated questions and never listened to answers.

'I had no idea there were Jews still living in Karcag,' I said.

'Who told you there were no Jews here? Whoever it is, is wrong. There are one or two Jewish-owned businesses along the main street; there are Jewish doctors. Sure, it's different. Before the war, we lived in the houses around the synagogue, and the empty field beside it was a home for the Jewish elderly. After the Holocaust, survivors came here from the surrounding villages. The ones who didn't were sorry. In the 1950s, Jews were beaten, robbed and tortured in small towns. No Jew would live out in those places anymore.' He smirked. 'Aside from you. You must be crazy living in a small village.'

'And the synagogue still functions?'

'Only on the High Holidays. A rabbi comes from Budapest, and a few men arrive from Debrecen to make up a *minyan*.[110] Come back on Rosh Hashanah. I'll meet you in front of the synagogue, introduce you to people.' He laughed, a nervous sound. 'Me, I don't go inside. I don't believe in anything much. I was a communist; my wife isn't Jewish. Many Jews are like me today. My father was religious, and my grandfather, my great-grandfather, my great-great-grandfather. They were all clockmakers, generation after generation of clockmakers.' He paused. 'Not my daughters. They're modern. They go to university in Budapest.'

***

---

[110] A quorum of ten men (or women, in more modern synagogues) required for certain religious obligations.

PART FIVE : THE JEWS

*F*eig kept his promise. He waited for me on the synagogue steps, jittery, shifting from foot to foot. Before scooting down the road, he handed me over to Sára, a woman in her eighties, and her daughter Ági, a teacher of English and Russian.

Inside the synagogue were the original benches. The bimah, the raised reading platform, stood in the middle; women sat on the left, men on the right; and at the front, a few men *davened*.[111] But, despite such concessions to tradition, this seemed to be a social occasion, and most circulated, exchanging news.

I opened the scarred wooden desk in front of my bench, found shredded prayer books and destroyed Torah commentaries. On the inside of the desk's lid were the pencilled-in names of those who had passed through town in more peaceful times: Sándor Klein, 1927; István Silverman, 1924; József Grunbaum, 1934. I opened other lids: more trashed books, more names. Overtaken by the Holocaust, how many of those men had survived?

***

*Á*gi and Sára lived near the synagogue, in a house surrounded by a high garden wall. 'I was born sixteen kilometres away, in Kisujszállás,' said Sára. 'There were many Jewish families in the town, and there was no difference between Jews and Christians. All the young people would meet in a big courtyard and we'd talk, sing. We went to the same school; we lived in the same sort of houses. No one had running water at home, but that was normal back then. We had vegetable gardens and fruit trees, and we produced what we needed.

'I was a beautiful girl, and my parents expected me to marry a doctor, someone important, but I attracted the attention of an older boy. From the moment he saw me in that courtyard, he

---
111   *Daven:* to pray, in Yiddish.

Those Absent

dreamt of going out with me. Of course, my parents wouldn't allow that: he was too old, he wasn't a doctor, and his father was only a coal and wood merchant. To make sure we couldn't meet, my parents sent me to relatives in Mesőkövesd to learn to sew. Mesőkövesd isn't far, but back then rail journeys took a long time, so it seemed a great distance away.

'After March 1944, we were ordered to wear the yellow star. Then in April, early one morning, we were rounded up, old people, sick people, everyone, and we were brought to the cemetery. They took away our money and jewellery, then force-marched us to the Szolnok ghetto in the sugar factory. We were treated very badly by the Hungarian police.

'My brother and I were sent to a work camp in Austria. Our parents, all the other family members, went to Auschwitz. We would have been transported to a death camp, too, but the war ended. Still, it was too late for my brother. He was ill, and he died a month later.

'After the war, there were lists with the names of survivors. That young man who had wanted to marry me years before, the coal merchant's son, had also survived. After he saw my name, he wrote to me at the refugee camp and proposed: "I want one word: yes or no." We would never meet our in-laws because our parents were dead, his brother had died on the Russian front, but we were alive and we had to start again.'

To recreate families, survivors sought spouses to replace those murdered. The most unlikely married, old with young, people obviously mismatched. Brides made wedding dresses out of whatever they could find, passed them on to the next bride after the ceremony. But there were others, broken people, those who found no reason to continue.

'Jews didn't want to go back to the small villages where we

would be isolated. We came to towns like Karcag or Debrecen. Many wanted to go to Israel. My husband applied to emigrate, but the application was refused – the communists had all the power, and no one knew why some people could go, and others couldn't. Because we'd tried to leave, we were accused of being Zionists and were punished. A group of soldiers occupied this house. My husband and I, our two children, all of us had to live in this one small room for years.'

For others, it was worse. Jewish industrialists, bankers and directors, accused of being bourgeois exploiters, were deported to internment camps for 're-education'.

Those Absent

XLIII

As long as men lived in the wilderness, the excitement and glamour of the hunt had meaning in the context of survival, in promoting aggression against prey and predators. But agriculture and the domestication of animals gradually reduced hunting from a truly important activity, a vital part of the world's work, to a sport for people with time on their hands...men deprived of hunting as a major source of prestige, deprived of wild species as a major focus of aggression, began playing the most dangerous game of all. Men began to go after other men, as if their peers were the only creatures clever enough to make hunting really interesting. So war, the cruellest and most elaborate and most human form of hunting, became one of the most appealing ways of expressing aggression.

John E. Pfeiffer[112]

One morning, as Gizi and I chatted in her yard, a scrawny man appeared at the gate. Pointing to me, he held out an envelope. 'A letter from my uncle. He heard you were asking about Jews.'

The uncle wrote that he was born in Tiszaörs in 1933, and that his parents had been friends with a man named Lebovits from nearby Poroszló:

> He was an honest watchmaker who mended clocks, any gadget, any household item. He was clever with his hands – certainly my mother thought so, and her opinion could be trusted. Lebovits and his young wife (perhaps she had been his mistress) often came to visit my parents.
> One day, in October 1944, Lebovits and the woman showed up with a girl of around eleven, pretty, with long hair, beautiful eyes and a nice voice, but shy. We all sat in the family room, had lunch. Then they spent the next few days with us. My parents warned me not to tell anyone – not even

---
112 *The Emergence of Man.* John E. Pfeiffer, 1914-1999, American writer.

school friends – that they were there, because they were Jews and were hiding.

I remember hearing the Germans blow up the airport runway in Kunmadaras – the ground shook in Tiszaörs, fifteen kilometres away. I also heard the guns when the Third Ukrainian Front arrived. Right after that, Lebovits, the woman and the girl left our house.

The man stayed by the gate, uncomfortable, edgy. 'What happened to the Lebovits family?' I asked.

'My uncle can tell you. He'll be here in three weeks.' Turning, he sidled off.

Gizi sniffed. 'I went to school with that man. He was always a loser, and now he's just another village alcoholic.'

***

On October 15, 1944, as Soviet and Romanian armies advanced over the Great Plain, Regent Horthy announced Hungary's withdrawal from the war. Immediately following this announcement, an SS commando unit kidnapped his son and Horthy resigned. He was replaced, six hours later, by Arrow Cross[113] leader Ferenc Szalási.

This was the Hungarian Fascists' one heady moment of power. Revoking Horthy's armistice, troops were ordered to continue fighting. In a senseless frenzy of violence, barns with farm animals were burnt, women and girls raped, houses pillaged and destroyed. The corpses of soldiers, civilians and horses sprawled in the thick mud, or were crushed under felled telegraph poles and house walls. Retreating soldiers loaded booty – dishes, pots, pans, tables, pictures, clocks – onto carts, carried it away, then abandoned all along the roads.

Why had Lebovits, the woman and the young girl, appeared

---
113   The Arrow Cross, an ancient symbol of the Magyar tribes, signifies the racial purity of true Hungarians.

Those Absent

in Tiszaörs at this moment? How had they avoided the ghetto and deportation? Had they been hidden until new denunciations necessitated flight?[114] Could they have been the village Jews who hid under a haystack? Perhaps, having heard Horthy's proclamation of peace, they thought persecution was over. Did they join the thousands of refugees walking west? Jews found in those endless columns were arrested for Von Ribbentrop, offended that so many had survived, shipped another forty thousand to the death camps.

Weeks passed, but the uncle never appeared. Ági and I sent him a letter, and he wrote back: he had been feeling poorly and hadn't been able to travel. Ági and Ágnes obtained a list of Poroszló's earlier Jewish residents, but found no repairer of watches, and no one named Lebovits. Again, we wrote to the uncle; again, he answered. His health hadn't improved. He would contact us when he felt better. There was no further word from him.

***

*H*itler had assured German-Hungarians that as *Volksdeutsch*, ethnic Germans, they would be lords of the Reich's Eastern Colony. Convinced of superior racial heritage, some changed their names back to the original German, took up high positions in government[115] or volunteered in the SS units.[116] Another 50,000 were forcibly recruited into the SS.

Although only one third of ethnic Germans had overtly demonstrated loyalty to Hitler's Germany, at the end of 1944,

---
114 Holocaust scholar Tomasz Frydel discovered that some Polish peasants killed Jews they had been hiding after other Jews, caught by the Germans, informed on their rescuers.
115 From 1932-1936, the Prime Minister of Fascist Hungary, Gyula Gömbös, was an assimilated Swabian.
116 Others were conscripted until almost one-quarter of Hungarian Germans were fighting in SS units.

an anti-Swabian campaign began. In former Austro-Hungarian lands (Hungary, parts of Czechoslovakia, Romania, Yugoslavia and Ruthenia), 170,000 'traitors' were expelled in a wave of ethnic cleansing dubbed the 'exchange of populations'. They left in horse-drawn wagons or on foot, carried what was essential, buried the rest for the day when they could return.[117] The few who remained were forced to give their homes, possessions and fields to incoming ethnic Hungarians who, expelled from surrounding countries, had also lost all.

A more terrible fate was reserved for 600,000 Swabians, Hungarians with German-sounding names, military personnel, farmers, field workers, Jewish survivors of the labour battalions, and passers-by who were in the wrong place at the wrong time. Told by the Soviets they were needed for clean-up work, they were marched to waiting trains and transported to the gulag, where torture, rape, illness and starvation were part of everyday life. Two hundred thousand died before repatriation began in 1947. Treated as war criminals, their experience was not to be discussed during the communist regime. They received no compensation, no sickness benefits.[118] Only in the 1990s, were monuments erected.

***

*P*erhaps the painting Misi sold to Udo had been a hidden Swabian treasure. Or was it pillaged from a Jewish house, a manor, or a comfortable middle-class dwelling? Forgotten, left to decay in some damp attic, mouldy cellar or clammy barn, it was little more than a memory. Misi was decidedly shifty when I asked about its provenance.

'I'm not allowed to tell you. Sure, there's not much left, but

---
117 It has been estimated that some 11,000 people perished along the roads.
118 Hungarian Central Statistical Office, cited by Ágnes Huszár Várdy *in Forgotten Victims of World War Two: Hungarian Women in Forced Labour Camps.*

it's probably valuable. Go get an expertise in a museum or someplace like that.'

The gold frame was rotted, but there was enough flaking paint on the canvas to show it had been an exquisite, romantic landscape, perhaps eighteenth century. On the left were sumptuous trees, a clear river, soft hills and a radiant sky: on the right, tatters of disintegrated rag.

PART FIVE : THE JEWS

XLIV

He who keeps quiet is half a fool; he who talks is a complete fool.

Yiddish proverb

Outside, heavy snow fell, cutting off back streets, but in kocsmas, the atmosphere was amiable; did harsh weather pull people together? Perhaps, with most foreigners gone, this was again a Hungarian village. When the temperature sank to minus twenty Celsius, the water taps froze. Sándor, the veterinarian, made his rounds on foot, for there was no other way of tending to ailing cows, pigs or sheep in backyard barns. Those with no indoor plumbing carried metal cans to the communal pump on the main road. I joined them, for my outside tap was also frozen. No one grumbled; smiles were complicit, particularly from those who ignored me in easier times.

Heinz and Odette were amongst the few Germans who remained over the winter. On warmer days, Odette and I cycled over the plain, but bad weather forced us to walk. She, a simple, good-natured widow, had abandoned Germany fifteen years before. 'What's there for me?' Her one son, having received his heritage, had nothing to do with her, and after years in Hungary, she had little in common with her friends. For her, this was home, although she had never wanted to integrate into local life, and she knew no Hungarian other than the word for bread. '*Kenyér, kenyér,*' she'd shout at the local shop. And when a thick loaf was passed over the counter, she was proud of her linguistic talent.

My questions about the past confused her. 'Why do you want to know all that?'

'Because it's interesting.'

Those Absent

'Not for the rest of us, it isn't.'

I often returned home with her, accepted the hot drinks, homemade schnapps and soups prepared by her partner, Heinz. He, overweight, stiffened by arthritis and unable to walk any distance, was grateful for company. Passionate about history, he knew much, but all his information was off-key and distorted. He had been in the Hitler Youth Movement and was still proud of the association. Certainly, he regretted Germany's defeat and, pulling out his photo album, he showed me photos from the 1950s when, tall, limber, blond and blue-eyed, he'd proudly worn the high boots of the SS: he was letting me know how things stood. Like former SS officers I had encountered years before, he felt the need to confess to a Jew that there had been excesses committed in 'the enthusiasm of youth.'

One evening, he invited me for dinner with a few older Germans, also permanent residents. It was glacially cold outside, and if the thick stew was too salty, the wine terribly sweet ('cheap but good quality,' he insisted), the room, warmed by a wood-burning stove, was cosy. And soon, all were trudging down the worn conversational path so loved by expatriates.

'The Hungarians, they speak like machine gun fire. You can't understand a word they say.'

'Useless to learn the language. If you're a child, it's okay. You can practice it every day in school. When you're an adult, it's different.'

'What's the point? People don't want to understand when you make an effort.'

'All Hungarians want is to have a German or Austrian to hang on to, give them work, food, money, clothes.'

'You can't say that,' tempered Josef, a car dealer from the Rhineland. 'People have a different history here. When I first arrived back in '92, I was looking for a house to buy, and a farmer outside Tiszafüred who spoke some German offered to help me. I started going to his house to see him and – I remember this clearly – I saw someone who worked for him, an elderly man. He lived at the end of the house, in one tiny space, no more than a small closet. He had nothing, no possessions. He received a little pocket money once a year, but no salary, no pension. He wasn't allowed to eat with the family because they considered him too low for that. They threw him food, as if he were an animal. Basically, he was still a serf, and he belonged to his employer. Communism had come and gone, but people like that still existed. People who had been passed by.'

There was an uncomfortable silence. The story had been too great a departure from the usual.

'It's the fault of the Austrians,' said Lorenz, finally. 'When you see the overly generous tips they leave in restaurants, you know they're ruining everything. The Austrians always ruin things, no matter where they are.'

Heinz grunted. 'The worst are the English. In Germany, after the war, everything was forbidden. If we went out into the street, the English chased us back into our houses. "Get back inside!" they'd scream. "Get back!" They thought they could do whatever they wanted. They rationed everything: one loaf of bread for a family of three, although there was nothing else to eat. The English hated us then, and they hate us now.'

'You can't say that about all of them,' Annie tempered. 'You're talking about exceptions.'

'I'm talking about most of them. Most hated us. They preached hate. In March, the Americans were there. Then, in May, the English came.'

'They hated us because of Hitler,' said Josef.

Those Absent

'*Ja, ja, ja,* Hitler,' Heinz said, annoyed. 'But they were all the same, all the leaders. Churchill was as bad as Hitler.'

'That's true,' said Lorenz.

'All as bad, Franco, Mussolini, Churchill, Stalin, Eisenhower. All the same.'

'Did Churchill also build extermination factories?' I asked.

'What about the Allied POW camps!' Heinz shouted. 'German soldiers were tortured and shot in those places. They were starved, used as slave labour. Why? For revenge, also because the Allies could get away with it. Everyone knew what was going on, but who cared?'

Annie turned to me. 'We were terrified of the Allies. Before they arrived in our village, we were told the devil was coming. We hid in the forest for days, that's how frightened we were.'

'Then the Canadians came with their low-flying planes and mowed down German farmers who were working in the fields,' Heinz railed. "Or they marched through town and shouted to people, "What sort of job do you have?" Then they'd shoot them. A whole family was burnt to death in a house in our town, a Russian family. They were there temporarily, and the Canadians in their planes killed them. The house was burning, and one was calling out, "Help, help!" But they weren't allowed to come out.' He glowed triumphantly.

'I remember a pilot who ejected from his plane near our town,' said Annie. 'An American. His parachute got caught in a tree, and he couldn't get loose. He called for help: "Help me, help me!" We all came running. We were children, but we saw the men kill him, right then, right in front of our eyes. Then they cut the straps holding him up in the tree, and everyone grabbed his parachute. We wanted the fabric because we could make clothes out of it. We needed it, you see.' She was apologetic. 'It was good fabric, white silk. But it was macabre all the same. Horrible.'

'The English!' Heinz was not to be diverted. 'Hypocrites, all of them. When Jews tried to go to England, they weren't wanted. The English didn't let them go to Palestine either, so they were sent to America, then Canada, South America, but no one wanted them anywhere. And when they took them out of the concentration camps, no one wanted them then either. Everyone blames us, the Germans. That's easy. But the French hated Jews too. And in Finland, they said there were no Jews, but they were lying. There were Jews in the Finnish army, and Jewish officers.' His fist pounded the table. 'Our German soldiers, our boys, had to greet Jewish officers. Salute to them.'[119]

Everyone looked uncomfortable.

'But most Germans hated Jews,' said Josef quietly. 'A woman who lived near us – she wasn't Jewish, but her husband and children were – and they were all killed. Why were Jews hated all over the world? Because everyone was jealous of them, that's why.'

'From the time we were little children, we always heard the same thing about the Jews,' said Annie. 'That they were evil. We didn't know any better.'

'When a Jew had a shop, he did anything to make money. Anything,' said Heinz. 'Jews, they aren't just a religion. And they aren't just a people either.'

'Which makes us what, exactly?' I asked.

Heinz grunted, heaved his huge body from the chair and went to make coffee.

***

---

[119] Several hundred Jewish soldiers in the Finnish army fought on the German side against the Russians.

Those Absent

*S*nowflakes, captured by street lamps, were transformed into sequins. There was no one around so late at night, no cars on the slippery main road. I arrived at the Deutsch house, stopped, peered at it in the dark. Waited. For what? What information did I hope to glean from a silent building? Its shutters were pulled down tight, and the high surrounding fence told no tales. It belonged to other people. Perhaps they had never heard of the Jewish grocer, his wife, and his children.

Out in the dark, the night dogs roamed, big woolly shapes. I called to them, those fearful creatures, despised strays. Never barking, they stared at me, then slunk soundlessly into the shadows. Vanished.

Coal and wood smoke curled into the air, icebound trees glistened, and the evening was beautiful.

PART FIVE : THE JEWS

XLV

If the ghetto didn't exist, I'd have no shirt and no trousers.
Hungarian Folk Song

*I*n Toronto, I went to the Baycrest Home for the Aged, where the Hungarian Circle met. When I asked about the Old Country, most ignored me. Others were suspicious.

'What do you want to know?' one woman challenged. 'Why ask all these questions?' I was dredging up a past none cared to remember.

'You want to know what life was like for Jews?' asked another. 'There was always anti-Semitism. When I was a little girl, a neighbour, a friend of the family, slapped my mother on the face – this was in 1940, and people could do that kind of thing. After, when we returned from the camp, everyone said that Jews hadn't suffered during the war, that we'd had it easy.'

By her side, a wizened man smiled. 'Every summer, my parents rented a tiny house in a Swabian village. Those Swabians were real anti-Semites, everyone knew that, but Jewish kids flew our kites in a certain field, and the Swabian kids flew their kites in the same field. We all got along. One day, someone came and asked, "How come you Jews are playing together with Swabians? Aren't they anti-Semites?" And we answered: "Not in the summer."'

'Can anyone tell me about the post-war pogroms?'

'Pogroms after the war? I never heard of that,' insisted one man. 'After the war, everything was wonderful. They gave money back to the Jews. The Russian army was protecting us and giving us rights. While the Russians were there, there was no problem with being Jewish, and no one said bad things.'

Those Absent

There was a long silence. These people wished me gone. Feeling guilty, ghoulish and ashamed, I was ready to retreat.

Just then, perhaps exasperated by the assuaging words, a man rose to his feet. 'No one here wants to talk about what happened? If you don't, I will, because I was born in Kunmadaras. I grew up there. It was a normal Hungarian community, and we were typical Jews of that time: my grandfather was religious, but not my father, not me. We were assimilated, we spoke Hungarian, and we lived like other Hungarians.

'I went to school in Kunmadaras, and every afternoon when class let out, the Christian boys would be waiting to beat us up. If we Jewish kids managed to hide, the Catholic boys beat each other up. Sometimes the Protestants and Catholics would beat each other up, but believe me, if there were any Jews around, Catholics and Protestants got together to beat us up. Still, you could say that everyone was friendly with everyone else.

'My grandfather had six sons in the military, and five fought in the First World War. Then, one day, they were all kicked out of the army because people suddenly decided Jews were enemies of the country. I was sent to Auschwitz with forty relatives. Only a few came back, and me, my father, my sister. My sister left to start a new life in Budapest. My father and I stayed in Kunmadaras.

'Then, in April 1946, someone said that Jews had kidnapped a Christian child for Passover and killed it for its blood. A few men bought a pig, put its blood in a dish, covered it with a linen cloth and said it was the child's blood, and that they'd found it in Weinberger's barbershop. Then they went into his shop to murder him. Why? What was the real reason? Because he'd tried to get back his possessions after the war. All this came out afterward, after the police arrested the men responsible for starting the rumour.

'And, while Neulander lay dying on the floor of his haberdashery, the mob carried everything away, but the police made no move to stop them. I remember seeing two terribly injured people, a husband and his wife, the Kleins. They had returned from the death camp six weeks before.

'There was a priest who knew beforehand what was going to happen. He could have influenced people, told them blood libels were something leftover from the Middle Ages. He could have stopped the pogrom before it started, but he didn't.'[120]

***

*I*n March 1945, 650,000 acres belonging to expropriated Swabians, 8,000,000 acres formerly owned by the aristocracy and the church were redistributed among 640,000 smallholders. Once again, the programme of land reform was doomed to failure. Many new farmers had been labourers with no experience in independent work. Poorly equipped – tools had been requisitioned during the war, and fifty-nine percent of the country's workhorses had perished – they were unprepared for the new market controls. Unable to meet government delivery quotas or pay taxes, 400,000 farmers were prosecuted for endangering public supplies.

Faced with economic chaos, the government took advantage of the still-virulent anti-Semitism and denounced Jewish speculators, black market traders and 'capitalist criminals'. Communist anti-Fascist myth forbade any mention of Jewish suffering or of the extermination camps, and the National Peasant Party leader, József Darvas, stated that 'no one may

---

[120] In 1990, László Ötvös, a Protestant minister published his account, *A madrasi antiszemita megmozdulás*. Ötvös claimed the pogrom had been carried out by people from elsewhere, not by the people of Kunmadaras he was so fond of. This version is preferred to the more painful truth.

Those Absent

claim privileges on the basis of suffering,' that 'a certain group should not demand preferential treatment'. Anti-Semitic caricatures, those used by the German Nazi Party, were again disseminated.

Three hundred and seventy-one Jews had lived in Kunmadaras before the war. Of those, 175 had died in deportation. Only 75 chose to return to the town. The synagogue still stood, but historical Jewish life was over. Jewish businesses, the bakery, the kocsma, were still open, and the ironmonger and pharmacist were selling the merchandise of the murdered owners. Neighbours, friends and acquaintances were the same people who had watched and jeered when Jews had been driven off to the ghettoes, who had taken part in the violence and plundering. Objects once belonging to Jewish families – lamps, pictures, clothing, quilts, pots and furniture – were now in neighbouring houses; animals they had owned were nestled in neighbourhood barns.[121] One joke told of a Jew meeting a Christian friend on the street:

> *'How are you?' asked the friend.*
> *'Don't ask,' answered the Jew. 'I just got back from the camp and, apart from the clothes you have on your back, I've got nothing left.'*

Retrieving belongings without police intervention was difficult.[122] Those who willingly returned possessions were resentful: Jews were always better off; they were profiteers and exploiters. Weren't hundreds of thousands of Christian Hungarians still in Allied or Soviet captivity? Yet here were the Jews, reclaiming their property! Hadn't the defeat been their fault? Hadn't most Hungarians suffered during the war?

---
121   Some, when forced to return animals, demanded compensation from the Jewish owner.
122   The restitution of property followed a normal procedure in Budapest, but not in towns and villages.

PART FIVE : THE JEWS

Perhaps the extermination camps and gas chambers were Jewish inventions and, like wealthy Christians, they had spent the war in Budapest, or in some cushy, foreign haven. 'Look at how well Jews are doing now, running the black market, sponging off Hungarians.' If a Jew dared suggest he had suffered more than a Christian, he was beaten or slapped.[123]

'When the Jews came back, they had nothing,' said Eszter Kabai Tóth, a Kunmadaras resident. 'Now they're eating white bread, while I toil the fields with my nose to the ground.'

Illiterate, a victim of poverty and ignorance, Tóth had no concept of the Holocaust. Hadn't the previous administration redistributed Jewish goods? Wasn't local government now in the hands of the National Peasant Party and the Smallholders Party?[124] Didn't that mean power was in the hands of the poor, and that everything belonged to the community? Wasn't that the principle? What she did know, said Tóth, was that two Kunmadaras Jews had given money to a young Christian girl and sent her to Sándor Kohn's tobacco shop to buy cigarettes. Once there, she was forced into the basement where several men tried to kill her and take her blood. Fortunately, she had escaped.

Another town resident, Zsigmund Tóth,[125] member of the Slovakian fascist HLINKA and responsible for several pogroms, said: 'Christian children disappeared when I lived in Slovakia. When that happened, we hung Jews from lampposts. How long

---

123 *Hungary: The Assault on the Historical Memory of the Holocaust.* Randolph L. Braham,
124 The Communist Party was unable to attract many voters in rural areas, for many remembered Béla Kún's hated 1919 Soviet Republic. To gain power, the communists resorted to intrigue. Merging with the National Peasant Party, they destroyed the Smallholder's Party, arrested prominent politicians or forced them to leave the country.
125 No relation to Eszter Kabai Tóth.

Those Absent

will you tolerate them making salami out of your children here?'[126]

A police officer in Karcag also heard that Jews were kidnapping Christian children, killing them, and using their blood for kosher sausage:

> *The rumour was circulating all over this part of the country. In one kocsma, everyone claimed it had happened in the town of Böszörmény. In a kocsma down the road, people claimed it had happened in Fegyvernek, or Csendes. People kept coming to me, repeating the story and thinking they'd rise in my estimation. One market day, a woman told me her seven-year-old daughter had been kidnapped by Jews. I did nothing because I knew it was a rumour. A week later, the daughter reappeared: she'd been with relatives in the west of the country. So you can say I didn't drum out the news about Jews kidnapping children.*

Most who heard the stories of kidnapped children knew better, but wasn't it more agreeable to believe myth than admit complicity in pillaging, deportation and murder? Hadn't Arrow Cross propaganda labelled Jews subhuman parasites, that genocide was the only way of dealing with them? How could parasites be Hungarian citizens? Wasn't the communist press urging revenge on exploiters who stockpiled food and gold, who used Christian blood in the Passover ceremony?

***

*I*n June 1945, János Nagy, a pro-German teacher in Kunmadaras, was accused of having collaborated with the nazis and arrested. But Nagy was a respected figure, and the charge

---

[126] In September 1946, a pogrom was narrowly averted in the town of Hajdúszoboszló. In July, a pogrom broke out in the city of Miskolc. Influenced by official anti-black-market propaganda, 25,000 workers from nearby foundries marched into town and killed two Jews supposedly selling flour above the legal price. The next day, the same mob captured and killed the Jewish police officer who had tried to protect the victims. Anti-Jewish riots also took place in the Soviet Union and the new satellite countries of Romania, Slovakia and Poland.

created backlash, particularly amongst those who had been his students. At his trial one year later, members of the local Smallholder's Party and their supporters arrived at the Karcag courthouse with a petition demanding entry to the courtroom, and that Nagy be found innocent. Both ultimata were refused. When Nagy was sentenced to three-and-a-half years of forced labour, people were enraged. Who was responsible for such injustice? The capitalists! The Jews! The courts, even the police, were controlled by Jews.

"They should be murdered by any means possible,' said Zsigmund Tóth.

Anti-Jewish sentiment was running high when all returned to Kunmadaras. Aware of the danger, local Jews asked for police intervention. It was not forthcoming. Unhindered, the crowd marched through town, encountering Communist Party secretary Ferenc Takács who had testified against Nagy: 'You are paid by the Jews, you traitor.'

Because Takács was armed, the police were able to bring him to safety. Not so Ferenc Wurczel, a Jewish Social Democrat who had also testified against Nagy. He was severely beaten and left with head injuries, broken teeth and cracked ribs.

The next day was market day. Stalls selling vegetables, fruits, clothing, chickens, milk and cheese were set up as usual; women were shopping. Zsigmund Tóth was also there, alongside Gergely Takács, secretary of the local Smallholders Party. It was Tóth who shouted: 'When are we going to begin? It's almost eight o'clock.'

Egg merchant Sándor Csoli Klein, a Holocaust survivor, was at his stand. Also present was Eszter Kabai Tóth. Taking off her wooden shoe, she began beating Klein, throwing eggs to the ground and screaming: 'The Jews took away my brother's

Those Absent

son and killed him!'

Two women, Gizella Makó and 'Russian' Júlia Bánhegyesi, joined in the violence, and when Vilmos Fisch, a Tiszazentimre Jew, came to Klein's assistance, he, too, was beaten.

'Let the bloody Jews perish,' Gergely Takács shouted. 'They sponge on Christian and Hungarian citizens.'

Klein and his wife ran from the market square to the town outskirts, but were overtaken by two pig herders; Klein's skull was smashed in seven places, his wife's in three.

Grabbing garden tools, iron bars, sticks, a horse's leg bone, fence posts, anything they could find, and yelling 'Today the Jews, tomorrow the bourgeoisie,' a lynch mob of men, women and children swarmed down the road to merchant Ferenc Kuti's home. Huddled inside, how relieved Kuti and his family must have been when the police arrived.[127]

'Kuti the Jew is inside,' screamed the armed horde. 'He has a gun! He's dangerous!'

The officers entered the house. 'Do you have a gun?' they asked.

'No,' said Kuti. 'I have nothing. No gun.' Did he think that by showing good will and vulnerability he would be saved?

The representatives of law and order stepped outside, announced: 'He has no gun.'

And the crowd thundered in, beat and stabbed Kuti: 'That will teach you not to make sausages with the flesh of Hungarian children.'

Swelling to 400, the throng moved through town, destroying Jewish houses, shops and gardens, pillaging. Dragged from the attic where they were hiding, barber Ernő Weinberger and his wife were beaten and left in a ditch. And in Neulander's clothing shop – he was president of the Jewish community –

---

127   Some accounts say one police officer arrived, others claim there were three.

PART FIVE : THE JEWS

Eszter Kabai Tóth urged: 'Kill the Jew.'

Later, an ambulance did arrive to take the dying Neulander away, but the mob protested. 'Jews shouldn't be carried in Hungarian ambulances'. And when Neulander's wife tried to climb in beside her husband, the driver pushed her into the melee. 'Take this woman away. I don't want to watch while she dies.' And she was dragged through the street by her hair.

In Rosenberg's clothing store, all helped themselves. Sára Kerepesi, resentful because forced to return looted booty, thrashed Mrs Rosenberg: 'That's for the quilt.'

On foot on the road to Kunmadaras, Károlyi Rosinger heard of the danger. Wisely, he began heading back to Karcag, but two railway workers caught up with him and beat him to death. 'We're killing you because you take our children.'

In one outlying farmhouse, shepherds cut a Jewish child's throat. Seeking help in town, the family arrived at the home of a Christian friend, a colleague. 'Go away,' he shouted. 'I want nothing to do with you.'

***

*T*he police station in Kunmadaras remained closed throughout the pogrom. Officers had known what was about to happen, had seen several hundred people brandishing weapons. Did they believe Jews had murdered Christian children? They took meat and sausage from Jewish homes as 'evidence.' Later, police arriving from Abadzalok, Kunhegyes, Szolnok and Karcag found a bloodstained throng outside the closed station.

'We need help. Arrest the Jews. Save our children.'

'Jews started the whole thing.'

'They attacked the townspeople.'

'Weinberger wanted to recover a mirror and a quilt!'

Those Absent

Four Jews died; another twenty were badly wounded. Despite the rumour of kidnapped Christian children, no one searched for them: all had been too intent on looting. One hundred and twenty people were arrested and 90 of them were known to have pillaged Jewish houses in 1944. Fifty-nine, mostly agricultural day workers and housewives, were charged. Eight were held directly responsible.

Witnesses at the trial could scarcely believe their eyes; the women were nicely dressed, well coiffed, respectable wives and mothers; the men wore dirty, torn clothing, were barefoot. Illiterate, intimidated by authority, most were so primitive it was impossible to obtain coherent statements from them. How could such people still exist in 1946? None understood they were guilty. Jews were rich; they owned all the buildings; they worked for the secret service. Local people had simply taken justice into their own hands.

'Why did you beat Rosinger to death? You never had any problem with him. He'd always been well-liked.'

'Because the Germans gave me Rosinger's furniture, and he wanted it back. He wanted his cows back, too.'

'I beat the Jews to death because everyone else did.'

One man claimed he was innocent because the steel rod he'd used to commit murder was hollow and couldn't be considered a weapon.

Eszter Kabai Tóth, unable to give her birth date, said she was around forty-one. When taken to Sándor Kohn's cellar where, she had claimed, several Jewish men had tried to kill a Christian girl, she whispered in an investigator's ear: 'Don't tell the Jews, but it was a lie.'

Three defendants, Zsigmond Tóth, Gergely Takács and János Nagy were sentenced to death; two others were condemned to fifteen years' hard labour, confiscation of their property and expulsion from Kunmadaras. Three policemen were given five years imprisonment, and four youths were sent to reform schools. The rest were acquitted.

The death sentences were eventually commuted: one murderer was freed; another had his prison sentence reduced to two years and two months. Ferenc Kuti's wife received death threats, and local party representatives called on Jews to leave Kunmadaras if they couldn't adapt to the town's 'democratic way of life.'

In the 1980s, the story stirred some interest, but much time had passed. What had really happened? Right wing politicians claimed Tóth had been a Soviet agent; that intelligence services had known a pogrom would take place; that the accusation of blood libel had been a deliberate move to provoke chaos and give the Soviets a reason to take control. Those on the left insisted that the pogrom, a resurgence of fascism, was an attempt to destroy the nascent people's democracy.

***

*I*n 1994, in a documentary film, locals were asked about the post war pogroms in both Kunmadaras and Szegvár.[128] One of the condemned claimed he remembered nothing; a son excused his father. Some people expressed solidarity with the Jews; others gave credence to the blood libel accusation.

Kohn's daughter passed a copy of the film to Ági, and together with Udo, we watched it. The road where Rosinger was murdered was the one I had taken from the train station on the day I first arrived. The wheeled water pump near Kata's house was where the 'friend' had refused to help the desperate

---

128 *Midőn a vér (As the Blood)*, written by János Pelles and produced by Edit Kőszegi, Sándor Simó, András Surányi at Hunnia Stúdió, Budapest, 1994.

Those Absent

family. The wide courtyard of the long low yellow building to the left of the park is where several hundred men and women gathered, bent on murder. And Kuti's house on the grassy crossroad island is one I admired for its fine woodwork and broad terrace.

Later, Karcsi, Enikö, and several of her friends also asked to see the film, so we gathered in Ildikó's apartment, and Enikö translated for Udo: 'I want to make certain I understood everything the first time.'

'Why didn't anyone talk about this when we were in school?' Enikö shouted. 'People shouldn't be allowed to forget.' She hoped her mother would be equally outraged.

But Ildikó wasn't interested. 'If the people in Kunmadaras had done something like that, I'd have heard about it.'

Józsi gaped at his wife. 'What do you know!' he bellowed. 'You're not from here. You're from Püspokladány. Of course, the people here in Kunmadaras would do something like that. They were primitive back then, and they're still primitive now.'

Furious, Ildikó turned away.

'I'm glad I asked Enikö to translate,' said Udo to me. 'The first time we saw the film was with Ági. Because she's Jewish, she might have given me a slanted version of the story.'

PART FIVE : THE JEWS

XLVI

The Hungarian Jews have managed to concentrate in their hands all the commerce of this rich country. In the villages they exercise the calling of shopkeepers and innkeepers, combined with that of bankers and usurers. The country Jew carefully hides his hoard of gold, until some fine day when he emigrates with his cash box into the town, where he then sets up on a grand scale.

Victor Tissot

*P*éter, an exceedingly thin man with shaved head and tattooed arms, came from Budapest to speak with Ágnes. He was originally from Tiszaörs, had been raised there by his mother and grandmother. One night, when in his teens, he'd had a dream in which he'd heard music unlike any he'd ever known. The sounds, haunting yet familiar, had stayed with him. Then, by chance, he heard Jewish music on the radio.

'Traditional music, sung by a cantor. It was the music from my dream, and I wondered if anyone in our family could have been Jewish, although we are Catholic. I asked my mother and grandmother, but my question angered them. They began screaming: "How dare you suggest our family had anything to do with Jews! We've always been Christians. Always!"

'Because their reaction was so extreme, I knew something was wrong. After that, each time they left me alone, I started going through all the closets, drawers, cupboards and boxes, looking for family papers, anything. And I finally discovered records showing our Jewish family had converted to Catholicism.

'I confronted my mother and grandmother, showed them what I'd found, but they yelled at me, denied any link with Judaism, claimed the papers were false, that they had been planted in our house to discredit us. Eventually, I understood their reaction: Jews have been persecuted for so long, and my mother and grandmother feared the terror would start again.'

281

Those Absent

Now Péter was studying Hebrew and learning about Judaism. 'I'm hoping to be admitted to a Budapest yeshiva. I want to become a rabbi.'

His mother and grandmother still lived in the village, right on the main road, only a few doors away from where the Deutsch family had lived. They continued to deny Jewish ancestry. 'Don't bother going to see them,' Péter warned me. 'They won't speak to you, and they won't be nice about it.'

***

In the 1945 elections for the National Assembly, the majority vote had gone to the Smallholder's Party, but power was in Soviet hands under Marshal Kliment Yefremovich Voroshilov. Over the next year and a half, with the help of forcible removals, purges, torture, show trials and executions, the communists consolidated their hold on power. New elections were held in May 1949, and voters were presented with a single list of the combined parties. A new constitution, produced three months later, was almost identical to that of the Soviet Union. The country was renamed the People's Re,public of Hungary.

The Hungarian Communist Party leader was Mátyás Rákosi (born Mátyás Rosenfeld), the squat, bald son of a Jewish village grocer. A minister in Béla Kún's short-lived 1919 regime, Rákosi had passed eighteen years in Horthy's prisons. Liberated in 1940, he went to Moscow and became 'Stalin's best disciple,' although most of his Hungarian comrades had been exiled to Stalin's camps or murdered in purges.

He built a personality cult around himself, spewing out folksy parables in a bogus peasant's accent, making anti-Semitic remarks and eliminating rivals by 'cutting them off like slices of salami'. At his side were other lapsed Jews, vengeful men who had seen their families exterminated. Gábor Péter (Benjamin Eisenberger), a Jewish tailor, became head of ÁVO, the State

Security Department; KGB agent Ernő Gerő (Ernő Singer)[129] – his father had been a banker – was Communist Party secretary; Mihály Farkas (Hermann Lőwy), Minister of Defence; and József Révai (József Lederer), Minister of Culture.

That so many were of Jewish descent confirmed the myth of the Jewish quest for world power. In reality, other intellectually eligible candidates were disqualified because of their pro-Nazi affiliations. However, lower-ranking members of the Arrow Cross Party were acceptable; their earlier crimes were forgotten in exchange for denouncing so-called subversive elements. Their anti-Semitism bothered no one. It was easier, said Rákosi, to make good communists out of little nazis than Jewish intellectuals.

To distract attention from the great number of Jews in government, the community was singled out for persecution: activists were arrested, and contact with world Jewry was curtailed. When Foreign Secretary László Rajk criticised the government's Stalinist policies, he was tortured, then executed with eighteen other people. Many Jews, finding themselves yet again the butt of hatred, were more than willing to give up their religious and cultural traditions; their children never knew their families had once been Jewish.[130]

---

129 As 'The Butcher of Barcelona,' Gerő was known for his purge of Trotskyist groups during the Spanish Civil War.
130 Csanád Szegedi, a right wing Jobbik Party leader known for his anti-Semitic and anti-Roma remarks, attended the first session of the European Parliament wearing the paramilitary uniform of the banned Hungarian Guard. In 2012, it was discovered that his grandparents were Jewish – his grandmother had survived Auschwitz, his grandfather, a Jewish labour battalion. They had kept their Jewishness hidden, certain there would be another Holocaust. Asked to leave the party, Szegedi sought advice from Lubavitch Rabbi Slomo Köves. Adopting the name Dovid, he began wearing a kippah, learning Hebrew and visiting Israel. He has had himself circumcised and now lives as a practicing Jew. His wife converted to Judaism but doesn't feel particularly comfortable in the synagogue. However, she finds the people there preferable to her husband's former Jobbik friends.

Those Absent

XLVII

What's on his mind is on his tongue.

Yiddish Proverb

On April 16, 2004, sixty years after the Hungarian Jewish deportations to the camps began, my photographic exhibition of the Holocaust opened in Tiszafüred. Many of the village Germans came to the opening. Despite his eternal loyalty to the Hitler Youth Movement, Heinz, dressed in his finest suit, came over to me after the speeches. 'I'm proud of you,' he said. 'We all are.'

Elderly Petra, she who had been imprisoned as a nazi collaborator, didn't attend. 'Every time you turn on the television, that's all you hear. I'm sick and tired of the Holocaust.'

Tattooed Endre put newspaper articles about the exhibition in my mailbox. 'The whole village is proud of you.'

I passed Edit the cheese-maker on the street. 'We saw you on television,' she said. 'We saw you twice. And we read the articles in the newspapers, too.' She paused, squinted like a woman with a sneaky secret. 'You know, before the war, there were several Jewish families in this village. I don't remember their names, but their children went to the Catholic school.'

'Why would they do that?'

'They had no choice. It was the one school in the village. Jews paid taxes to the church, and the church took care of us all.'

But when I questioned her further, Edit shook her head, glanced down the empty road. 'That's all I know.'

More Jewish ghosts appeared. Old András waved me over to his garden gate. 'You wanted to know about Jews who lived here. I remember them,' although a few years earlier he had denied their existence.

PART FIVE : THE JEWS

'Tell me more.'

Nervously jiggling from foot to foot, his paunch was a trembling jelly over stumpy thighs, and his flaccid face blotched sheepish pink. No doubt sorry he'd offered me information, he began hiding behind his usual, almost incomprehensible pidgin Hungarian mixed with pidgin German. 'Me child. No remember.'

'But you remember some things.'

'Wife, she remember. László Schreiber had mill, make flour. Altman, Imre Altman. Ignaz Schwartz, he live in house of German woman, Brigitte. Another Jew, we children call him Jewish Péter. No shop. House. Inside house, Jewish bar.'

An entire community was surfacing. 'Where? Where was the Jewish bar?'

'Still there. Bar still there. Beer bar, sörözö, on back street. House new. Jewish woman living near church, too. Lizi Farkas across from Deutsch family: Zoltán Deutsch, his wife Juliska, four children. Deutsch have grocery shop on main road. Good people, Deutsch. One Jew, Jordan, out on Puszta farm, have many chickens. House gone. All Jews gone.'

Country Jews [131]

---
[131] Photo courtesy of the Museum of Hungarian Speaking Jewry, Safed, Israel.

Those Absent

'So many.' Why had everyone denied their existence?

'Doctor, too, Dr Sándor Steiner. Good man, rich. We children, follow Steiner in street, call out, "Money, money. We want money." He take coins from pocket, throw on ground.' András giggled without a hint of shame. 'Joke, only joke. We children. Children do things. Sometimes problem with Jews. One like another man's wife… happens everywhere. Everywhere good Jews, bad Jews. Germans same, Russians same. Good and bad.'

'What happened to them all?'

He raised his hands, a gesture of helpless acceptation. 'Some Budapest, some Karcag. Others Auschwitz.'

'Why did everyone turn against them?'

'Propaganda. We work land; Jews have shops. In Tiszafüred, Jews have shops, in Kunmadaras, everywhere in Hungary. Here, people poor. Some ten hectares, some five, some one half hectare. We no rich. Have gardens, vegetables, fruit.' He stopped, scratched his rumpled neck, then leaned in closer. 'Life better in communist time.'

PART SIX:
Change

Hungarian Jewish Farmers[132]

One of the worst economic disasters was the flooding of the Nagylengyel oilfields in western Hungary...In the summer of 1955 Rákosi had been warned that over-production would cause a risk of water entering the wells; in spite of this he had raised the plan by 200,000 tons over the previous peak production. When he was warned by the experts that the danger limit had been reached, his only answer was to raise the target in the 1956 plan by another 100,000 tons. The wells were flooded, and oil production reduced by half.

Dora Scarlett,[133] 1959

---

132   Photo courtesy of the Museum of Hungarian Speaking Jewry, Safed, Israel.
133   *Window Onto Hungary*. Scarlett was a British writer and broadcaster who, heavily involved in the Communist Party, went to live in Budapest. Soon disillusioned with communism, she left the country.

XLVIII

The Magyars are by no means a grasping people, and are always satisfied with whatever is given them, returning a hearty 'Thank you,' no matter how small the gift, which by the way, they have the good taste never to look at in your presence.

Nina Elizabeth Mazuchelli, 1881

*L*ocal interest focused on a bald man from Budapest, a falsely amiable person with a piranha's smirk and new black Mercedes – he owned a construction company, was said to be on excellent terms with important politicians. He and an invisible partner bought up a few adobe houses on a back street, destroyed them, and began erecting a pretentious structure with twenty pillars on a wraparound terrace. Work stopped when half-finished.

With the same ghostly colleague, he began constructing a hotel on the main road. Three stories high with a reception area, several dining rooms and 'fake antique' windows criss-crossed by gold vinyl bars, it impressed many: 'He's putting this village on the map. Tourists will come, and money will finally start circulating.'

'He's Mafia. Knows how to work the system.'

A few pretended scorn; most were admiring.

'It's about time we had a decent, modern restaurant here,' said the Germans.

Then all work stopped. Red breeze block walls remained bare; wind slapped plastic sheeting on unfinished doors and windows; scraggy grasses struggled for survival in a yard of rubble, hardened cement, crumpled polystyrene and cans of dried-out paint.

The bald man's next interest was a graceful ruin on the main road: 'A great place for a restaurant, something with character,' said Margit, the kocsma owner. But, after purchase, it remained empty, collapsing.

'There's a reason. Something to do with subsidies.'

'Misused subsidies,' said those more realistic. 'That's what happens when you're friends with the right people in Budapest.'

'Corruption. That's routine in Hungary,' said Misi. 'Builders are corrupt, promoters are corrupt, the medical system is so corrupt you have to pay doctors under the table if you want decent treatment. And if you do end up in hospital, you're expected to bribe the nurses and everyone else who works there.[134] And who are these corrupt capitalists with wealth, power and important positions? Former communist politicians and officials.'

Udo's face twitched with dark distrust 'The communists might be disguising themselves as capitalists, but communism is still a real danger.' These days, he was ever on the lookout for menace, a consequence of his new job. The print shop he previously worked for had folded, and he now travelled through rural Austria selling (to naïve bumpkins) costly electric blankets guaranteed to quash deadly electromagnetic waves and offer protection from cancer, rheumatism and pain.

'How can electric blankets destroy electromagnetic waves?' I asked. 'They have to be plugged into an electrical circuit. It sounds absurd to me.'

He was smug, even superior. His faith in the tenets of what seemed to be a pyramidal sales para-religion was reinforced by all-night sensory deprivation sessions, dangerous trial by adversity exploits, and in-group humiliation when sales

---

[134] Because of low pay, Hungarian physicians accept 'gratitude payments' or tips that patients give for medical appointments. International patients are expected to be exceptionally generous.

remained stagnant or fell. His political opinions had swung from right to extreme right: Jörg Haider was a good man or he wouldn't have been received at the Vatican by Pope John Paul II; European leaders were condemning Haider wrongly, just as they'd done with Kurt Waldheim.

I wasn't disappointed when group-bonding activities reduced Udo's visits to Hungary.

***

*T*he bald man bought another earthen house and brought in a team of workers from Budapest. Then, to local surprise, instead of destroying the house, he restored it with traditional materials, planted grape vines along the wood-pillared terrace. There were new reports: he was leaving his third wife, coming to live here with his three children, his mistress and her three children.

We'd seen the mistress in the baths. Impassive, beautiful and slender, she wore tiny bikinis. He, square, rough and rustic, was adoring. Visibly in love, they gazed at each other with fevered eyes, were often locked in languid, passionate embraces. And when the house was ready, hearsay did prove correct: the mistress moved in.

She sometimes strolled through village streets, her shiny nut-brown hair swinging over her shoulders. Not hostile, she was reserved, for wealth and the love of a powerful man kept her separate from others. She was also much envied, and I noticed how often people passed her house, peering over the gate to catch sight of her as if she were a star, a great celebrity.

'No one knows anything about her or where she came from,' said Gizi, who itched for titillating gossip.

Every weekend, the bald man arrived from Budapest in

his big black Mercedes. People grovelled in his presence, for corruption and influence gave him rank. The couple lent a neon Hollywood glow to our humble village.

Those Absent

XLIX

There are, in this area, houses with roofs made of dried grass, although this has been forbidden for at least fifty years; but the inhabitants are so poor they have never had enough money to cover their roofs with straw. The second last house of this street isn't much larger than a gypsy hut. The old municipal sweeper who occupied it died two years ago. He was a widower. His whole life, he fought against rotting grass roofs and mouldy walls. He left this world when he could no longer stand his misery. His slum stayed empty until the day when it was designated as the residence of the wife of the 'kulak' Istok and their two daughters, their own coquette, three-room house was taken away and given to Berger who wanted it... Accused of having sold two pigs on the black market, Mátyás Istok had been taken away and no one had ever seen him again. Their lands were confiscated and incorporated into the state farm...The hut had one room and a woodshed...and was inhabited by five people.

Gusztav Rab,[135] 1959

'Our little village has existed since the Stone Age,' said Panni, the librarian. 'When the first Magyars came into the country, here is where they settled. When I was a girl, there was a sawmill where logs were made into windows and doors; there was a small factory where they made lovely roof tiles. Nowadays, doors, windows and roof tiles are industrial products made in Austria and they're too expensive for us.

'My parents, grandparents and great-grandparents were dwarf holders,[136] and we grew table grapes and gooseberries. We worked our fields by hand, put down manure each year and the earth was lovely, light and brown. The grapes were such excellent quality, you couldn't find better anywhere, and

---
135 *Voyage dans le Bleu*. Gustave Rab, 1901-1963, Hungarian author.
136 Dwarfholders were those with little land, often too little for survival.

we sold all we produced in the market. We made wine, we had ducks and geese, and our whole family could live on what we earned.

'Then collectivization began. Officials showed up, told us we could no longer sell in the market. That everything was to be sold to the State. You had to obey. They came to your house, examined what you had, and then took everything away. They went out to the land that had always been ours, ripped out every single grapevine and gooseberry bush, then planted wheat and corn, and sent my father to work for the water company.

'But out in those fields, the earth isn't good for wheat and corn. My sister, mother and I, took our bicycles, rode out and had a look. Where row after row of fat gooseberries and grapes had grown was just stunted wheat, shrivelled corn.

'Such stupid people were in charge of collective farms. They knew nothing about local agriculture, climate or quality of the soil, but they wouldn't listen to people with good sense or experience. Older peasants were pushed aside. No one cared about their wisdom.

'By 1961, ninety-five percent of agricultural land belonged to collective farms managed by engineers, technicians and economists. There was one man in our village who said, "No, I won't give up my fields, not the tiniest bit of land." And he was taken away. We found him a few days later, he was hanging from a tree. The authorities claimed he'd killed himself, but we knew that was a lie. When the men cut him down, they found every one of his bones had been broken. How could he have walked to a tree and hanged himself? He had three little children and a wife, and they had to survive without him, but he was used as an example to show what would happen to us if we didn't cooperate. I was only a young girl, but I remember it perfectly.

'After that, everyone gave up their land without protest. People stopped planting fruit trees or planning for the future. Some went to work in the cooperatives, but there weren't jobs for everyone. Others were sent off to the mines, or the factories, and they came home on Sundays. Later they returned for official holidays, or when it was time to put flowers on family graves. But their life was so hard. They were country boys and only knew country traditions. So many died in the cities, the factories and the mines.

'Later, if we handed in papers showing that the land had been ours, we got compensation, but they gave so little money, you couldn't buy a handful of sugar. We never dreamed the system would change, that communism would end. Some people were smarter. They didn't exchange their papers, and they're the large landowners today. But the men who tortured and murdered people? They're still here, living side-by-side with us.'

***

During the revolution in 1956, I managed to sneak into Austria, like 200,000 other Hungarians,' said Dénes, the Englishman, as we sat in the kocsma, sipping pálinka. 'They took me to a refugee camp, and those were terrible places, with fascists and communists living alongside the victims of fascism and communism. People killed each other there. Sometimes Hungarian officials showed up and tried to get people to come back by promising them special privileges if they became informers. The best thing to do was find another country that would take you. The Brits were looking for miners, so I lied, claimed I'd always done that. I ended up in a Derbyshire pit but couldn't stick it. I knew how to make things, so I opened an ironworks, did well.'

Sentenced to eighteen and a half years' imprisonment for desertion, he could only return to Hungary when communism ended. Building a modern holiday home at the village end, he began buying traditional houses and tearing them down. It was a bone of contention between us.

'You want me to restore old houses? What for? There's no beauty in those rotten places. I'm buying the land for my sons, as an investment.'

'Do your sons ever come here?'

'Maybe one day they will.'

'Are they interested in this country?'

Momentarily discomfited, he lifted his glass. 'A new building is better than those adobe things you're so fond of. Come to my house for coffee tomorrow and I'll show you. Just don't come early.' He grinned, anticipating the destruction to be wrought by the day's pálinka.

***

Dénes's two-story concrete and cinderblock house stood in a yard of poured concrete. I waited until noon before knocking, but my arrival took him by surprise, for alcohol had smudged out all memory of our rendezvous. The night before, he'd fallen asleep in a ditch. Upon waking, unable to find his house keys, he had spent an icy five hours shivering on the back seat of his car. Hungover, sickly, he ushered me indoors.

And because he hadn't had time to prepare for the visit, I'd caught him out. This new house possessed central heating, a large central entry/dining room, a living room and several upstairs bedrooms; yet, despite half a century in England and marriage to an Englishwoman, Dénes employed the house in

Those Absent

the ancestral way. Shamefaced, he admitted he lived in the kitchen, slept on a trestle bed beside the ancient wood-and-coal-burning stove. It was the only heat source he used. 'Old traditions die hard.' Or perhaps this new building, a status symbol underlining success, was no more than a raspberry directed at the former communist authorities.

'Old houses? They remind me of the places we were forced to live in during my youth. You can't imagine what our life was like. Under the communists, our family was persecuted because my paternal grandmother had been a baroness. We didn't have money, we didn't have land, but that didn't matter. We had to be punished. We couldn't live in one place, but were constantly moved from one freezing wretched hovel to the next.

'Kids from aristocratic families had their social class marked in school documents, so classmates and teachers harassed us, and I wasn't allowed to go to university. But when they called me up for military service, they made me an officer – an officer was always an aristocrat. You see? Typical communist thinking: It never made much sense. Not that the Yanks were better, persecuting commies in their own country, but when we needed them during the '56 revolution, where were they?

'When I was a kid, I had friends who were also being persecuted, and there was nothing we could do about it. We used to meet in the mulberry grove – don't bother looking for it, because the communists cut down all the trees for firewood. Because we met there, we gave ourselves a name: The Mulberry Gang.

'There was one woman in particular, the most powerful, vicious communist in the village. Everyone was frightened of her. We hated her so much, we decided to assassinate her. Beside the school, there's a little lane that runs down to the marshes. We found hand grenades down there after the war, left by retreating Germans who had to get away fast, and we had contests to see who was the best at dismantling them. We weren't afraid. Sometimes we'd take the grenades, go chuck them into the river to get fish. It wasn't a good thing to do, but that's how it was.

'Anyway, we decided to blow the woman's head off. We watched her for a long time, knew all her habits, knew that she walked past the mulberry grove at the same time each evening. Then we decided that instead of killing her with a grenade, it would be better to shoot her. We had a gun, because my father had once been an engineer, and he had one hidden away. Each one of us in the Mulberry Gang vowed we would take the gun and shoot. That way, it wouldn't be one person who was guilty. We were in it together; we wouldn't betray each other. It would be a political assassination.

'The night we planned to kill her, we waited in the mulberry grove with the gun, but for some reason, she didn't pass by. That one night, by pure chance, she didn't go home. After that, we lost our nerve. We didn't want to get caught. We got scared.'

Dénes and I went to see the latest house he had purchased and was planning to demolish. Its roof was sinking, but it was a beautiful building, well over a hundred years old, once a family's pride and joy. Thick, whitewashed walls were healthy and solid, and sun filtering through solid double windows turned beams and wide-planked floors golden. But Dénes was immune to the beauty. All would soon be a heap of earth and straw rubble in a wasted field.

Those Absent

L

Two apple trees spread their branches in the back of the yard, not far from the shingled cottage. One was an old tree, disporting its years and the profusion of its branches in the sky. Next to it stood a small, sprightly tree, evidently having the old one for its grandsire. Here the fledgling light lingered, whirled round in silver swirls between the branches of the two trees, on which the snow squatted in thick streaks like the fat bacon that comes to the poor man in the fairy tale. The light gathered there, coming to a rest between the snowy branches. It swayed and fluttered, as if trying out its wings.

Áron Tamási,[137] 1946

'Life is getting more difficult and older people are suffering,' said Edit. 'We can't afford anything. The price of gas is rising. How will we keep warm in winter? I can't bake bread, because I have to think about how much heating the oven will cost. Being in the EU hasn't improved our lives.'

I had come to Edit and László's house to buy cheese, but there were no pungent bundles hanging in the kitchen or the larder. I felt uncomfortable asking why. Had new EU laws discouraged undeclared home production? Perhaps few sought the rustic homemade cheese, preferring 'modern' goods in plastic packaging.

'Look at this.' László pushed a glossy supermarket brochure across the table. 'We get these every week. Show me one Hungarian product.'

Edit and László had lived through a time when large socialist enterprises had been subsidized at the expense of the population. Now, at the expense of the population, the government was encouraging global companies with promises of low – or no – tax, paid holidays, cheap or free land and

---

137 *Pinions of Poverty.* Áron Tamási, 1897-1966, Hungarian writer.

poorly paid local employees willing to work long hours.

'In Budapest everything is fine, but what about us?[138] What about what we produce out here in the country, the hams, sausages, vegetables, butter and onions? They've already built three huge supermarkets in Tiszafüred this year, and they're building a fourth. Why?'

Up-to-date supermarkets filled with international products were the utopias of Germans, Austrians and Swiss, and they snapped up, with relief, the familiar foods from home. However, shopping in them was financially impossible for most locals. Dazed, cowering families would clump together in the aisles, gaze with wonder at the proffered goods, then leave these epicurean palaces empty-handed.

'Many of us don't have cars to drive out to the supermarkets,' said Edit.

'How can we keep up?' László asked. 'The communists were better than the EU.'

***

*I*n the steamy kitchen, windows sweated, and moisture dribbled down the lacquered walls. Misi was preparing dinner, boiling smoked ribs in water spiced with an onion and white pepper. With a slotted spoon, he fished a few from the pot, put them on plates for Udo and me. 'Try those.'

They were greyish and gristly, and I began peeling off the rubbery exterior. Although Hungarian national cuisine has found favour all over the world, (rich Hungarian desserts are considered the equal of those from Vienna), I still failed to appreciate its boiled or deep-fried meats, sugared pasta, chunks

---

[138] Today, Budapest is once again a glittering city with vast shopping malls offering luxury goods, concert halls, theatres and busy cafés. Money from the European Union has gone into construction and renovation projects. This attracts tourists, but also lines the pockets of developers. Most are personal friends of Viktor Orbán.

of raw pork lard on bread, pastries made with duck and goose fat.

'What the hell are you doing?' Misi shouted. Whisking my plate away, he pushed the fat into his mouth. 'Good food's wasted on you. Fat's the best part.'

'For clogged veins and arteries?' Heart disease, stroke and hypertension were the leading causes of death in the region.[139] 'Have you been to the cemetery recently? Seen all the graves of people in their 50s?'

'That's crap. Fat is healthy. You need fat. Look at Gizi. See how much weight she's gained? She's getting nice and round, all because of my cooking. Women with fat are more fun in bed. You westerners understand nothing.'

On the table was yet another glossy catalogue. Once our mailboxes had been stuffed with sickly coloured flyers offering bargain pots and drab work clothes, but these modern versions proposed chunks of industrial furniture, bathroom fixtures, televisions, computers, lacy bras, garter belts and thongs. The last four pages were devoted to photos of barely clad young women arching forward, legs spread suggestively, full-lipped mouths open in red provocation. They weren't selling their own opulence, nor were they proposing pornographic film carnality. They were merely advertising makeup.

'It's getting like the West here,' said Misi. 'People here are so fucking stupid. They're demanding lawns, not gardens. They want to buy apples and tomatoes, not grow them. They want to show the neighbours how modern they are. They want something new? They go to a bank, borrow money. In the old days, families had a couple of kids, and when it came time for the oldest son to get married, everyone went out and built him a

---

139   Hungary has one of the lowest life expectancies in the EU (the Borgen Project, 2017).

house. When the second son got married, he stayed home, and he and his wife took care of the parents. When they died, he got their house and everything in it. No bank, no loan.

'Today, parents have to give expensive gifts to teachers if they want their children to graduate. They give expensive motorbikes and cars to their children to encourage them to acquire. When those kids go to the city, they buy them apartments. Then these same kids go to the bank, take out a loan for a bigger car, a house, a bigger television, and that makes the parents proud and happy. In the end, everyone belongs to the bank. Or else they steal. Little people steal little things, big people steal big.

'You hear what everyone is saying? They all want to become big capitalists, but that life was better under the communists. The communists? They did such stupid things. They went into the pharmacy, closed it down, took over the house of someone they didn't like, and said: "now this house is going to be the pharmacy." They took small shops, closed them, closed the kocsmas, took over people's houses and said, "this is where the taverns will be." They came into my father's workshop – he was a leather craftsman and employed three people – and said, "It's finished. You're closed." And they sent my father to grow vegetables.

'In this village, they called in a swineherd, a guy so ignorant, he couldn't sign his name, could only make an X. And they turned him into a party big shot and made him mayor because the bosses running the show could do what they wanted with him.

'There was a horrible woman with tree trunk legs. She was high up in the party, and everyone tried to sleep with her. One day, there was a meeting at the party headquarters, and my grandfather happened to be sitting on the bench outside. This

Those Absent

woman comes out of the meeting, and she's glowing with power. She sees my grandfather sitting there, goes up to him, and says: "You know what, Márton bácsi? I have the whole village in my hands." And my grandfather, like me he had a big mouth, so he says to her: "Madame, you know what you have in your hands? A pile of shit."' Misi roared with mirth. Then sobered.

'Still is a pile of shit. A backwater. People have the mentality of serfs. What did those big shots do when the revolution broke out in 1956? They ran to the fields and hid in the little huts where people press grapes. Some guys came in a truck from Karcag and dumped a load of guns on the marketplace, but someone else hid them in a basement. One group of so-called revolutionaries stormed the school, ripped the red star off a classroom wall and tried to put a big crucifix in its place. "Now we can pray again," they said. But they hammered in the nails so hard, the porcelain Jesus shattered into a million pieces. Four other men went to the village centre and pulled down the statue of Stalin. Another guy got drunk, went into the kocsma with his horse – a huge workhorse – ordered a pálinka for himself and a beer for the horse. That was about it for the revolution in this village.

'Then, when the revolution failed, all the ÁVO scum who hadn't been killed in Budapest were sent here, to the country, to become police officers or part of the Peasants Watch Committee. The four men who'd ripped down the statue of Stalin were told to appear at the commissariat in Tiszafüred at six o'clock. When they arrived, they were beaten. And the police told them, "You be here tomorrow at six." And they were beaten again. Every day it was like that. They had to come, be beaten. Finally, one man, he couldn't stand it any longer, and he killed himself. But the people who did that are still around, living well, happy. They've simply changed their political ticket.

'Look at Robi the insurance broker. He's the perfect

Hungarian. He takes money for insurance policies, puts it in his own pocket. When something goes wrong, a fire, a burglary, people discover they aren't insured. What happens to him? Nothing. He takes kickbacks, files false claims for his friends, but his family is in politics, so no one asks questions. He renovated his house, built a guest room with toilet and shower, bought another house, renovated it into a guesthouse, bought a big new car, all with money he made illegally. This same guy, what was he doing when he was young? He was head of the communist youth group. I asked him about that: "how could you do that back then, and be a big capitalist today?" And he said: "Well, that was the thing to do in those days; now it's different."

'It's the same with the church. Under the communists, if you went to church, you became an outcast. Informers stood across the street and watched who went in. Now, the most corrupt people go to church with their families. Why? Because the big shots in the Fidesz Party – those same guys who were good communists in student days – are suddenly going to Catholic mass so they can win over religious voters. The communists murdered a hundred million people, but no one was brought to trial because they would implicate people higher up, those who had given the orders: today's big capitalists and right-wing politicians.'

Udo had been sitting in his chair, eating his ribs, drinking wine and quietly misunderstanding Misi's diatribe in English. Now he roused himself. 'Socialists and liberals cater to the Turks,' he said without the slightest flutter of irony. 'The Muslims forced us to take down the crucifixes in our school classrooms. They're taking away the freedom of our Catholic Church.'

Those Absent

LI

Wife, learn to look up to your man
And whatever he does, don't complain:
If he goes to the pub, know your place
If he knocks you about, shut your face
Though he skins you alive, heigh-ho,
Though he skins you alive!

Folk Song

*T*he bald man from Budapest bought the spa baths, the communist style canteen and the thatched adjacent hall used for dinners and dancing in the summer. He planned to modernize all.

'It won't happen,' said Udo, his rosy spectacles well in place. 'The Hungarians are too smart to destroy what they have. They don't want modernity. They love tradition.'

The row of separate spa cubicles, once the province of libidinous communist bureaucrats, were the first to go. Then, work stopped, and the baths became the lieu of all night drunken parties – orgies, insisted some – for the bald man's rowdy Budapest friends. The Germans, showing up for their early morning swim, were confronted by smashed bottles and filth. It became a major topic of conversation and inspired much exaggeration, even tall tales.

'Disgusting. Now that Hungary is in the EU, they have to keep things up to standard.'

'You never know what diseases you'll catch by going in the water.'

'When Helga's sister was here a few weeks ago, she combed her hair after getting out of the water, and the comb turned black.'

'Monika knows someone who has been ill ever since bathing here.'

PART SIX : CHANGE

But the baths had been mismanaged for years. Money received for distributing hot water to surrounding houses had filled, not village coffers, but the mayor's pocket. Private homes had been built with it; it had financed foreign holidays. Only the pockets had changed.

One Saturday evening, I went with Heinz, Udo and Odette to the village kocsma where a musician played pop tunes on a synthesizer, and a spotty youth stressed an electric guitar. Now a regular production, this was popular with the locals.

When the bald man arrived, he did so with a retinue – five strutting muscle men, and a cluster of meek flunkies. Like any king, he would never travel lightly. The mistress went to sit at a back table with their Budapest friends. By now, villagers had grown used to her, and she had changed considerably. Dressed in leather, her hair cropped short, she was no longer so lovely, dreamy or romantic.

The bald man had been drinking. Loud, aggressive, he shouted and bragged. Sometimes losing his balance, his heavily muscled body slammed against the counter. The lackeys grinned obsequiously. Then, for no reason, he turned, smashed the weakest, a mere youth, to the floor and kicked him hard. The boy doubled up in pain.

'Now Feri,' said Margit, the kocsma owner, 'if you want to do that, go outside.' She smiled with good-natured indulgence. She knew the bald man well. How? Why? There were ties and complexities in the village that I, an outsider, would never grasp.

Mortified, the boy rose, stared pleadingly at his tormentor. Loyal, servile, what had he done to deserve such punishment? Gleeful, the bald man swung again, tried to knock him down. And missed.

At her table near the back, the mistress was weeping. Now

she rushed to her lover's side, began pleading with him. He ignored her. The boy, the lackeys, the musclemen, the bald man, all went outside. The beseeching mistress, with appeasing but useless gestures, followed.

'Not the first time that's happened,' said Misi who was, as ever, by the slot machine. 'He has a reputation for being violent. He beat his ex-wives, now he beats this new woman.'

I wondered if people still envied her, knowing the price she paid for the pretty house, the expensive Mercedes and the lush life. The bald man was dangerous, but important. How important? Who knew? A small-time corrupt capitalist? Someone close to the powerful in Budapest? No one would dare oppose him.

PART SEVEN:
After

Only the buffaloes, the ninety-seven buffaloes, had been forgotten or left behind. Why? This has never been cleared up. The large red buffalo herd...were surprised by the flood. And then began the unbelievable: they began to fight. The deadly fight of the red buffaloes that lasted a week. Many watched in the first days, then lost interest. The buffaloes wandered day and night in the water, towards the southeast until one only could see them as black dots on the horizon of high water... And there must they sink.

Adelbert Muhr[140]

---

140 *Theiss Rapsody.* Adelbert Muhr, 1896-1977, Austrian journalist, writer, translator.

Those Absent

LII

But thanks to my invention, my capitalist friends and I were able to bring the government to its knees.

Erno Rubik[141]

Although I had planned to be away from Hungary for a short while only, eighteen months passed before I returned. Villagers, catching sight of me, hurried down the road to greet me or doubled back on their bicycles. András, my neighbour, graced me with his rapturous, yellow, two-incisor smile and filled my arms with ruddy apples. In the kocsma, all bought me drinks and (briefly) treated me like a (very minor) returning celebrity. And Annie, she who had told me about the parachutist's execution, presented me with thick woollen socks.

'I knitted these for you because I knew you'd be back. But don't stay long. We're too dull for you, and life here is too provincial. You are meant for more exciting things elsewhere.'

There had been many changes. Large PVC windows and roll-down shutters had replaced many wooden double windows; more houses had vanished and been replaced with new ones in cement and embellished with 'Spanish-look' grillwork, rounded arches and railing-less suspended balconies on upper stories.

---

141   Erno Rubik, b.1944, Hungarian architect and inventor of the Rubik's cube.

PART SEVEN : AFTER

A newly elected village mayor was ordering grass to be cropped close and ditches to be kept tidy. If they refused, recalcitrant house owners would pay a fine: a suburban image was being sought. Ducks, chickens and geese no longer pecked in the grassy verges; no cows padded along streets at dusk; there were no yapping herder's dogs. People no longer gossiped by the dairy, and that hut had been pulled down. Other than the cement floor, there was no trace of it.

'EU rules say that bringing milk to the dairy on bicycles is unhygienic, so no one has a cow anymore,' Gizi explained.

'Last year three hundred pigs in village,' added András. 'This year few.'

'True,' Gizi explained. 'Because now you have to bring them to the slaughterhouse, but that costs money. And you're no longer allowed to collect the blood for sausage.'

'Life difficult,' András muttered gloomily. 'Communism better.'

The modern green house next door had gone through more modernization: the garden, stripped of fruit trees, shrubs and vegetable patch, had become a close-cropped lawn surrounded by a chain-link fence, and decorated with expensive plastic toys. The family car was new; there was a satellite dish antenna; there were 'American-style' doors and windows. The couple spent spare time listening to disco music or sitting in front of a television behind new ruffled 'French chateau' curtains. Their daughter wore frilly frocks in pastel colours or pristine white and never played outside.

'How do they do it?' Gizi asked sourly. 'Where do they get their money? She's the daughter of a kocsma owner and doesn't work; he's a small-town fireman. Obviously, he takes payoffs.'

Those Absent

The romantic phase with Misi had passed. Well fed on his cooking, she was plump but less enamoured. 'I'd love to meet a foreigner, someone wealthy. I thought I could be happy with Misi, but he owes me money. He talks about marriage, but I told him that before you marry, you have to earn a living.' She sighed. 'I always thought he was strong, but now I realise he needs people to tell him what to do. I feel sorry for him, and for me too. My ex-husband was like that. A weak man.'

The antiquated communist style restaurant where I had sat so often with Dénes, the nearby reed-thatched hall where Udo and I had passed evenings, were both gone, burnt to the ground. Villagers said the bald man had destroyed them for the insurance money.

'Everyone knows it was arson, but inspectors were paid to drop the investigation.'

The baths had been sold to a surly man and his sour wife. They'd cut down all the ancient and beautiful trees; in their place was an asphalted parking lot. Now the bald man owned a new restaurant a mere fifty metres away. I caught sight of him sitting on a chair outside, bored, waiting for clients, for time to pass. Beside him was the equally apathetic mistress. Both had grown surprisingly stout, fat-cheeked and unglamorous.

The main road was busier than ever, linking a new motorway extension to the Romanian border. Rumbling trucks made house walls tremble and crack.

'These buildings have been standing for a hundred years.' Attila contemplated his buckling front wall. 'They won't last another twenty.'

There was talk of European Union subsidies for a ring road, a speedway outside village boundaries, beyond grassland and abandoned wells. Out there, in the wetland paradise of birds, it would threaten rare plants, amphibians and invertebrates.

'Don't worry,' said Csaba, the (secretly) pro-European bartender.. 'EU money given to Hungary always ends up in private pockets. Millions are squandered on corruption, and you won't find one businessman who hasn't paid bribes. That's the system, that's how things work here.'

In 2006, the Prime Minister, Ferenc Gyurcsány had said, in a private audience, that nothing had been done since the fall of communism, that it was time to make changes. Leaked to the public, this declaration had destroyed the left's credibility. Encouraged by Orbán, demonstrations and riots had followed. Fidesz had since won local elections in various regions, and listening to local opinion, it seemed possible that the party would win the next general election.

'We need someone like Viktor Orbán to put this country in order,' said Gizi. 'He's no racist, no anti-Semite.'[142]

Few in the country seemed bothered that Orbán was favouring cronies with lucrative posts, that party members were helping themselves to public money, that Orbán and his treasurer had used party funds for private profit. Who cared about the misuse of EU monies? What did a European Commission in faraway Brussels really do? Only impose new and unpleasant regulations. Here, there was little or no European identity: only

---

142   In 2010, Viktor Orbán's Fidesz Party won sixty-eight percent of Hungary's parliamentary seats. With the support of powerful landowners, the wealthy elite and the Catholic church, the openly xenophobic nationalist government has waged hate campaigns against Jews, liberals, homosexuals, the poor, the homeless and refugees. It has removed people of 'questionable loyalty' from the theatre, opera, museums and the media. To consolidate its hold on the country, Fidesz changed the constitution, instituted new electoral rules, limited the number of independent TV and radio stations, and reduced their range to a 75-mile radius from the capital. It also took over provincial newspapers. By 2018, there were no independent papers outside Budapest.

Those Absent

Hungarian national identity was enduring, stable, and familiar.

***

Misi invited me for dinner, 'To make sure you haven't forgotten what real food is.' When I arrived, he was deep-frying fatty pork in pork fat. The kitchen was a sauna of grease.

'You been following what's happening? What's going on with Transylvania? A few years ago, you mentioned Transylvania and the Trianon Treaty, and the communists arrested you. Now, you bring up Trianon and everyone says, "Oh, forget that." Why should we forget it? We're going to take Transylvania back, wait and see.'[143] The slotted spoon in his hand swished through the air and splattered fat. 'It belongs to us, the Hungarian people. No one defends Hungarians, not even other Hungarians.'

'There was always a Hungarian majority in Transylvania,' said Gizi. Squeezing her rounded hips between hefty chairs, refrigerator and unrelenting enamel sink, she began setting the table.

'When the Trianon Treaty was signed in 1920, there were almost a million more Romanians than Hungarians in Transylvania,' I said. 'But the big landowners and lawmakers were Hungarian.'[144]

Gizi glared at me. 'That's not true. We weren't taught that. That's not written in any Hungarian books.'

'Probably not,' I conceded. 'But that doesn't make the information false. Anyway, everyone here keeps telling me they don't like Transylvanian Hungarians.'[145]

---

143 Orbán has since granted Hungarian citizenship to ethnic Hungarians in Romanian Transylvania and the surrounding countries, has granted money for Hungarian-language education, social, cultural and religious programs. Hungarian passport holders can also apply for welfare payments from Hungary.
144 Romanians probably comprised around 57.5% of the population.
145 In 2016, in a study conducted by Závecz Research, one quarter (24%) of Hungarians questioned stated that they would not allow a Transylvanian Hungarian to live next door to them.

PART SEVEN : AFTER

'I don't believe you. What people say that?' Misi spattered more fat. 'We're part of Europe now, and the European Union should be helping us take back our territory. The Hungarian kingdom was a thousand years old when Trianon took it apart. Just look at the Jews. Someone tries to take what they have, and they fight back. They don't care what anybody says. But the Hungarians? We were occupied by the Turks for 150 years, then by the Austrians. Then comes Trianon, and most of our country disappears. Why? Because the French and the other Europeans cater to Romanians, and to Croats, Serbs and Slavs.'

'At the time of Trianon, the minorities in Hungary were being treated badly,' I said.

'Foreign sentimentality! Look at Serbia now. These two Hungarian guys came out of a disco, and a bunch of Serbians beat them up. Then what happens? The Hungarians get nineteen years in prison. I saw that on television. If you watched Hungarian television, then you'd see what's going on. Believe me, Jews always talk about suffering, but what about Hungarians? Why do we owe the Jews anything? They always do well, but the Hungarians don't know how to help themselves.' Misi stopped shouting. Ogling Gizi, he went over to her and, with his free hand, pinched her soundly on the rump. 'Nice and fat. She feels like a real woman now.'

Thoughts of Transylvania and injustice had been vanquished by lust.

***

*T*he last house Dénes had bought, the one we had visited together, was gone. Another village memory vanished, another empty lot where weeds trembled in a nippy wind. I was hoping to see Dénes again, listen to tales told with his drunken good humour and cranky charm. Perhaps all of us were.

Those Absent

'He told us he'd be back in March,' said Margit, the kocsma owner. But it was now April, and like Eugene O'Neill's misbegotten in Harry Hope's saloon,[146] we could only wait.

'I saw Dénes when I went to England with my daughter last summer,' said Gizi. 'We stayed with friends near London, but the trip cost me so much because my daughter kept making me buy things, a video camera, a computer, a television that doesn't work here in Hungary because it's another system. Buy, buy, buy. She doesn't know the value of money. Then we went up north to see Dénes. When I arrived, I called him and, right away, he said he'd arrange for me to stay with close friends of his. I was surprised, because he always said I could stay with him if I came to England.

'The friends were nice about it, and they invited Dénes to join us for dinner. When he showed up, he was so different. I tried joking with him, but he was stiff and cold. We all drank wine, but he stayed sober. I asked if I could come visit him, but he said his house wasn't tidy enough. When he left, my hostess said she'd never been to his home, although she'd known him for years. It was so strange seeing him like that. He wasn't the Dénes we know. He had become the model priggish Englishman, more English than the English.'

***

*H*elga gave a surprise birthday party for Beate. Most of the German-speakers were there, and all had baked cakes for the occasion. 'With German flour and German yeast. You can't trust Hungarian products. Not the same quality.'

'Not the same price either. Things have become too expensive here since joining the EU.'

'But it's still the same dirty little country,' said sour Marlis.

---
146   *The Iceman Cometh.* Eugene O'Neill.

'Don't know how to make a sidewalk correctly,' Gerhardt complained. 'Weeds still pushing up in between the cracks.'

'Or keep ditches clean, no matter what they're told to do. Took me two months to dig out the one in front of my house and line it with cement. People complain there's no work, but they can't do simple jobs.'

'You've noticed the little chapel up on the hill has been restored,' said Herbert to me. 'It was my special project, and I'm proud of the result.'

'They were letting that chapel fall apart,' said Beate. 'It was disgusting. The Hungarians don't take care of their buildings. They're too ignorant to appreciate something beautiful, something of historical worth.'

All harrumphed their indignation.

'Have any of you wondered about the mound the chapel is on?' I asked. 'Or why there's such a high knoll in the village when the surrounding countryside is unconditionally flat?'

Everyone stared at me.

'The mound is a kunhalom, and they're quite unique. They indicate that there was a Neolithic or Bronze Age village here. Or perhaps this kunhalom was a burial place for noble Sarmatians or Scythians, or it was used for sending news over the plain, or it was a tribal border marking. Aren't any of those things more interesting than a rather banal nineteenth century chapel?'

There was a hostile silence: I wasn't going to be rewarded for such irregular thinking. Only Herbert appeared disconcerted; a self-styled historian, he liked to have all the answers.

It was Helga who took up the challenge, steering conversation back into comfortable waters. She smiled at me. 'We took up a collection, had a priest come in and say the prayers in German, not Hungarian, when the restoration was finished. It was lovely.'

'Of course it was lovely,' said Sophie, the perky reactionary octogenarian all adored. 'You can't do anything with these people. Take my neighbour. Walter and I saw the husband with another woman, didn't we, Walter? Walking down the road with her, just like that. The next thing we knew, he'd packed his bags and abandoned his wife and his three lovely children. So beautiful, those children. How can you leave beautiful children? But Hungarians, that's what they're like.'

'Ugly children are another story altogether,' I said.

But even this little group was changing. Two women had died, and several couples were putting their houses up for sale, for they missed home comforts and growing grandchildren. They were unable to understand the Germans and Austrians who were now moving into this area. Starting businesses, soon speaking fluent Hungarian, that younger generation considered themselves Europeans in a European country. Fully integrated, they snubbed these older, myopic residents, rejecting their invitations to coffee, cake and mudslinging, or to the clannish gulyás evenings.

'They think they fit in here, but they'll soon see,' said Heinz sourly. 'Can't make head or tail of Hungarian. Get one vowel wrong, and people pretend they don't understand a word you're saying. Hungarians have a bad attitude.'

PART SEVEN : AFTER

LIII

I lay down the lyre. None should now
Expect a song of me – that's done.
I'm not as I was long ago.
The better part of me has gone

János Arany[147]

The blue-eyed naïve and easy-going Udo no longer existed. Smug, certain, far right xenophobia moulded all his opinions. Although he was a house owner in a foreign country, Hungary, he believed foreigners had no place in Austria. Bringing his food from Austria in plastic containers, he abandoned the scruffy casual clothes he had once worn when here. Even his movements were strangely robot-like as he patrolled his terrain, trimming shrubs into regimental lines, cropping grass bathmat short, thereby grinding into bloody pulp the tiny tree frogs that had once thrilled him. Nature had to be controlled!

He, star hawker of electric blankets purported to quash electrical waves, was deeply loyal to his boss (leader), who loved him 'like a father', who honoured him and other top salespeople with in-group trips to the Gulf States and Finland. Outside social contacts were discouraged, but Udo's eldest daughter had joined the company and was proving to be a most admirable seller; he hoped his eldest son would do the same.

Resisting my arguments, Udo was adamant. He wasn't selling snake oil to country bumpkins; he wasn't exploiting ignorance. He was a healer.

***

Kata still spoke to me in annoying pidgin, as if I were too dull to understand much else. She showed me her latest acquisition:

---

147   János Arany 1817-1882, Hungarian journalist, writer, poet and translator.

a large screen television. Her house had also been renovated; the blue front terrace with its row of wooden frame windows had become a shiny structure in white plastic.

More sophisticated, she dressed elegantly. She had spent time with her daughter in Canada, hoping perhaps to have the same luck – a rescuing romance, a new house with modern conveniences. Things hadn't panned out that way, but she was happy and doing well, working for someone highly placed in a house out by the baths.

'Very, very, very important man.' Her eyes glowed with clear-cut pride.

'I think I know who you mean,' I said. 'You're working for the man who claims to know his wines.'

'Yes, many good wines. Many guests, important guests, important politicians from Budapest.' She giggled. 'So interesting.'

'What about Karcsi?'

'Sick, very sick. Drink too much. Maybe soon die.'

'And Ildikó? How is she? Do you still see her?'

'Ildikó busy. Works in big hotel. Berekfürdő.'

***

'Ildikó has changed,' said Udo. 'You'll be disappointed. I went to see her a few months ago with Ibolya, but she barely acknowledged us.'

Nonetheless, Udo and I drove out to Berekfürdő. How could good-natured Ildikó have changed so radically? Certainly, it was Udo's new perception of the world that tinged all with hostility.

The sleepy spa town, with its villas and dirt roads, was transformed. The glass factory had closed and was a desolate ruin; modest holiday villas had been renovated or replaced.

PART SEVEN : AFTER

Spurting waterfalls, cement dragons, egrets and turtles enhanced the baths for a better class of tourist, and billboards promised a future with tennis courts, a football field, a stage for pop singers and conjurers. Clients would soon avail themselves of a weight spa, a Finnish sauna, massage therapists, manicurists and pedicurists: nothing like the rustic scene of a few years before.

Hotels had sprung up, and their American-sounding appellations indicated that life in this part of the world was fast and up-to-the-minute: California Hotel, Florida Beach Pension, The Beach Hotel, Green Island, Riverside. Although there was much talk of falling water tables and desertification, funds were being allocated for other new spa hotels and mineral baths in the area.

We drove to the far end of town where once a dirt lane had led to the canal. How often I had sat here, watching glittering snakes slip into the luxuriant undergrowth. The lane, the vegetation and the snakes were gone. All had been replaced by a chain link fence and a large 'international' hotel with roll-down shutters, and decorated, here and there, by a bit of rustic-looking wood. Taking a crazy paving walkway, we crossed an Astro-turf lawn and went into the reception area. Two perfectly groomed but inimical young blonde women inspected us over the top of a high counter.

'Can I help you?' one asked in perfect German.

'We're going to the bar for a drink,' said Udo.

The two young things, imbued with a heady sense of power, shot us looks of derision. 'No,' said the first. 'This is a private hotel.'

And this was New Hungary with all the grandeur of a consumer magazine, the depth of a cell phone conversation and the aesthetics of a video clip.

'We can't go into the bar?'

'No.' They busied themselves with cards and brochures.

'Is Ildikó here?' I asked in Hungarian. 'We're here to see Ildikó.'

The women glanced at each other. 'This is a private hotel,' they said in unison.

'Aren't they all,' I acknowledged.

They didn't stop us when we headed down a corridor in textured yellow cement.

The overheated dining room was filled with well-dressed, bored-looking couples; the women were all blondes, the men, impatient-looking. Hearing an electronic wheeze, I turned. Surrounded by microphones, sound boxes, and an endless twist of thick electrical wire, here was Józsi, seated at his synthesizer.

We went over to him. He had always been effusive… but not now. He didn't call out our names as he had always done. Nodding politely, he launched into the intricacies of *Hernando's Hideaway:* pa-pump, pa-pump, pa-pump-pump-pump…

'I told you so,' muttered Udo.

Where was Ildikó? In the kitchen? At a central buffet stood a slender woman with coiffed, dyed-black hair and perfect make-up on a smoothed face. She threw us a vague, disinterested glance. I went over to ask her where Ildikó was.

Then, suddenly, I realised this was Ildikó. A new Ildikó, self-assured, chic. Part of New Hungary. Restyled, remade. Counted in. She glanced at me with little warmth. Presented her cheek for the obligatory kiss but did not air kiss me back.

'You look wonderful,' I said. 'So sleek. Sophisticated.'

She smiled, a two-second smile, then turned away. Udo had been right: she didn't want us here. Once, as foreigners, we'd been welcome in her kocsma. Now we were not quite the right foreigners: minus froth, minus elegant impatience, minus big bucks.

I Did It My Way followed us back along the long corridor.

***

'I've tried to give my children a feeling of how things used to be, but they're not interested,' said Attila. 'Society has changed, and what happened back then has no meaning for them. They're only interested in cars, computers, telephones, in anything they can buy. Governments have encouraged people to get stupid and consume.

'I remember life after the revolution in '56. ÁVO was gone; the terror was finished. Sure, people were still being arrested and executed, and you couldn't talk about politics in public because it was too dangerous, but there was a feeling of solidarity. We'd hang around with workers, or the son of a powerful man whose shoes cost more than the clothes the rest of us wore, but that didn't matter. What was important was the closeness we felt for one another. People don't have that anymore, and no one understands what you're talking about when you mention it.

'A few months ago, I went to my class reunion in Budapest. Fifty years had passed since I'd seen my friends, and I was looking forward to being with them again. But everyone was so rigid. They were trying to show each other how important they'd become, as if a good image was all that mattered. No one was friendly to me, not even those who had been my best friends. No one said, "Come to my house, have a coffee, meet my wife." It was as if we were strangers. Now I regret I made the effort to go see them. It would have been better to remember the companionship.'

Those Absent

LIV

...the minds of the young had been filled only with illusory ideals and chauvinistic slogans. From the turn of the century, his generation had been fed with self-congratulatory theories, which had so misled it that any criticism was at once dismissed as unpatriotic.

Miklós Bánffy[148]

A few Roma were in the kocsma on this damp and chilly afternoon, several men and three young women. Young, fashionably dressed, they played billiards in the back room, drank beer or cola. I stood in the doorway, watching the drizzle while Udo and a red-haired, freckled, Celtic-looking individual smoked. Soon the Roma, their game over, paid and left the kocsma. A laughing, merry group, they crossed the wet main road, disappeared behind dripping trees and a scrabble of hedge.

'Brazilians,' said the freckled Celt. He smirked, waited for a reaction.

I stared at him, not understanding. Did he mean the group had come from South America, or was it a reference to their darker skin, exotic looks? Was this a new euphemism?

'Gypsies,' he clarified. Shook his head. 'Not good.'

'What's not good?' I asked testily.

Udo, who had understood, murmured anxiously in German: 'Don't say anything. Don't argue with him. You can't convince anyone here, anyway.'

'Which is no reason for keeping my mouth shut.'

'Steal, steal,' said freckle-face, resorting to idiot-level pidgin Hungarian. How could a mere foreigner understand a grammatically correct sentence?

---

148 *Transylvanian Trilogy: The Writing on the Wall.* Count Miklós Bánffy, 1873-1950, Hungarian member of parliament, minister of foreign affairs, writer.

'That's not true,' I said. I was angry.

'Don't bother. Please,' said the "New Udo" with panicked urgency.

'This sort of conversation is unacceptable,' I insisted. 'People can't spew out hate and feel smug about it.'

'No good, Gypsies. Steal. No good.'

'There are good and bad Roma, good and bad Hungarians. There are good and bad people everywhere.' A simplistic argument, but I was preaching to a simple-minded man.

He was merely surprised, that I had come to the group's defence. He'd been so certain I'd chortle and sneer along with him. 'But they're Gypsies,' he answered in a tone reserved for dull and wayward children. 'Gypsies are not people.'

Those Absent

LV

When you sweep the house, you find everything.
                                    Yiddish Proverb

I went to visit my neighbour, jelly-bellied, two-fanged András. He was now alone and lonely, for his wife had died, and his health had deteriorated. Unable to drive his putting tractor out to the far plot near the Puszta's edge, he no longer tended to his allotment, his bees, his garden.

I stood at his house gate but didn't need to ring the bell; several ratty-looking dogs threw themselves wildly against the grillwork and made a hellish racket. András lumbered into sight, stiff, bandy-legged, painfully navigating puddles, every movement torture. But he was pleased to see me, and he urged me to come in out of the rain. There were things he wanted to tell me, he said. He had stories from the old days.

We worked our way over the courtyard's thick batter of mud. I had never been inside his house, and the shabbiness of the kitchen startled me. Renovated in the sixties, dirt was deeply ingrained in the linoleum floor, and walls were grimy. The dreariness was emphasized by the day's clammy chill and the lack of heating.

We sat at a table covered with cracked plastic, a few feet from a blaring television. András grinned. No. It was more of a leer, one that fully exposed his appalling dentition. 'Kiss, kiss,' he said. Lifting his arms, he made the gesture of clasping me in his arms.

It was my fault. I should have known better. I had breached etiquette by coming into a man's lair instead of remaining at the gate for a chat, despite foul weather. Such brash behaviour he took as a sign of availability.

PART SEVEN : AFTER

'No,' I said.

'Why no kiss?' He seemed genuinely surprised.

'You said you had stories about the old days.'

Thwarted, he stared mutinously.

'Tell me the stories,' I urged. But getting no reaction, I stood, prepared to leave.

He stopped my retreat. 'You ask Deutsch family. Jews in village.'

'Yes.' I again sat, waited to hear what he would say, although I had since obtained the names of other local Jewish inhabitants from Yad Vashem in Israel: David András and Miklós Vörös who, like Dr Sándor Steiner, had died in the labour battalions; Lájos Neubauer, missing in Slovakia; Mózes Szalpéter, shot in Auschwitz; Mendel Deutsch, dead in Germany; Imre Altman, murdered in Mauthausen.

'My wife deceased,' said András. 'She know Jews here.' So he had nothing to tell me. The subject had been a lure to keep me inside.

'How are you managing on your own?' I asked, resigned to trite small talk.

'Hard.' He looked sorrowful. 'Not so young. Eighty-six.' The sorrow quickly transmuted into a leer. 'No kiss for me?' He didn't lack determination.

'No kiss,' I confirmed.

'Me child know Jewish doctor. Dr Sándor Steiner.' He stopped, ruminated for a minute or two. About what information to give me? 'Steiner live other side of village. Little, low house, not brick. We love him, Dr Sándor Steiner. Rich. Old man when he die here.'

'He died in a labour battalion on the front,' I corrected.

Those Absent

András stared blankly, as if he had no idea what I was talking about. Perhaps he didn't. Or he believed in the fairytale ending.

'Me child. Jews always rich. Smart people. In Kunmadaras, many shops near market place. Make good money. Dry goods shop owned by Jew Hirsch. Good salesman, Hirsch. Peasant women sell butter, fruit, milk, eggs on market. Come to Hirsch's shop. "Come in," say Hirsch. "Come look." Women look, see pretty things. Hirsch say: "Take, take. Pay next time." Hirsch rich. Jewish bakery in Kunmadaras. My aunt live Kunmadaras, get bread market days. I go. Jewish baker, he say to aunt, to me, "Wait ten minutes. Good, fresh bread come from oven. Wait."'

'This was before the war?'

'Before. Baker die in war.'

'What did people say when the Jews were deported?'

'Me, child. We don't like Jews die in Auschwitz. Go away in wagons. Soldiers here do job, do what told. We think, oh Jews go to Tiszafüred, Budapest, not Auschwitz.'

'Then people plundered the Jewish houses.'

'No! Not everyone. Deutsch house, people go in. Cupboards, chairs, books, good furniture. Plates. Nice. Deutsch family not poor. Nice furniture. Some people break, some people take cupboards, chairs, everything.'

'You saw this?'

He shifted nervously in his chair. 'Me, child.'

'You are eighty-six. You were in your twenties then.'

'Me young child.'

'No, you were an adult.'

'Maybe.'

'Tell me more.'

PART SEVEN : AFTER

'Me young soldier, one Jewish friend. Neulander. After war, come back Kunmadaras. Me see Neulander on street. "Hello, hello!" Later Neulander go live Israel. He write, tell me.'

'Neulander?' Navigating through the gobbledygook of truncated pidgin was as difficult as untangling the contradictions. 'Neulander never went to Israel. He died in the Kunmadaras pogrom.'

András shook his head with violence. 'I don't know. I don't know.'

'You don't know about the pogrom? You don't know that Neulander was murdered?'

'Me, child.'

'Were you in Kunmadaras on the day of the pogrom?'

He wasn't looking at me, but staring out onto the sludgy garden. 'Aunt come from market, see me on road, say, "Don't go. Killing Jews. Bad, very bad." We like Jews. After war, Jews do well. Get rich. We, no rich. Little houses, little land. Nothing to eat. Jews, different. Always different.'

'That's why Jews were killed in Kunmadaras? Because people said they were rich?'

'Jews come back. Weak. Everybody say Jews need blood. Must get strong. Normal, normal. Need children blood, but this not good, not good. Our children, Hungarian children. Must stop Jews. People saying must stop.' He was pleading.

'You helped stop the Jews because you believed they needed children's blood?'

András shook his head, confused. His sagged cheeks were mottled, ugly. 'Children blood. Bad, bad.'

We sat in silence. Did he expect understanding? Absolution?

There was a quick rap at the door, and a woman stepped

into the kitchen, András's niece. She carried a heavy back pot filled with soup. She smiled. 'It's nice of you to come visit my uncle. He's been so lonely since my aunt died.'

András grunted with great relief. He no longer had to deal with me, with my questions. 'Soup, soup, soup. Warm soup.'

'It's so good that you speak Hungarian,' said the niece. 'We can be friends. Come and visit me in my house one afternoon. It would make me so happy.'

PART SEVEN : AFTER

LVI

We had not gone far, when suddenly ahead stretched a great irregular lake, in which groups of trees and woods were reflected, and to the left a large cathedral stood on a little island. We stared in astonishment – there behind was the farm and settlement we had left, rising like a small Venice from still, calm water. Then the lake began to shift its quarter, to dry up in parts and spread again in others... so this was the fata morgana, and a most luxurious phenomenon it is. No matter that one knows the scientific explanation – that the trees will prove to be a herd of sheep or pigs, the cathedral a tiny village church miles and miles away – it is most cheering, and as good as a draught of water to a thirsty man...

Margaret Fletcher

Gyula, the construction worker, came down the road and saw me stowing things in my car. 'Are you leaving for good?'

'No, I'll be back,' I answered, although I knew I might not be.

'Don't you care about us? Don't you love Hungary anymore?'

'Of course I do,' I said, and meant it. But it wasn't this new, sanitised version I was attached to.

He threw his arms around me, hugged me, as if my departure mattered to him.

Black József, disconsolate, brought me another stuffed animal: an almost headless, completely eyeless and grubby orange cat. 'So you won't forget us.'

Attila appeared next, and he watched me morosely. 'This is your country. You'll miss it if you go because you belong here. You're as chaotic as the Hungarians.'

Heartsore, dreary, I knew he was right. I would miss the dry earthy feel of a house with adobe walls; I would miss these people with their foibles and the weightiness of their country's

Those Absent

complicated history. I would forever long for the broad expanse, the commotion of local birds and frogs, the grace of snakes, the plodding ungrateful turtles I had rescued on the main road, the fragrant winds and the almost incandescent Puszta light.

But so much had vanished: the itinerant merchants, the women sitting along ditches, telling tales and filling sacks with onions, the topsy-turvy shops, the shoddy bars. How I had loved the riotous weeds, the squabbling fowl and the puffing cows that nibbled village vegetation as they rumbled home. Rough and untidy, less consumer-oriented, that world was what I had sought. What was left of it was disappearing so quickly. Perhaps my illusions were what I missed most.

With Dog and Werewolf, my newest adopted stray, I took the track leading out of the village, left behind red rooftops, passed feudal plots, the irrigation canal and the fields of stunted corn. Came, finally, to shaggy Puszta and a hollow of boggy marsh where constant wind made reeds and grasses twitch. The air was musky, the light fragile.

Here, where horse skulls had once protected dead chieftains, I conjured up phantoms – Gepid, Hun, Iazyge, Avar, Kuman, Kabar, Magyar, Mongol – but none appeared. If ever they haunted their prior territory, today they were absent.

Then, unexpectedly, the sun came out, strong, too intense. Fields, grasses, the track, all seemed to shift in its brightness. On a varnished horizon, water appeared, an iridescent, wobbling sea. And high shadowy mountains, and great billowing trees. The silvery hint of a castle.

None of it was real. This vague and temporary offering was all that was left of the famous *fata morgana*, a modern version, modest and timid because altered by pollution. But a gift, nonetheless, and I accepted it with gratitude.

PART SEVEN : AFTER

Those Absent

Acknowledgements

This book couldn't have been written without the tales, humour, knowledge and musical ear of the late Attila Szabo. He never hesitated to answer, with great patience, my questions, and to make a vanished world come alive. His wife, Paula Szabo, added hospitality, biting wit, and a humorous view of society.

I am much indebted to writer Hava Oren who went through this manuscript with a fine-toothed comb and made everything better with her suggestions, corrections, and childhood memories. Thanks also to Barry James for his excellent comments, to Bernard Tisserand and Robin Roger who read or listened to earlier versions of this manuscript, offered advice and much encouragement, and to author, historian and scholar Robert A. Rosenstone for his unique way of presenting history.

I am particularly indebted to Ágnes Szegő, Ági Elek, and Eva Samery for sharing their knowledge of Jewish life in Hungary; to Maria Majoros who gave me a clearer view of local society; and to the very many villagers who, often unwittingly, offered me their stories.

My work was made easier by the assistance and interest of the staff of the Toronto Reference Library the National Széchényi Library (Országos Széchényi Könyvtár), the Bibliothèque nationale de France, the Maison de la Culture Yiddish in Paris, and particularly the Memorial Museum of the Hungarian Speaking Jewry in Safed, Israel. The Memorial Museum also gave me permission to use many of their archival photos in this book. I am equally grateful to the Canada Council for the Arts and the Ontario Arts Council whose work in progress grants greatly helped in carrying out this project.

And many thanks to Alex Green at Claret Press for all his suggestions, and to my publisher Katie Isbester for her ongoing faith in my work.

JILL CULINER

About the Author

Born in New York, raised in Toronto, Jill Culiner, writer, social critical artist, and photographer has spent most of her life in France, England, Germany, Hungary, Turkey, Holland, and North Africa. Her photographic exhibition about the First and Second World Wars, *La Mémoire Effacée*, toured France, Canada, and Hungary under the auspices of the French Ministry of Foreign Affairs and UNESCO. Her non-fiction, *Finding Home in the Footsteps of the Jewish Fusgeyers* won the Joseph and Faye Tanenbaum Prize for Canadian Jewish History and was shortlisted for the ForeWord Magazine Award. Her biography of a nineteenth-century rebel Yiddish poet and singer, *A Contrary Journey with Velvel Zbarzher, Bard*, was published by Claret Press in 2022.

She presently lives in a 400-year-old inn in France that is so chaotic and strange, it has been classified as a museum.

Web sites: http://www.jillculiner-writer.com
http://www.jill-culiner.com
Blog: https://jewish-histories.over-blog.com
Podcast: https://soundcloud.com/j-arlene-culiner

About the Book

An incredibly evocative book about the lost Jews of Hungary, part history, part detective story, part personal memoir, it brings to life a cast of characters fitting for a Dickensian novel, deals with the fallibility of memory, with the nature of prejudice and persecution, and with the past as both history and fiction.
Dr Michael Talalay, Writer, Lecturer, Regents University London

Those Absent is a fascinating literary journey, exposing anecdotes of rural life and anti-Semitism in the late nineteenth century to modern days. An intriguing and frank investigation of the region's daily life, its common beliefs and rarely mentioned truths. Highly recommended.
Mel Cederbaum, Executive Director, Toronto Workmen's Circle

Jill Culiner vividly recounts her relentless six year search for the truth about the fate of the Jews who returned from the Nazi death camps to Kunmadaras. Part memoir, part travelogue, part history, part elegy, this multi-layered homage to the Great Hungarian Plain embraces its majesty and tragedy at virtually the last possible moment.
Robin Roger, psychotherapist, writer, reviewer

The long history of hatred toward the Jews combined with the exploitation and misery of the peasants have forged Hungarian identity. Jill Culiner's Central Europe is plagued by the same demons that led to the tragedies of the past century.
Dr Marcel Calvez, Emeritus Professor of Sociology, University of Rennes.

In a narrative of village life, coarse xenophobia and cruelty contrast with acceptance, friendship and laughter. The horror of the past is concealed, yet Culiner finds compassion in human failure.
Penny-Lynn Cookson, Art historian, writer.

www.ingramcontent.com/pod-product-compliance
Lightning Source LLC
Chambersburg PA
CBHW041312110526
44591CB00022B/2885